International Political Economy Series

Series Editor
Timothy M. Shaw
University of Massachusetts Boston
Boston, USA

Emeritus Professor
University of London, UK

The global political economy is in flux as a series of cumulative crises impacts its organization and governance. The IPE series has tracked its development in both analysis and structure over the last three decades. It has always had a concentration on the global South. Now the South increasingly challenges the North as the centre of development, also reflected in a growing number of submissions and publications on indebted Eurozone economies in Southern Europe. An indispensable resource for scholars and researchers, the series examines a variety of capitalisms and connections by focusing on emerging economies, companies and sectors, debates and policies. It informs diverse policy communities as the established trans-Atlantic North declines and 'the rest', especially the BRICS, rise.

More information about this series at
http://www.palgrave.com/gp/series/13996

Stuart S. Brown • Margaret G. Hermann

Transnational Crime and Black Spots

Rethinking Sovereignty and the Global Economy

Stuart S. Brown
Moynihan Institute of Global Affairs
Maxwell School, Syracuse University
Syracuse, NY, USA

Margaret G. Hermann
Moynihan Institute of Global Affairs
Maxwell School, Syracuse University
Syracuse, NY, USA

ISSN 2662-2483   ISSN 2662-2491   (electronic)
International Political Economy Series
ISBN 978-1-137-49669-0   ISBN 978-1-137-49670-6   (eBook)
https://doi.org/10.1057/978-1-137-49670-6

*To Melvyn Levitsky and Bartosz Stanislawski
who inspired this project and book*

ACKNOWLEDGMENTS

We are indebted to Ambassador Melvyn Levitsky and Bartosz Stanislawski who started the Mapping Global Insecurity Project that forms the basis for this book. Ambassador Levitsky taught a course in the Maxwell School that became affectionately known as the 'Drugs and Thugs' class in which many of our professional and doctoral students enrolled. Bartosz was one such student who did a doctoral dissertation on the concept of the black spot after spending time in Ciudad del Este, Paraguay. He began the study of these geopolitical locations with funding from the Moynihan Institute of Global Affairs and laid the foundation for what has followed.

The project on which this book is based is a multidisciplinary endeavor composed of students and faculty with interests and expertise in economics, forensic science, geography, law, political science, psychology, and public policy working together. We have benefited enormously from these interactions. Among those to whom we owe a particular debt of gratitude are Jonathan Adelman, Bethany Eberle, Isaac Kfir, Angely Martinez, Keli Perrin, Catriona Standfield, Laura Steinberg, and Corrine Zoli. We have also benefited from the help that students enrolled in the Maxwell School's Master of Arts in International Relations Program have provided. They have been critical in writing and updating the in-depth case studies that form the backbone of this book. Specifically, we would like to thank Marc Barnett, Taylor Brown, Jane Chung, Chris Conrad, Jessica Kesler, Paige Kisner, John Rastler, Bree Spencer, and Tim Stoutzenberger.

The project on which this book is based was supported by grants from the US Department of Defense, SRC Inc. (formerly the Syracuse Research Corporation), and an SU Chancellor's Research Initiative grant as well as annual funding from the Moynihan Institute of Global Affairs where the Mapping Global Insecurity Project is housed. Persons in these institutions have been especially supportive of the research presented in this book, in particular, Ben Riley and Bob DelZoppo. We are most grateful not only for their financial support but also for the stimulating discussions we have had with them and the challenges they have posed to us as we moved forward. Erik Wemlinger at SRC has also been invaluable in helping us streamline our data collection efforts and build relational databases. Our research is better for their help and encouragement.

This book was made a reality by Palgrave Macmillan's International Political Economy Series editor, Tim Shaw, who believed early on in the importance of our topic and research, serving as a discussant on an ISA panel focused on black spots, and has been very supportive throughout the process. We also owe a debt of gratitude to Christina Brian who, at the time, was the Editorial Director for Politics and International Studies at Palgrave Macmillan. She encouraged us when we needed it and has been interested in what we were doing from the start. Moreover, we are indebted to Zaklina Nocevski who diligently helped with all the last minute details so necessary for completing the manuscript and the rest of the staff of the Moynihan Institute of Global Affairs who took on extra tasks to allow us the chance to work uninterrupted on the book.

Finally, we are both most appreciative of the understanding and encouragement of our families. Stuart thanks Rachel, Evan, and Jackie for their love and support. Margaret (Peg) is grateful to her son Chris who, with expertise in the field of urban planning, provided valuable input to the project, and to her daughter, Karen, who ensured that she included grandchildren and balance in her life.

CONTENTS

ACRONYMS

DDoS	Distributed Denial of Service
DRC	Democratic Republic of the Congo
EFIG	European Financial Intelligence Group
FARC	Revolutionary Armed Forces of Colombia
FATA	Federally Administered Tribal Areas
FATF	Financial Action Task Force
FTZ	Free Trade Zone
GDP	Gross Domestic Product
ICE	US Immigration and Customs Enforcement
IMF	International Monetary Fund
ISIS	Islamic State of Iraq and Syria
ISP	Internet Service Provider
ITU	International Telecommunications Union
IVTS	Informal Value Transfer Systems
MB	Megabyte
MENAFATF	Middle East and North Africa Financial Action Task Force
MNC	Multi-National Corporation
MONUSCO	United Nations Organization: Stabilization Mission in the Democratic Republic of Congo
NEG	New Economic Geography
NGO	Non-Governmental Organization
NPPS	New Payment, Products, and Services
OECD	Organization for Economic Cooperation and Development
OSESG	Office of the Special Envoy of the Secretary-General
PKK	Kurdistan Workers' Party
TBML	Trade-Based Money Laundering
TCO	Transnational Criminal Organization

UNEP	United Nations Environmental Programme
UNODC	United Nations Office on Drugs and Crime
UNRWA	United Nations Relief and Works Agency
UWSA	United Wa State Army
UWSP	United Wa State Party
WISE	World Information Services on Energy

LIST OF FIGURES

LIST OF TABLES

CHAPTER 1

Introduction: Setting the Stage

"It is a dream come true for criminals and terrorists to find a place where no one can look for them, and where they can mix with, ally with … and work with minimum interference from legal authority" (Levitsky 2008: 392). These safe havens have been called a variety of names from 'dark corners' (Crane 2008) to 'geopolitical black holes' (Naim 2005)—areas governed by transnational criminal, terrorist, and insurgent organizations that are outside effective state-based government control and are sustained by illicit economic activities. They are modern-day versions of the pirate islands of the seventeenth and eighteenth centuries. The Daniel Patrick Moynihan Institute of Global Affairs in its Mapping Global Insecurity Project has, to date, identified 150 such places around the globe and completed in-depth case studies of 80. We call these geographic locations 'black spots,' recognizing that they represent particular locations that do not fit within our usual definitions of a state. Much like the black holes in astronomy that defy the laws of Newtonian physics, these black spots defy the world as defined by the Westphalian state system. In effect, they provide us with a map of the world as viewed through the eyes of organizations engaged in transnational criminal activities. These black spots are the nodes connecting and facilitating the illicit activities of such organizations and their trafficking in drugs, weapons, people, money, natural resources, household goods, and violence.

One such black spot became the focus of attention during the US War in Afghanistan—the Federally Administered Tribal Areas or FATA.

© The Author(s) 2020
S. S. Brown, M. G. Hermann, *Transnational Crime and Black Spots*, International Political Economy Series,
https://doi.org/10.1057/978-1-137-49670-6_1

Located on the border between Pakistan and Afghanistan, FATA is outside the effective control of both governments—indeed, that is one of its advantages in the view of those involved in transnational criminal activities. But this region is not ungoverned—it is governed by structures that facilitate a black market in drugs, weapons, and natural resources, exploiting the area's geography, poverty, corruption potential, and closeness to a conflict zone. Other examples of black spots are the dual cities Tabatinga and Leticia on the border of Colombia and Brazil, the Pankisi Gorge in Georgia, the Bekaa Valley in Lebanon, Kismayo in Somalia, the Wa State in Myanmar (Burma), and the Tohono O'odham Reservation on the US border with Mexico. Among the 80 black spots we have mapped and studied in depth and which will figure prominently in this book, 18% are in Africa, 20% in Asia, 19% in Europe, 16% in the Middle East, 21% in Latin America, and 6% in North America. Table 1.1 contains a list of these 80 black spots by region.

Although often differing in scale—from a neighborhood to a city to a mountain valley to a province, 90% of the black spots that we have studied so far are located on, across, or around national borders. They are found in what has aptly been called the 'borderlands' (van Schendel 2005). Such border areas offer opportunities for avoiding legal entrapment, marking as they do the extent of a particular state's legal zone of influence. And in so choosing, the black spots are overwhelmingly (90%) found in areas along these borders where corruption is prevalent and that can be described as involving geographically and/or jurisdictionally challenging terrain. Three-quarters came into being because they are on traditional trading routes—think about the 'silk road' of old linking Asia to Europe, the trails through the Amazon in Latin America, the routes across the Sahara desert, and the sea routes of the privateers. Some 86% are located near conflict zones in areas that are ethnically heterogeneous.

The 80 black spots studied here are governed by rules and norms that are either imposed (42%) or embedded (53%). In other words, there is a governance framework in place to guide behavior. A major tenant of this governance structure is to remain 'invisible' or off the radar of the international media as well as national and international law enforcement. Moreover, counter to ours and others' expectations, black spots are not a phenomenon of the post-Cold War era and the demise of the Soviet Union. Close to 60% of the 80 black spots were in place well before 1991 and 41% have come into being since 1991. As we will show,

Table 1.1 Black spots studied by region

Africa:
Tri-border Area, Algeria/Mali/Niger; Equatorial Guinea; Guinea-Bissau; Niger Delta, Nigeria; Tri-border West Africa (Sierra Leone/Liberia/Guinea); Goma, DRC; Kisangani, DRC; Lubumbashi, DRC; Mbuji Mayi, DRC; Shinkolobwe Mine, DRC; South Darfur, Sudan; Barawe, Somalia; Kismayo, Somalia; Ilemi Triangle, Kenya/Sudan/Ethiopia
Asia:
Little Wahhabi, Dagestan; Chuy Valley, Kazakhstan; Fergana Valley (Kyrgzstan/ Tajikistan/Uzbekistan); Rasht Valley, Tajikistan; Azad Kashmir, Pakistan; FATA, Pakistan; Gilgit Baltistan, Pakistan; Muzaffarabad, Pakistan; Kashgar, China; Tachilek, Myanmar (Burma); Wa State, Myanmar (Burma); Mae Sot, Thailand; Strait of Malacca; Surabaya, Indonesia; General Santos City, Philippines; Sulu Archipelago, Philippines
Europe:
Gudauta, Abkhazia; Kodori Gorge, Georgia; Pankisi Gorge, Georgia; Samegrelo, Georgia; South Ossetia; Transnistria; Zenica, Bosnia and Herzegovina; Novi Pazar, Serbia; Presovo Valley, Serbia; Sandzak Region, Serbia; Kosovska Mitrovica, Kosovo; Urosevac (Ferizaj), Kosovo; Scampia/Secondigliano, Naples; Ceuta and Melilla, Spain; Marbella, Spain
Middle East:
El Arish, Egypt; Rafah, Gaza Strip; Netanya, Israel; Bekaa Valley, Lebanon; Ein el-Hilweh, Lebanon; Hezbollah Territory, Lebanon; Nahr el-Bared, Lebanon; Abu Kamal, Syria; Erzurum/Kars/Igdir Triangle, Turkey; Hakkari-Van Provinces, Turkey; Sirnak Province, Turkey; Dubai, United Arab Emirates; Saada Province, Yemen
North America:
Kahnawake Reservation, Canada; Kanesatake Reservation, Canada; Akwesasne Reservation, Canada/US; Blackfeet Reservation, US; Tohono O'odham Reservation, US
Latin America:
Altar, Mexico; Chetumal, Mexico; Ciudad Juarez, Mexico; Los Zetas Territory, Mexico; Michoacan State, Mexico; Nogales, Mexico; Sinaloa State, Mexico; San Pedro Sula, Honduras; Darien Jungle, Panama/Colombia; FARC Territory, Colombia; Marquetalia Republic, Colombia; Nueva Loja, Ecuador; Tabatinga-Leticia Corridor, Brazil/ Colombia; Manaus, Brazil; Ciudad del Este, Paraguay; Encarnación, Paraguay; Pedro Juan Caballero, Paraguay.

---

those in place prior to 1991 often resulted from borders being mandated in areas that divided particular ethnic groups and tribes, separating these groups and tribes jurisdictionally from one another and giving rise to a variety of insurgent groups and organizations. The Durand Line which was drawn by the British in the late 1800s to demarcate the border between Pakistan and Afghanistan is one such example. It cuts through the Pashtun tribal areas and the Baluchistan region and has facilitated the development of a number of black spots including FATA noted earlier (Walker 2011).

DISCOVERY OF BLACK SPOTS

How did we discover this phenomenon we have called a black spot? This project grew out of a dissertation in political science done as part of the Moynihan Institute's study of transnational crime (Stanislawski 2006), which involved fieldwork in Ciudad del Este in the tri-border region of Paraguay, Brazil, and Argentina. This research project was based on ethnographic observation of what went on in this particular community as well as 'conversations' (informal interviews) with people in the area engaged in what appeared to be illicit activities and officials of the Paraguayan government with responsibility for security and law enforcement. It became quite apparent across the period of study that the economy of the city was built around illicit activities and not under the control of the central government. But the city was functioning effectively with a thriving economy. Indeed, Ciudad del Este was being governed by collaborating transnational criminal organizations.

Based on this research and an extensive review of literature on the behavior of transnational criminal, insurgent, and terrorist organizations; of what goes on in supposedly ungoverned territories and so-called failed states; and of various types of illegal trafficking, we developed a set of questions to ask of other identified potential black spots to explore if Ciudad del Este was 'one of a kind' or whether there were other such functioning areas like it. We focused on the following four sets of questions that our literature review and experience suggested were important to examine. Each set explores a different area of analysis: (1) What are the conditions that lead to the development of black spots and their sustainability? (2) How is state authority challenged and/or undermined by a black spot? (3) What kinds of insecurity do black spots produce and/or export to the outside world and how? (4) What defensive moves have national and international legitimate authorities made in response to black spots? The questions posed in each of these areas of analysis have become the foundation for a coding manual used as a guide in doing an in-depth case study of each black spot. The answers to these questions form the data on which this book is based. The coding manual can be found in Appendix A.

Employing research assistants from around the world, we asked them to identify some geopolitical areas in their countries that seemed outside central government control and generally were known to engage in illicit activities. They were quick to nominate areas with such a reputation.

We, then, had them use open source materials (e.g., Benavides 2015; UN Office on Drugs and Crime documents; US Department of State reports; BBC Monitoring; Agence France-Presse; International Crisis Group reports; STRATFOR; Economist Intelligence Unit reports) and write a case study of the particular area, answering all the questions in the coding manual that we had identified out of the study of Ciudad del Este and our more general literature review. Such a procedure—called structured, focused comparison (George 1979; George and Bennett 2005)—provides the researcher with an in-depth case study of a black spot based on a common set of theoretical ideas but also enables that same researcher to develop a quantitative database that facilitates comparison across cases since the same questions were asked of every case. We learn what is unique to a particular case as well as what is common among the cases. Once completed, a case study is updated regularly to explore if anything has changed and, if so, how. This process allows us to take advantage of new open source materials and yearly updates. Importantly, those writing the in-depth case studies often speak the language or languages relevant to those in the black spot and can monitor local open sources as well as those done at the national and international levels. An example of an in-depth case study is found in Appendix B. Summaries of a sample of the case studies are available in a special issue of the *National Strategy Forum Review* (Stanislawski 2011).

VALIDITY PROBES

Because we are heavily reliant on open source materials in identifying black spots, we have been interested in validating our observations and designations through research in the field. Several of the project's research assistants have visited areas identified as black spots in addition to Ciudad del Este mentioned above. Among these have been the Akwasasne Reservation that crosses the border between Canada and the US along the Saint Lawrence River (Spencer 2011); Marbella, Spain (Roberts 2016); and black spots along the age-old Balkan trading route that goes through Kosovo, Serbia, and Bosnia and Herzegovina (Stoutzenberger and Barnett 2016). They have done initial ethnographic work comparing what they see on the ground with what was discovered by other research assistants via open source materials.

Moreover, we have been fortunate in attracting practitioners to become part of the project who in their jobs have dealt with illicit organizations in particular black spots. One was a Pakistani customs officer who reviewed our case studies of black spots in that part of the world which he had observed and visited, corroborating what we found. Indeed, our identification of black spots in the Latin American region benefited from the on-the-ground experience of a German police official serving in that country's drug enforcement agency and a US National Guard member's interactions with Central American military.

Mapping Illicit Behavior

Recognizing early on that black spots were dependent on one another if they were to be economically viable, we became interested in learning which were engaged in 'production' (the source of the illicit activities in which the organizations governing them were engaged), which were involved in 'transit' (they transported items), and which were 'distribution centers' (destinations where items were sold or distributed to other entities to sell). While most (85%) were involved in the transit of some type of illegal activity, 58% were the sources or producers of the items being trafficked and 40% were locations where distribution took place. By mapping from where, through where, and to where trafficking occurs, we can capture relationships among the black spots and envision how an integrated illicit economy works.

An important part of this mapping exercise involves identifying the illicit activities emanating from each black spot and tracing where they go as well as noting what flows into the black spot as other commodities flow out. Indeed, most of the flows are transactions—for example, drugs for weapons, drugs for money, people for money. Can we identify how critical a particular item is to a black spot's economy? In other words, what is the frequency and intensity of the flow of drugs, weapons, people, and so forth? Can we use open source materials to monitor variation in these flows? These are questions we are exploring as we map the black spots and examine the connections among them. Of interest also is learning what happens to the flows when national and international law enforcement try to disrupt one part of an interlinked network of black spots.

Most of the 80 black spots that we have studied to date are involved with the illicit economy surrounding the trafficking in drugs and conventional weapons—for roughly three-quarters of them, these are dominant commodities. Trafficking in people is next at 53%, and 37% are engaged in identifiable money laundering activities. Some 42% of the black spots are involved in terrorist activities. In fact, almost half (46%) of the black spots on which we have case material engage in the trafficking of drugs, weapons, *and* people—they engage in all three. These black spots have become what Miraglia and his colleagues (2012) have called nodes in a transnational interconnected network formed around the distribution and marketing of more than one item; they are flexibly able to shift and adapt with the markets for these items.

In effect, black spots share some common characteristics with multinational corporations (MNCs). Both are driven by the goal of profit maximization. Moreover, both types of organizations are non-state actors, that is, not necessarily bound by sovereign borders or owing allegiance to a particular state-based government. And both utilize the advantages afforded by globalization—notably product fragmentation and advances in information and communication technologies—to produce, enhance, and transport their product to the customer. Furthermore, in order to minimize their costs, they both must consider the availability of labor, the ability to secure raw materials and/or intermediate products, and transportation. But they differ when it comes to the rule of law. Whereas MNCs welcome some degree of regulation in locations where smaller firms are hired to implement specific tasks and with regard to insurance purchased to compensate for unforeseen delays or failed contracts, black spots do better without state governance and regulation. Actors in the black spots are likely to build in all sorts of redundancies to facilitate the movement of products while insuring the absence of state interference. Bribes, kickbacks, and protection monies are ways of facilitating lack of detection as are the establishment of legal front organizations as well as enhancements to the quality of life of residents in the black spot in a way analogous to 'corporate social responsibility.'

Given the parallels between MNCs and black spots, we are interested in using what we know about MNCs and their global supply chains to learn more about how a black spots network might form and the problems it might confront. A pertinent question is, have increased globalization and, in turn, the retreat of the state (Strange 2010) along with the spread of technology and the lower costs for transportation and communication facilitated the building of global networks among the black spots much like has happened among MNCs? A major focus of this volume is to begin to address questions like this one. Indeed, as we began to map the flows of such things as drugs, weapons, and people among black spots in a region, we learned quickly where other black spots were located. We encountered holes in the network and redundant routes were exposed. These apparent breaks in the network often led to the identification of a new black spot—either governed by the same transnational criminal, insurgent, or terrorist organization or a group affiliated with them. We also learned that it is possible to geographically map black spots networks and their associated flows of insecurity within and across regions of the globe. And in the process of mapping these connections, we realized that we were studying the applicability of ideas regarding corporate global supply chains to black spots networks. We were learning whether what we know about corporate global supply chains operating within the legal economy held any lessons for us regarding what is happening in the illicit economy.

Consider two studies that students related to our research project have completed focusing on a particular black spots network and law enforcement's attempts to eradicate or change its behavior. The studies examined the effects of Plan Colombia—an arrangement between the US and Colombia that mandated reduction in the flow of drugs from Colombia into the US (Rastler 2013; Adelman 2014). The data from these studies show how transnational criminal groups used redundant routes and locations to keep the drugs flowing, how they enhanced their sales to Europe as the flow to the US decreased, and how these same organizations relocated to other black spots when their original locations were interdicted. Plan Colombia did not reduce drug trafficking, it just allowed for what is called 'squeezing of the balloon,' that is, the relocation of those involved in transnational criminal activities to other black spots using the redundancies and flexibilities that have been built into the network in this particular Latin American area. This black spots network had ready alternatives to interdiction and, like MNCs, could relocate their suppliers, transportation, and distribution centers as problems arose.

WHO GOVERN BLACK SPOTS AND HOW ARE THEY FUNDED?

There are several implications of mapping the global illicit economy that we will address and examine separately. First, our completed, in-depth case studies suggest that black spots are governed by different types of actors. Some 41% involved insurgent groups, 31% terrorist organizations, and 28% transnational criminal organizations acting on their own. Among these are insurgent groups like the Uighurs in China, terrorist organizations such as al-Shabaab in Somalia, and transnational criminal organizations like the

Sinaloa Cartel in Mexico. Do the black spots in which we find these various types of actors engage in different kinds of illicit activities? Are the black spots governed by each type found in different parts of the globe? What kinds of motivations and goals drive their illicit behavior? And what happens when transnational criminal organizations are mixed into the governance structures in a black spot with an insurgent or a terrorist organization? How do these coalitions function, who is in charge, and how is power shared? Do such coalitions have an impact on the types of illicit activities that flow to and from such black spots?

Then there is the issue regarding how black spots are financed. After all, black spots are used by illicit actors as places of business. They need operating capital to grow their business, their own wealth, their influence, and their ability to engage in corruption on a national and international scale (Calvery 2012). At the same time, such actors need to minimize their transaction costs, lower the risk of detection, store values securely, and maintain liquidity. And there is the need to 'clean' money that has been obtained illegally, to lend it legitimacy so that it can be used in the licit global economy without drawing the attention of law enforcement officials. What can we learn from the black spots about how money is laundered in the illicit economy? Some 49% of the 80 black spots studied to date offer illustrations of how the illicit actors governing them approach gaining operating income and transforming such illegally acquired funding so that it is regarded as legal.

ARE THERE BLACK SPOTS IN CYBERSPACE?

A third area of interest arises out of our observation on the importance of borderlands to facilitating the presence of black spots. Such borderlands, as we noted earlier, enhance the ability to avoid legal entrapment. But what about cyberspace where there are no borders and there is shared governance between state and non-state actors? With 48% of the world's population linked into the internet by 2017, it has become a giant marketplace. And not only is it a giant marketplace but it allows for instantaneous communication worldwide. Cyberspace seems designed for crime and criminals. It is essentially borderless and provides illicit actors with transnational access to large numbers of people and computers where contact is instantaneous. Moreover, there often is confusion regarding just who is legally in charge (Adams and Albakajai 2016). In effect, do we find black spots in cyberspace?

ORGANIZATION OF THIS BOOK

This book begins with an examination of the concept of a black spot and how it challenges our notions of sovereignty and provides us with an alternative or 'new' map of the world (Chap. 2). That discussion is followed by an exploration of the parallels between multinational corporations and black spots—between the global licit and illicit economies—exploring the implications of the new economic geography literature for the illicit economy (Chap. 3). Although most discussions of trafficking commodities such as drugs, weapons, people, and natural resources tend to focus on each type separately, we are interested here in what we can learn about the illicit economy by mapping the flows of all such phenomena as they interact in black spots networks (Chap. 4). Consider what is traded for what, if regions differ in the commodities appearing in the illicit economy, how redundancies are built into networks to insure there remains an accessible market should changing routes or focusing on a specific commodity be mandatory. And what can we learn about the black spots that form the key nodes in the networks—the spaces that are involved in production and transportation as well as distribution? Are the crucial geopolitical places with the most redundancies the capitals of the illicit economy?

Once we know something about black spots and their networks, it seems appropriate to inquire about who governs the black spots and toward what ends (Chap. 5). How do those governing the black spots define sovereignty and can we map their goals and strategies as they become involved in the illicit economy? And just how is money acquired and managed in the illicit economy defined by the black spots (Chap. 6)? We observe a range of techniques from using informal banking systems such as the Hawala to establishing front organizations such as trucking companies to changing money into stable commodities like gold and art. Do black spots differ in the choices that are made regarding the methods used to launder money? And, lastly, are there black spots in cyberspace, an arena that is essentially virtual (Chap. 7)?

All these issues are addressed as the reader moves through the book. We end with an overview of what we have discovered about the nature of black spots as well as how they are governed, financed, and operate. In this concluding chapter (Chap. 8), we also explore some of the challenges that are raised by what we have learned for those interested in doing further mapping of black spots networks, for those involved in law enforcement, for those concerned with globalization's impact on ideas regarding sovereignty, and for the relevance of the new economic geography to the illicit economy.

Throughout the book, we use examples from the 80 in-depth case studies and their updates that are listed in Table 1.1. The data that have resulted from asking the same questions of each case form the basis for the various percentages and tables found across the chapters. Readers interested in specific black spots can contact the authors for copies of those specific cases. We welcome others using the coding manual to do their own in-depth case studies, to update a particular case of interest to them, or to report on experiences that they may have had on the ground in a particular black spot or black spots network. In this volume, we are laying the foundation for the study of black spots; it is intended to be the beginning of the process of rethinking sovereignty and the global economy.

REFERENCES

Adams, Jackson, and Mohamad Albakajai. 2016. Cyberspace: A New Threat to the Sovereignty of the State. *Management Studies* 4 (6): 256–265.
Adelman, Jonathan. 2014. Modeling Insecurity Flow Dynamics in Response to Degradation of Illicit Groups' Safe Havens. Paper Presented at the Annual Meeting of the International Studies Association, Toronto, Canada, March 26–29.
Benavides, E. Ben. 2015. *Open Source Intelligence (OSInt) 2ool Kit on the Go.* Online Book, Creative Commons.
Calvery, Jennifer Shasky. 2012. Combating Transnational Organized Crime: International Money Laundering as a Threat to Our Financial System. Statement before the Subcommittee on Crime, Terrorism, and Homeland Security, Committee on the Judiciary, United States House of Representatives, February 8.
Crane, David M. 2008. Dark Corners: The West African Joint Criminal Enterprise. *International Studies Review* 10: 387–391.
George, Alexander L. 1979. Case Studies and Theory Development: The Method of Structured, Focused Comparison. In *Diplomacy: New Approaches to History, Theory, and Policy*, ed. P.G. Lauren. New York: Free Press.
George, Alexander L., and Andrew Bennett. 2005. *Case Studies and Theory Development in the Social Sciences.* Cambridge, MA: MIT Press.
Levitsky, Melvyn. 2008. Dealing with Black Spots of Crime and Terror: Conclusions and Recommendations. *International Studies Review* 10: 392–395.
Miraglia, P., R. Ochoa, and I. Briscoe. 2012. Transnational Organised Crime and Fragile States. OECD Development Cooperation Working Papers, Paris.

Naim, Moises. 2005. *Illicit: How Smugglers, Traffickers, and Copycats Are Hijacking the Global Economy.* New York: Anchor Books.

Rastler, John. (2013) *Don't Forget the Drugs: The Impact of Plan Colombia's Cocaine Flows on US National Security.* Master's Thesis, Hertie School of Governance, Berlin.

Roberts, Elise. 2016. Notes from Marseille, Rotterdam, and Marbella. Memo, Mapping Global Insecurity Project, Moynihan Institute of Global Affairs, July 23.

Spencer, Bree. 2011. Akwesasne: A Complex Challenge to US Northern Security. *National Strategy Forum* (Special Issue), 20 (3 Summer): 45–50.

Stanislawski, Bartosz H. 2006. Black Spots: Insecurity Beyond the Horizon. Unpublished Doctoral Dissertation, Maxwell School, Syracuse University (Retrieved from ProQuest Political Science. UMI Number: 3251822).

———. 2011. Black Spots: Breeding Grounds for Terrorism and Transnational Crime. *National Strategy Forum* (Special Issue), 20 (3 Summer): 5–10.

Stoutzenberger, Timothy and Marc Barnett. 2016. Trafficking Trends in the Migrant Market. Paper presented at the annual meeting of the International Studies Association, Atlanta, March.

Strange, Susan. 2010. *The Retreat of the State: The Diffusion of Power in the World.* Cambridge: Cambridge University Press.

Van Schendel, Willem. 2005. Spaces of Engagement: How Borderlands, Illicit Flows, and Territorial States Interlock. In *Illicit Flows and Criminal Things: States, Borders, and the Other Side of Globalization,* ed. Willem van Schendel and Itty Abraham. Bloomington: Indiana University Press.

Walker, Philip. 2011. The World's Most Dangerous Borders: Afghanistan and Pakistan. *Foreign Policy,* June 24.

PART I

Theoretical Foundations

CHAPTER 2

Geopolitics and Transnational Crime

How do those engaged in transnational crime view the world? Suppose we could interview the leadership of such organizations and ask them to provide us with a map of the world through their eyes, what would it look like? Would it include states and their border crossings; be focused around places where illegal goods are produced, transported, or distributed; be defined by traditional trading routes; showcase areas that are safe havens and generally outside the reach of law enforcement; display spaces where potential commodities and employees are available; and/or delineate zones of influence and who governs them? Although such maps are implied in discussions of transnational crime, surprisingly little attention has been paid to the geopolitics of the illicit global economy (Keefe 2013). In fact, generally these areas are not studied until a major uptick in crime or a security breach has occurred. For example, consider the highlighting of the Federally Administered Tribal Areas (or FATA region) in Pakistan during the US-Afghan War post-9/11 or of Hezbollah Territory in Lebanon after the war with Israel in 2006. What can we learn about the world as those involved in transnational crime envision it by examining the 80 black spots we currently have studied as part of the Mapping Global Insecurity Project? After all, as Neocleous (2003: 418) observed, "the earth has no political form. We need to ... appreciate the political function of maps in constructing rather than merely reproducing the world and in creating rather than merely tracing borders." Maps represent interpretations of what counts geographically to their creators.

© The Author(s) 2020   15
S. S. Brown, M. G. Hermann, *Transnational Crime and Black
Spots*, International Political Economy Series,
https://doi.org/10.1057/978-1-137-49670-6_2

BLACK SPOTS AS GEOPOLITICAL BUILDING BLOCKS

Typically, geopolitical maps are built around states, often noting topographical terrain along with the borders defining the territory belonging to the state as well as its capitol and large cities. And much of the study of what happens in the world takes a state-based perspective. Indeed, the theories and debates common in international relations are focused on the interactions among states. We use states' names—the US, Russia, China, and Germany—or their capitals—Washington, Moscow, Beijing, and Berlin, respectively—in discussing what is going on in the world. But what about non-state actors—multinational corporations, regional and international organizations, transnational non-governmental organizations, transnational criminal organizations, terrorist organizations, and insurgent organizations—who seem to be playing an ever-increasing role in what is happening? How do they see the world; what does their map look like? As Strange (2010: xv) has commented, "it is imperative to look seriously at the power exercised by authorities other than states. Not only have such collectives brought about structural changes in world production … they continue to constrain options open for states."

The purpose of this book is to map the world through the eyes of those non-state actors involved in transnational criminal operations. Specifically, we are interested in learning more about the locations that they use in carrying out their activities as well as the ways these places help them to exploit the constraints states try to impose on them. Can we trace the flows of illegal commodities through knowledge of such a map? In other words, is there a logic to the design of the locations that such organizations choose to operate from that facilitates the production and flow of what is produced as well as thwarts the laws set up by the world composed of states? Why do those engaged in transnational criminal activities choose such places as Urosevac, Kosovo; the Kodori Gorge, Georgia; Abu Kamal, Syria; the Wa State, Myanmar; Kashgar, China; the Shinkolobwe Mine in the Democratic Republic of the Congo; the tri-border area where Algeria, Mali, and Niger intersect; the Darien Jungle, Panama; or the Akwesasne Reservation on the border between the US and Canada in which to operate and to engage in the export of narcotics, illegal weapons, undocumented people, stolen natural resources, terrorist activities, and so forth?

We will use Williams' (2001: 106) definition of organizations involved in transnational criminal activities. He notes that they are the "illicit counterparts of multinational corporations" with their activities thought of as "commerce by other means." Like multinational corporations, they are engaged in profit maximization and, thus, in seeking geographic locations from which to operate that are particularly "congenial and can function as a staging area or transshipment point or even a base of operations" (Keefe 2013: 88). Although there has been a recognition of the possible existence of such geographic locations—note the use of terms such as 'geopolitical black holes' (Naim 2005), 'criminal enclaves' (Sullivan 2013), 'states within states' (Lamb 2008), and 'dark corners' (Crane 2008)—these places have received relatively little systematic study. Given that some estimates put the illicit global economy as presently accounting for between 15% and 20% of the world's GDP, "you would think that tallying the major geographic centers of this thriving shadow market would be an easy and uncontroversial exercise" (Keefe 2013: 88).

So what do we mean by location or place? Geographers talk about place as a "natural location that has social and psychological significance insofar as it grounds political interests and projects in the settings of everyday life" (Agnew 2009: 35). Places facilitate the building of local to global relationships that, with current access to transnational capital and distance-spanning technologies, allow sub-national political units to provide governance activities to citizens that are usually reserved for and monopolized by states. In other words, places are generally locations in geopolitical space that are linked with other sites around a specific activity or set of activities. They have borders, they have rules, and they offer protection and other services to their residents. As Sullivan (2013) observed, they offer a kind of sovereignty to those residing in the place. Indeed, "politics … is constituted geographically out of place-making activities in which the national is only part of the overall spatial architecture" (Agnew 2009: 39). Consider the range of types of places that have been identified as 'sovereign' entities across history from the city-state to the pirate island to the feudal castle to the tribal village.

We build here on Guttmann's (1973) ideas about the linkage between notions of territory and those of political power—or, in other words, ideas about statehood and national sovereignty. Like him, our focus is on the balance between an emphasis on security and stability and an emphasis on opportunity in considering how important notions of a specific territory are at any point in time. An argument can be made that across history we see an oscillation between these two. At times stability and 'secure borders' (territory) have the upper hand while at other times 'opportunity' comes to the fore and we have a movement toward escaping borders and boundaries and expanding one's view and activities (political power). In many respects, the places where those engaged in transnational crime locate exemplify this oscillation. An examination of the 80 such locations studied here shows that criminals do, indeed, seek places where they have authority, are in charge of security, and can offer some stability to the local residents. But they also look for places that provide them with easy access to markets and the redundancies necessary to deal with regulations intended to prevent them from taking advantage of these markets. In effect, they are interested in some form of territorial sovereignty while also being able to take advantage of the opportunities offered by globalization.

EXPLOITING TENSIONS BETWEEN STATE SOVEREIGNTY AND GLOBALIZATION

In fact, those engaged in transnational crime do appear to take advantage of the tensions that we have just described between security/stability and opportunity in their choices of places to locate. As we discussed in Chap. 1, 90% of the black spots studied so far are near international borders. Indeed, 56% of these are also near an internal border—a provincial or regional boundary. These non-state actors have become adept at using border areas to their advantage, exploiting the jurisdictional tensions that arise between state (or territorial) sovereignty and globalization. As Speth and Haas (2006) have noted, sovereignty is no longer a 'sanctuary' for states. In effect, globalization has decreased the ability to control what crosses borders in either direction. The argument is made that competition now is for market share not territory (Strange 2010; Shelley 2014). Organizations engaged in transnational criminal activities exploit this increased porousness of borders by locating where they can easily move back and forth between states and link with others involved in similar enterprises. Having places along borders provides such organizations with a certain degree of invisibility as they fit in with all the other movement occurring around them.

Abraham and van Schendel (2005: 25) refer to these areas as borderlands—"spaces formed by the intersection of multiple competing authorities" that straddle an international border. They argue that such locations almost by definition provide opportunities for those engaged in transnational crime and pose a constant threat to state governments. Consider the fact that 75% of the 80 black spots lie along traditional trading routes—the Silk Road, the Balkan Route, the Trans-Saharan trade routes—which have been used historically to define the borders of countries, often geographically dividing up peoples and cultures and making the border into a borderland. Then there are border cities like Tabatinga, Brazil and Leticia, Colombia—the Avenue of Friendship dividing them serves as the international border. Called the Tabatinga-Leticia Corridor, it is a major gateway for drug and resource smuggling in the Amazon River Basin.

Consider as well the geographically challenged borders that run through gorges, along mountain ranges, in deserts, and even through the middle of rivers. All are difficult for state authorities to police and, in some cases, it is even hard to define exactly where the border is. Some 72% of the black spots studied so far are found in these geographically challenged border areas—25% in mountainous areas, 24% in deserts, and 23% in jungles. For example, there is the Fergana Valley in Central Asia; Rafah in the Sinai Desert; and Manaus, Brazil in the Amazon Rainforest. Another type of geographically challenged area is that where the borders of three countries come together at one spot or a black spot crosses over a border. This challenge is geopolitical as it focuses on who exactly has authority and sovereignty. One such tri-border area is at the corner of Algeria, Mali, and Niger in Africa; another is the Ciudad del Este tri-border region in Latin America (Paraguay, Brazil, and Argentina). Then there is the Akwesasne Reservation that crosses the border between the US and Canada and the Darien Jungle that crosses the border between Panama and Colombia. "The political geography of a borderland is never static" (van Schendel 2005: 57). Indeed, as Rabkin (2004: 23) has argued, sovereignty equals the "authority to establish what law is binding...in a given territory" be that by state authority or that of an organization engaged in transnational criminal activities.

This transnationality of border areas is not a new phenomenon. Globalization and its push to keep borders open has probably only sped up this process. Some 60% of the black spots under study have been in existence 60-70 years if not longer, being remnants of trading routes that have been there for ages. Many of the other 40% have appeared as the result of the demise of the Soviet Union and the redrawing of states and borders. There is evidence that many of these were functioning as black spots even during Soviet times. Indeed, 72% of the identified black spots have been fairly stable across time even with attempts by state authorities to halt their activities. The Abu Kamal black spot on the border of Syria with Iraq fits into the other 28%. It has pulsed across time, being closed down and then coming back to life as those in charge changed. A US Captain, whose task it was during the US-Iraq War to close down this border crossing that was allowing jihadists to cross from Syria into Iraq, complained that it was a waste of time. He observed that the transnational criminal and terrorist organizations they had just chased out would be back in full operation in a couple of weeks after the American military left. And, indeed, this black spot became the border crossing that allowed ISIS to build a caliphate between Syria and Iraq in 2014.

Those involved in transnational criminal operations use the opaqueness of the borderlands and the black spots located in such areas to provide them with a semblance of invisibility, to cloak what they are about. Or, at the least, it lets them cross a border should state authorities move to make them, their location, and/or their activities visible. The borderlands provide them with a cover—they can easily disappear into another jurisdiction. We have already referenced the Tabatinga-Leticia Corridor which provides ease of movement across the border from Colombia to Brazil and vice versa—all one has to do is cross a street that separates the two cities. Consider also the Nogales, Mexico black spot and the black spot involving the Tohono O'odham Reservation which is located on the US border with Mexico. The Nogales, Mexico black spot is highly visible; the Tohono O'odham Reservation, roughly 40 miles away from Nogales, is almost invisible. Movement between the two is relatively easy. Indeed, some 44% of the black spots under study here move back and forth between being visible and invisible using the borderlands as a cover until state authorities tire of focusing on them and move to another spot.

Taking Advantage of Weak State Authority

In addition to exploiting the tensions between sovereignty and globalization by setting up operations in borderlands, those engaged in transnational criminal activities also appear to select safe havens within states with weak institutions, those that have difficulty providing goods and services as well as policing and protection to citizens in all parts of their 'sovereign territory.' Several studies have found a relationship between weakness in the rule of law and the prevalence of organized crime within a state's borders (Buscaglia and Van Dijk 2003; Sung 2004; Van Dijk 2008; Van Dijk and Spapens 2014). The correlation in one study was -.79 (Van Dijk and Spapens 2014: 219). The weaker the police institutions and criminal justice systems, the more organized crime flourished. Examining our 80 black spots, we find them located in 44% of the countries noted in these studies to have weak rule of law but in only 11% of those with strong policing and justice systems. In the studies just referenced, countries like Serbia, Pakistan, and Mexico ranked among the weakest in rule of law and among the highest in 'composite organized crime.' All three have more than one black spot among our 80.

Note, however, as the UN Office on Drugs and Crime (UNODC 2010) has observed, these groups and organizations are interested in locating in weak but not failed states. They want some of the advantages of a "functioning state such as modern infrastructure and communications, a banking system, and enough rule of law to make life generally predictable" (Keefe 2013: 102). In fact, using recent fragile states indices (see Fund for Peace 2015), we find that 62% of the 80 black spots studied to date are in states that would be classified as weak—they offer some risk but are not at the most risky or 'alert' stage. In other words, these states show signs of weakness but also offer some predictability. Only 9% of the black spots are in the least fragile states; the other 29% are located in 'as if' or 'almost' states like the FATA region in Pakistan. As observed previously, the Pakistani government has dealt with this area as if it were a separate state. Consider also South Ossetia on the border between Georgia and Russia and parts of the Democratic Republic of the Congo far from the capital like Lubumbashi and Kisangani. These areas are building their own institutions and during such a process organizations engaged in transnational crime can become part of that political authority.

Then there is the matter of corruption. "Corruption is not only a facilitator for ... illicit non-state actors but provides an enabling environment" making possible the purchase of cooperation from a range of officials to ensure the ability of the non-state actors to remain operational (Shelley 2014: 86). Some have likened this to the 'Robin Hood curse' (e.g., Zartman and Aronson 2005: 269; Peters 2012: 8; Shelley 2014: 86). No one really wants a conflict to end if, as a consequence, it puts a stop to the provision of goods and services to the citizenry who are benefiting from such activities. In effect, corruption makes feasible the cross-border movement that facilitates those engaged in transnational criminal activities plying their trade(s) and keeping their safe havens provided for and safe. An examination of the 80 black spots studied here indicates that there is strong evidence of corruption in 90% of the cases. Discussions in the open source materials on which the in-depth case studies are based often focus on how easy it is to corrupt those important in limiting what such illicit non-state actors want to do. Studying a recent Transparency International survey of the perceptions of corruption in states around the globe indicates that 44% of these black spots are found in the top one-third of states perceived as most corrupt, 41% in the second third, and only 15% in those states perceived as least corrupt (https://www.transparency.org/news/feature/corruption_perceptions_index_2016). In other words, organizations involved in transnational criminal activities find safe havens where corruption is an important facet of how politics and the economy run.

Such organizations also appear to want to locate their operations where they will have access to cheap and exploitable labor. But, perhaps even more important, they seem interested in locations where they can control what happens and where there will be little interference from state authority. For these reasons, many argue that these organizations seek areas where there is little or less state capacity, in other words, less access to jobs and public services (e.g., UNODC 2010; Keefe 2013). "In the absence of the state, non-state actors step in … offering services to citizens to advance their objectives, which are not just the welfare of the citizens" but the making of "major inroads with populations who otherwise might be repelled by their violence" and the nature of their operations (Shelley 2014: 80). Some 69% of the black spots under study are found in such areas. The illicit non-state actors offer jobs for much better pay than is often available and some stability, but under their control. Consider what Hezbollah does for the citizenry in Southern Lebanon—'its territory.' It is the government there, it is the rule of law. Then there is the Shinkolobwe Mine in the Democratic Republic of the Congo—a closed mine that is a relatively easy source of illicit cobalt, nickel, copper, and uranium and is surrounded by 10,000 potential miners in small villages. Corrupt public officials and transnational criminals have kept the mine functioning. As one miner said, "we do this because it is the only way we can make money."

Some 86% of the 80 black spots under study are located near where there has been a recent conflict, be it a war, civil war, or violence between opposition groups. These data, too, support the notion of choosing locations where there is weak state governance and little law enforcement. Moreover, the economies in these areas are often in shambles and there is very little legitimate employment. Desperate to support their families, people are easy prey for participating in transnational criminal activities that locate in their communities and offer them something to do. Such locations also facilitate the trafficking in people as there is often a flow of displaced persons. We note that 53% of the black spots located near a conflict zone are also involved in trafficking people. Such trafficking can be to facilitate illegal immigration, prostitution, or indentured servitude. The Balkans area has a number of such black spots in Kosovo and Serbia as well as Bosnia and Herzegovina as have the Middle East and North Africa. El Arish in the Egyptian Sinai is an example of one such black spot trafficking in people from the failed and fragile states in Africa to Israel and Europe.

Taking Advantage of Differences in Interpretations of What Is Illegal

Of interest here is "a distinction between what states consider to be legitimate ('legal') and what people involved in transnational criminal activities consider to be legitimate ('licit'). Many transnational movements of people, commodities, and ideas are illegal because they defy the norms and rules of formal political authority, but they are quite acceptable, 'licit,' in the eyes of participants in these transactional flows" (Abraham and van Schendel 2005: 4). In effect, what passes as criminal in one state may be legal in another and vice versa. Think about US corporations that locate their 'official' headquarters outside the country to avoid certain taxes; the fact that raising coca is a staple means of employment in Ecuador but illegal in the US; that people seek political asylum but do so by paying 'smugglers' to help them cross the borders; and that ships use flags of convenience such as those of Liberia and Panama to avoid having to meet certain regulations. And then there are the illicit-licit transformations that occur when money made from smuggling drugs is used to create a legally, registered company or stolen diamonds are accompanied by a provenance that says they are legal and meet all regulations. In effect, "prohibition is at the hub of transnational crime... More than any other form of state intervention, it is prohibition that has a particularly destabilizing effect upon the whole sphere of the illegal" (Serrano and Toro 2002: 15). State regulations make definitions of what is licit and illicit situational.

Those engaged in transnational criminal activities locate in places that allow them not only access to particular commodities, people, and ideas but that also provide them access to markets where their goods are likely to be appreciated even if considered illegal. "Never in history has there been a black market defeated from the supply side. From Prohibition to prostitution, from gambling to recreational drugs, the story is the same. Supply-side controls act, much like price supports in agriculture, to encourage production and increased profits" (Naylor 2002: 11). Not surprisingly, illicit non-state actors locate in places that facilitate the production, transportation, and distribution—the flows—of illicit goods and services to markets where they are prohibited *but* desired. Generally these destination markets have been in countries in the developed world.

Illegal drugs are a focus of 80% of the black spots that we have studied as they facilitate the flow of such commodities into Europe and the US. For example, the network for getting heroin to Europe follows the Silk Road trading route established so long ago. The black spots become the production, transportation links, and distribution centers that move the illegal drugs to market. Note also that 74% of the 80 black spots are involved in transactions having to do with conventional weapons; these areas tend to surround conflict zones and places where arms are sanctioned or embargoed. And 61% are involved in the smuggling/trafficking of people with the flows typically moving from the Global South to the Global North. Almost 40% of the 80 black spots deal in trafficking of a variety of household items including art and jewelry. Generally these networks focus on markets where there is recognition of the value of specific goods even if fake. Some 39% of the black spots are involved in the harvesting and smuggling of natural resources; the largest network for this activity is located in Africa. Moreover, 40% of the black spots that find themselves strategically located across the globe are engaged in money laundering—that is, helping those in other black spots make their illicit money licit.

Public acceptance of state regulations appears to be an important factor in how successful those involved in transnational crime are going to be in finding markets. Thus, for example, the less acceptable citizens find state prohibition against the use of marijuana, the greater the opportunity for those engaged in transnational criminal operations to exploit the situation and find a clientele. State borders stand as the last line of defense in asserting control and enforcing regulations. If those engaged in transnational crime use a black spots network to breach international borders, they challenge the territorial notion of a state's sovereignty and its rule of law. "The border stands precariously between the legitimate sovereignty of the state and a shadowy outer world of more or less organized crime" (van Schendel

2005: 40). Such seems particularly the case if there are citizens of a state who do not accept or do not understand the reasoning behind the regulations the government is promulgating.

Consider the US farmers interested in having Mexican and Central American help in planting or harvesting their crops as the US government puts up a border wall and reinforces its border patrol. In such cases, there are illicit non-state actors located in areas across the border ready to facilitate the flow of those needed for such tasks, no questions asked and money exchanges hands. Or note the following observation in *The Economist* (2015: 37): "Dubai, the biggest entrepot in the Gulf, has long been the back door through which smugglers have entered Iran to swap goods and cash in breach of Western sanctions." With the P5+1 Iranian nuclear agreement, these same 'smugglers' planned on becoming the front door too. These so-called border games (Andreas 2000) bring into sharp focus how easy it is with a black spots network to take advantage of differences in definitions of what is legal/licit and illegal/illicit between state authorities and their populations. Knowledge of how to play these games is inherent in the choice of a black spot on the part of those involved in transnational crime and in the linkages they forge with other black spots.

Selecting the 'Right' Safe Haven

In the previous sections, we have been building a case that those involved in transnational criminal activities look for certain types of places from which to operate. Their map of the world seems to take into account international borders and the ease of movement across them, access to traditional trading routes where activity is fairly constant, areas in weakly governed states where the citizenry is not well served by the government and can be incentivized to give authority to other than the government, locations where corruption is endemic, places that afford some challenge geographically and, thus, reduce the effectiveness of law enforcement, and areas that are nearby recent or current conflict zones where the people are forced to move as a result of the conflict. But we learned in doing the in-depth case studies that there is more to their map and it is to that 'more' we turn now.

Having found a general location—near a border, with weak state government, where corruption is endemic, an area geographically challenged with regard to effective policing, and a place with access to potential employees—how do those engaged in transnational crime narrow down their selection to a specific place? What else are they looking for? The 80 black spots that we have studied provide us with some clues. Surprisingly, there is no preference for a rural or urban setting; indeed, the largest percentage of these black spots involved a mixed setting or one that melded from urban into rural. The percentages are urban 30%, rural 32%, and mixed 38%. Some examples of black spots in urban areas are the Scampia/Secondigliano neighborhoods in Naples, Italy; Netanya, Israel; and Kashgar, China. Examples of rural choices are the Kodori Gorge, Georgia; the Bekaa Valley, Lebanon; and the Chuy Valley, Kazakhstan. The mixed terrain generally is in mountainous or forested areas like Goma in the Democratic Republic of the Congo near the Nyiragonga Volcano or the Tabatinga-Leticia Corridor on the border between Colombia and Brazil in the Amazon Rainforest. These data suggest that other aspects of the setting may be more important than the site's rural-urban character.

The black spots that we studied here tend to be located in places that have a heterogeneous ethnic community—two-thirds of the choices were for such locations. Ethnic heterogeneity is highly likely in border areas where the majority of these black spots are found. And heterogeneity facilitates the mingling of different types of people with no one necessarily standing out. Moreover, such heterogeneity presents the opportunity for linkages among black spots composed of similar ethnic and tribal groups and for the organizations involved to forge alliances. Such places make passing through without notice feasible. Ciudad del Este located in the tri-border area between Paraguay, Argentina, and Brazil—the place that began our project—is one such black spot that often hosts representatives of Hezbollah, the Chinese triads, and Japanese yakuza as well as Latin American transnational criminal organizations like the FARC (see, e.g., Cirino et al. 2004; Shelley 2014). The original heterogeneity of the area results from decades of immigration from conflict zones in the Middle East and Europe. It was (and still is?) considered "a paradise for fugitives on the run" (Shelley et al. 2005: 59).

It is noteworthy that the heterogeneous ethnic settings bring with them a degree of conflict. Some 60% of the heterogeneous black spots under study are conflictual in nature. Generally, such conflict is embedded in the setting which begs for some group or organization to arbitrate and control it. And it suggests that violence may be a way of life. Interestingly, when such places become black spots, those organizations choosing to locate in them use both the diversity in ethnicity and their own willingness to use violence to bring others into line. Indeed, 96% of the time any violence used is politically motivated and intended to insure control over the black spot and its residents. In many ways, through such behavior, the black spot becomes the 'sovereign territory' of the organization assuming political authority over the area. As Agnew (2009: 206) has observed in studying the effects of globalization, it "seems to be more geographically differentiating than homogenizing in its effects." At least for those engaged in transnational criminal activities, sovereignty has become a local phenomenon.

Access to transportation is also critically important in the selection of a place. There need to be multiple ways to exit the space and redundancies so that there is no dependence on only one way of ensuring commodities get to market. Roads, almost regardless of condition, are important—95% of the black spots under study are linked to the outside world by roads. Some 55% of these black spots have access to numerous roads. The other 40% have access to at least one road. The latter tend to be found in black spots in Asia and Africa. Next in importance are airports even if they are make-shift runways; 86% of the black spots studied here have some type of airport nearby. Also important is access to rivers. Some 67% of the 80 black spots are on or near water. Indeed, 41% have access to harbors and a wide range of freight and ships at their disposal. Only 42% of the black spots under study are located along or near railroads. Of the 80 black spots, 77% are located where there is access to *at least three* of these modes of transportation—generally roads, air, and water. Organizations involved in transnational crime choose places that offer multiple ways of coming and going from the area.

But, perhaps most essential, the places selected as black spots need to provide access to multiple kinds of illegal activities. The best places appear to be those that facilitate engaging in a range of activities and the possibility of trading off among activities if law enforcement gets too close or demand decreases with regard to a particular item or in a specific area. Note that 98% of the black spots under study are, in fact, in areas providing those in charge with multiple activities—for example, trafficking in drugs, people, and weapons, *not* just one of these. Having multiple activities allows organizations a selection in their choices of which other black spots to link with as they move their products to market and the ability to easily switch their focus should law enforcement get too close.

CONCLUSION

Figure 2.1 displays geographically where the 80 black spots that are part of this research are located in the world. Remember that Table 1.1 in Chap. 1 listed the black spots we are studying here by region of the world. Figure 2.1 presents the reader with a map of their locations and begins to define the map of the world as viewed through the eyes of those engaged in transnational criminal activities as well as to indicate how these organizations are using state territoriality and notions of state sovereignty to their advantage.

This chapter has begun the process of developing the theory behind how those engaged in transnational criminal activities map the world. Examining 80 particular safe havens that these organizations have adopted as places in which to locate their operations, we have discovered some characteristics of such black spots as we call them. We have learned that these black spots do, in fact, defy the Westphalian state system. Indeed, they are viewed by those engaged in transnational criminal activities as their sovereign territory—as areas that they govern and over which they have control.

These black spots tend to be in places where there is a lack of effective state governance—on borders, in fragile or weak states where corruption is common, near conflict zones. And they are in places that those involved

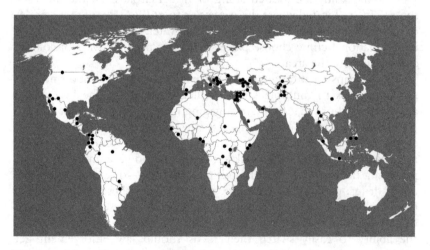

Fig. 2.1 Map of locations of 80 black spots in study

in illegal activities can control by themselves—that facilitate them creating their own informal rules and regulations and, as a result, providing governance for the place and its citizenry. The places afford such organizations a range of illegal activities and maximize the organization's opportunities to make a profit. Moreover, the locations offer these organization not only redundancies in what can be smuggled/trafficked/sold/laundered, but they also offer multiple ways to get illegal goods to market. Generalizing from what we have found, black spots (1) appear in areas that lack effective recognized state governance, (2) are controlled by illicit organizations that institute and institutionalize their own rules governing the area, and (3) facilitate the production, transport, and/or distribution of illicit transnational activities.

Globalization has granted organizations engaged in transnational criminal activities the same kind of freedom it has afforded multinational corporations. With the improvements in transportation, finance, and communications that have resulted from globalization, organizations engaged in transnational criminal operations are able to build the networks needed to maximize their profits. But, perhaps more importantly, globalization has enabled these organizations to identify and take control of locations—black spots—that allow for flexibility should law enforcement come too close. Globalization has given such organizations alternatives to interdiction. And instead of leading to a global governance system as predicted by its advocates, globalization has made possible the increased relevance of local areas. "Globalization is not working to produce a singular world but rather a much more differentiated one"; indeed, "globalization has been accompanied by a seemingly countervailing process of political-economic fragmentation" (Agnew 2009: 213). It is within this much more differentiated world that black spots and organizations involved in transnational crime exist and operate.

REFERENCES

Abraham, Itty, and Willem van Schendel. 2005. Introduction. In *Illicit Flows and Criminal Things: States, Borders, and the Other Side of Globalization*, ed. Willem van Schendel and Itty Abraham. Bloomington: Indiana University Press.

Agnew, John. 2009. *Globalization and Sovereignty*. New York: Roman and Littlefield.

Andreas, Peter. 2000. *Border Games: Policing the US-Mexico Divide*. Ithaca: Cornell University Press.

Buscaglia, E., and Jan Van Dijk. 2003. Controlling Organized Crime and Corruption in the Public Sector. *Journal on Crime and Society* 3 (1 & 2): 3–34.

Cirnio, John A., Silvano L. Elizondo, and Geoffrey Wawro. 2004. Latin American Security Challenges: A Collaborative Inquiry from North and South. In *Latin America's Lawless Areas and Failed States: An Analysis of the New Threats*, ed. Paul D. Taylor. Newport: Naval War College Press.

Crane, David M. 2008. Dark Corners: The West African Joint Criminal Enterprise. *International Studies Review* 10: 387–391.

Fund for Peace. 2015. *2015 Fragile States Index*. Washington, DC: Fund for Peace.

Guttmann, Jean. 1973. *The Significance of Territory*. Charlottesville: University of Virginia Press.

Keefe, Patrick Radden. 2013. The Geography of Badness: Mapping the Hubs of the Illicit Global Economy. In *Convergence: Illicit Networks and National Security in the Age of Globalization*, ed. Michael Miklaucic and Jacqueline Brewer. Washington, DC: National Defense University Press.

Lamb, Robert D. 2008. *Ungoverned Areas and Threats from Safe Havens*. Washington, DC: Office of the Under Secretary of Defense.

Naim, Moises. 2005. *Illicit: How Smugglers, Traffickers, and Copycats Are Hijacking the Global Economy*. New York: Anchor Books.

Naylor, R.T. 2002. *Wages of Crime: Black Markets, Illegal Finance, and the Underworld Economy*. Ithaca: Cornell University Press.

Neocleous, Mark. 2003. *Imagining the State*. Maidenhead: Open University Press.

Peters, Gretchen. 2012. Haqqani Network Financing: The Evolution of an Industry. Harmony Program, The Combatting Terrorism Center, West Point.

Rabkin, Jeremy A. 2004. *The Case for Sovereignty: Why the World Should Welcome American Independence*. Washington, DC: AEI Press.

Serrano, Monica, and Maria Celia Toro. 2002. From Drug Trafficking to Transnational Organized Crime in Latin America. In *Transnational Organized Crime and International Security*, ed. Mats Berdal and Monica Serrano. Boulder: Lynne Reiner.

Shelley, Louise I. 2014. *Dirty Entanglements: Corruption, Crime, and Terrorism*. Cambridge: Cambridge University Press.

Shelley, Louise I., John T. Picarelli, Allison Irby, Douglas M. Hart, Patricia A. Craig-Hart, Phil Williams, Steven Simon, Nabi Abdullaev, Bartosz Stanislawski, and Laura Covill. 2005. *Methods and Motives: Exploring Links Between Transnational Organized Crime and International Terrorism*. Washington, DC: US Department of Justice.

Speth, James Gustave, and Peter M. Haas. 2006. *Global Environmental Governance*. Washington, DC: Island Press.

Strange, Susan. 2010. *The Retreat of the State: The Diffusion of Power in the World Economy*. Cambridge: Cambridge University Press.

Sullivan, John P. 2013. How Illicit Networks Impact Sovereignty. In *Convergence: Illicit Networks and National Security in the Age of Globalization*, ed. Michael Miklaucic and Jacqueline Brewer. Washington, DC: National Defense University Press.

Sung, H.E. 2004. State Failure, Economic Failure, and Predatory Organized Crime: A Comparative Analysis. *Journal of Research in Crime and Delinquency* 41 (1): 111–129.

The Economist. 2015. Dubai's Bright Prospects: The Nuclear Deal's Other Winner, July 23.

United Nations Office on Drugs and Crime (UNODC). 2010. *The Globalization of Crime: A Transnational Organized Crime Threat Assessment*. Vienna: UNODC.

Van Dijk, Jan. 2008. *World of Crime: Breaking the Silence on Problems of Crime, Justice, and Development Across the World*. Thousand Oaks: Sage Publications.

Van Dijk, Jan, and Toine Spapens. 2014. Transnational Organized Crime Networks. In *Handbook of Transnational Crime and Justice*, ed. Philip Reichel and Jay Albanese, 2nd ed. Los Angeles: Sage Publications.

Van Schendel, Willem. 2005. Spaces of Engagement: How Borderlands, Illicit Flows, and Territorial States Interlock. In *Illicit Flows and Criminal Things: States, Borders, and the Other Side of Globalization*, ed. Willem van Schendel and Itty Abraham. Bloomington: Indiana University Press.

Williams, Phil. 2001. Crime, Black Markets and Money Laundering. In *Managing Global Issues: Lessons Learned*, ed. Chaneal de Jonge Oudraat and P.J. Simmons. New York: Carnegie Endowment for International Peace.

Zartman, William, and Cynthia T. Aronson. 2005. *Rethinking the Economics of War: The Intersection of Need, Creed, and Greed*. Washington, DC: Woodrow Wilson Center Press.

CHAPTER 3

The New Economic Geography and the Illicit Economy

In the previous chapter, we began exploring the world through the eyes of those engaged in transnational criminal activities and examined the effects that geopolitics has on their choices of locations from which to operate. Here we apply lessons from the new economic geography literature (hereafter NEG) to how locational decisions are made. NEG focuses on explaining the geographical unevenness of the economic landscape and the dynamics of spatial clustering (or dispersion) of economic activities or what is known in the literature as economic agglomeration. NEG provides fresh insights into where illicit actors are likely to cluster to produce, transport, and distribute illegal goods and services. In effect, through ideas concerning the economics of agglomeration, NEG alerts us to where black spots might form and work together to influence the nature of the illicit global economy.

BASIC TENETS OF THE NEW ECONOMIC GEOGRAPHY

Before Paul Krugman's pioneering work in the early 1990s, economic theory had difficulty explaining the spatial patterning of economic activity. Utilizing standard microeconomic assumptions, the Krugman-inspired NEG attempts to describe the forces driving the concentration of economic activity—or agglomeration—versus those forces that dictate spatial dispersion. In NEG, natural features in the landscape, known as 'first nature effects,' provide an initial catalyst for economic agglomerations.

© The Author(s) 2020
S. S. Brown, M. G. Hermann, *Transnational Crime and Black Spots*, International Political Economy Series,
https://doi.org/10.1057/978-1-137-49670-6_3

33

From our discussion of black spots in the previous chapter, think about international borders and traditional trading routes as examples of such first nature effects. While the natural advantages of particular locations may 'catalyze' economic clustering as we noticed in the 80 black spots under study, it is 'second nature' influences that provide the more direct and self-reinforcing drivers of agglomeration (Fujita and Krugman 2004; Fujita and Mori 2005). Where first nature effects initially encourage concentration, second nature influences serve to reinforce the initial clustering. For example, we have observed illicit actors tend to look for black spots on international borders but they go on to choose specific places along these borders that have ready access to roads, rivers, and airports, however crude, as well as places with multiple trafficking and smuggling opportunities. Having access to different modes of transportation and a range of possible illicit activities reinforces the original decision.

Second nature influences undergird the NEG's 'core-periphery' model (Krugman 1991). The model proposes that in the global supply chain of today, incentive compatibility drives firms, their suppliers, and their workers to cluster in centers of manufacturing. Krugman attributes the forces creating this manufacturing core to forward and backward linkages that reflect microeconomic decision making by individuals and firms. Workers (who are also consumers) seek to locate where there are a greater number and variety of goods and jobs while firms prefer to locate with access to the biggest markets. For a firm, it also makes sense to locate in areas where there is easier and cheaper access to the materials and intermediate inputs required for production. Initial clustering of firms and workers (consumers) has the effect of attracting additional participants in order to exploit the advantage of proximity and concentration. At the same time, a periphery remains around the manufacturing core as a result of immobile factors such as farmland, mines, and particular types of less mobile workers (e.g., farmers). And "if forward and backward linkages are strong enough to overcome the centrifugal force" generated by immobile factors and transportation costs, "the economy will develop a core-periphery pattern" (Fujita and Mori 2005: 381).

Likewise, the incentives to exploit forward and backward linkages could arguably motivate those involved in transnational crime to collect in particular locations. Much like customary firms, these individuals and organizations focus on transportation costs, the availability of workers with specific skill sets, and the ease of securing production inputs. But they also seek places where law enforcement is weak, where corruption is endemic, and where they can maximize the probability that their trafficking and smuggling operations will not be impeded on the way to market. It is critical to have access to potential alternative black spots near one's manufacturing core that can be exploited should law enforcement encroach. Note, for example, the dispersal of the black spots used by the FARC organization in Colombia once Plan Colombia went into effect. Once the US and Colombian governments started targeting their drug operations, FARC dispersed its activities to new black spots along the various borders of the country to facilitate ease of movement in and out of the Colombian government's legal jurisdiction (Rastler 2013). Indeed, coca cultivation spread to 23 provinces along Colombia's borders compared to being in only three when Plan Colombia was initiated (Adelman 2014).

Agglomeration need not be limited to a simple core-periphery structure as just described; it can occur at multiple levels of the global economy. Fujita and Krugman (2004) consider three spatial dimensions: international, regional, and urban, all of which are embedded within a unified complex global economy. At the international level, there is the North/South divide, with the core represented by the Global North and the periphery by the Global South. At the regional level, we find industrial clustering. Consider auto-manufacturing in Detroit, the computer industry in Silicon Valley, banking in Switzerland, or tourism in the Caribbean. At the urban or local level, economic clusters form within, for example, malls, downtown districts, and industrial parks. These various levels of agglomeration interrelate to form a comprehensive, spatially defined global economic system.

As with the licit economy, agglomerations can form at multiple levels within the illicit economy as well. At the international level, products tend to originate in black spots within the Global South, while markets predominate within the Global North (Passas 2001). At the regional level, for example, cocaine tends to be produced in the Andean region in Latin America and heroin in the southern parts of Afghanistan; money laundering is big business in places like Dubai; while Guinea Bissau is considered a narco-state. At the urban or local level, we have already discussed Ciudad del Este, in Paraguay on the borders with Brazil and Argentina as the black spot that got our research enterprise going. There are the Scampia and Secondigliano neighborhoods in Naples, Italy, locations that account for a large measure of the smuggling and trafficking of contraband into Western Europe. And there are the linked Rafah cities—one in Egypt and the other a border crossing into the Gaza Strip—and their tunnels that facilitate smuggled goods and services reaching those living in isolated Gaza.

MULTIPLE EQUILIBRIA IN THE NEW ECONOMIC GEOGRAPHY

From a NEG perspective, the rise of agglomerations at various levels of the global economy and the complex interrelationships among their constituent locations comprise a spatial general equilibrium. While such geographical positioning balances the forces of agglomeration and dispersion at a given time, periodic shocks can always disturb this arrangement, generating new spatial equilibria. Often the system exhibits multiple equilibria or, in other words, a multiplicity of potential geographical outcomes with the ultimate arrangement dependent on the reactions of the system's constituent actors. The existence of multiple equilibria infuses the economy with an 'evolutionary propensity' as it takes on new structures (Fujita and Mori 2005).

In the core-periphery framework, new agglomerations will periodically emerge while others shrink or disappear. For instance, workers in the population-expanding periphery may decide to form their own agglomeration because they are located at too great a distance from the core. Some workers and firms from the core may choose to defect and form a new core area at the edge of the periphery because of congestion and competition. Where forces tilt in favor of these new agglomerations and associated spatial restructurings of the system, the latter will always reflect "market potential derived from the underlying economics" (Fujita and Mori 2005: 382).

We suggest that at any given point in time the global pattern of black spots likewise reflects a spatial equilibrium. This physical positioning of black spots periodically shifts in response to market and policy shocks. Such shocks can involve, for instance, attempts at or actual interdictions that disrupt the means of getting a product to market, increased arrests, and a change in regulations that opens up a potential new market. Consider what happened when the US and EU countries became more successful at patrolling the waters off the coast of Somalia; piracy moved from East Africa to West Africa. When Plan Colombia did, indeed, limit cocaine shipments to the US, black spots emerged in Brazil and West Africa that facilitated increased shipments of cocaine to Europe.

Moreover, there seems ample reason to suspect that a constellation of black spots will exhibit multiple equilibria, involving the potential formation of new black spots or the reactivation of 'pulsating' locations. We noted in the previous chapter the black spot at Abu Kamal that is right at the border between Syria and Iraq and its continual pulsing character as the US closed it down during its invasion of Iraq and ISIS reopened it to insure access to oil and other commodities to finance its insurgent activities. We also noted the creation of new black spots with the demise of the Soviet Union and the re-drawing of states and borders.

Another implication of NEG is that agglomerations can defy the traditional boundaries of countries. On one level agglomerations may form around specific cities or regions within states, but they may also arise in the borderlands where two or more national boundaries converge. This tendency to transcend legal boundaries is one of the more noteworthy findings of our study to date. Remember that 90% of the black spots under study are located on or around legal boundaries in order to exploit neighboring jurisdictional discrepancies among states and/or to engage in arbitrage owing to differences in relative prices or legalities governing the commodities of relevance to the illicit actors involved. For agglomerations of illicit activity, location in a border area constitutes one of the catalyzing 'first nature effects' that NEG references. As Keefe (2013: 104) posited, simple geography may dictate that black spots are more likely to succeed in locations with ready access to multiple countries. Such a location diminishes accountability and increases the likelihood of finding "border authorities willing to take a bribe." Such a location may also exploit "a development disparity between neighboring countries and give rise to elevated levels of smuggling" as well as make obvious the "conditions of overlapping or contested authority inherently congenial to transnational organized crime" such as differences in what is prohibited or considered legal (Basu 2013: 324).

FURTHER INSIGHTS FROM THE NEW ECONOMIC GEOGRAPHY

In introducing NEG, we noted the existence of more and less mobile factors. Black spots arguably mirror this mobility/immobility construct with respect to the illicit economy. Mobile factors, by definition, tend to be located in black spots closer to final markets. Immobile factors anchor black spots to particular geographical spaces owing to the geographic specificity of certain illegal products. For instance, we note the spatial structuring observed around illicit drug production. Operations involving the growing and processing of coca leaves are less mobile, constrained by suitable land and climate. Black spots emerge around coca leaf cultivation and production areas such as the Andean region in Latin America because this is where the immobile factors are located. In contrast, marijuana and methamphetamine benefit from more flexible production location patterns. New technologies such as hydroponics for cannabis cultivation and laboratories for meth production facilitate greater mobility. As a result, the production of marijuana and methamphetamine can be located closer to the final markets where most consumers reside (Insulza 2013). In the illicit world, the degree of mobility that characterizes the production and distribution of a given commodity will typically reflect current efforts at interdiction in addition to the traits of the commodity itself. Such conditions may limit the sustainability of certain agglomerations, dispersing black spots and necessitating greater flexibility in the illicit economy.

NEG also suggests how interjurisdictional legal differences can impact decisions regarding location. Those involved in criminal activities are able to engage in arbitrage when they can supply a banned commodity to one country while sourcing it from a country in which the same good is legal or considered part of the 'culture.' Consider the trafficking in heroin from areas in Afghanistan where its use is legal to Europe where the drug is illegal.

Another feature of NEG models is a focus on increasing returns to scale at the level of the firm, which allows for a market structure involving monopolistic competition. Fujita and Krugman (2004: 143) outline the implications of this property: "Firms have market power and use it, but they are assumed to act in a purely unilateral fashion, never trying to organize cartels or even tacitly collude on prices. Every firm has a monopoly on its own distinctive product, but other firms can introduce products that are (imperfect) substitutes for that product." Think about restaurants located in a mall or downtown area that all compete against one another but do so by offering different types of food and even, for example, varieties of Italian cuisine.

Within the literature on illicit trade, the nature of competition remains the source of some debate. There is evidence that those engaged in transnational criminal activities can enjoy significant pricing power. Kopp (2004) characterizes the illegal economic system as a 'non-cartelized oligopoly,' with high transaction costs and high but not insuperable barriers to market entry, the latter generated by risk rather than technology. Yet, Hall (2012: 378) writes, "those cartels that do exist tend to be involved in extensive cross-border trafficking, but seem to have relatively limited, often vulnerable, spatial monopolies and rely on networking with other [illicit actors] internationally." With regard to market competition, Basu (2013) describes the illicit economy as a global supply chain aligned against competing chains built around similar commodities. And sometimes, he argues, violence among crime groups may emerge as a result of this competition. "Turf wars occur between rival drug trafficking organizations for control of fiercely contested smuggling routes that have access to prime transshipment points" (Basu 2013: 323). While the degree of competition within the illicit economy remains a fruitful avenue for further research, there seem to be sufficient grounds to justify the presumption of monopolistic competition. Those organizations utilizing black spots can enjoy a degree of market share precluded under conditions of perfect competition involving homogeneous products. However, new actors can emerge and put down their own stake, provided they are willing to accept the risks associated with the delivery of illegal products.

Location can also play a central role given the unusual complexity of logistics within the illicit economy. As we argued earlier, the production-related aspects of global supply chains witnessed in the licit economy, while present in the illicit economy, tend to be relatively less prominent. Competition among illicit actors is often more over control of particular black spots for purposes of securing transportation redundancies. Indeed, recall the importance to those choosing a black spot of the presence of roads, airports, and rivers/harbors and the redundancies such transportation possibilities offer in responding flexibly to interdiction efforts. In contrast, the logic dictating offshoring decisions relies more on the marriage between Northern firm technology and lower Southern wages, on the one hand, and the locational differentiation of lesser- and higher-skilled production tasks, on the other, and appears to be a less dominant concern facing illicit firms (see, e.g., Baldwin 2016).

Beyond NEG: Other Causes of Agglomeration

Moving beyond NEG which emphasizes, as we have observed, such concerns as forward and backward linkages and factor mobility, several other potential causes of agglomeration in the illicit economy merit consideration. For example, does illicit activity naturally gravitate away from governments and established economic activity? Alternatively, does it intermingle with the legitimate global economy, targeting areas that provide pre-existing infrastructure? According to Hall (2012: 376), "certain areas are seemingly little touched by processes of economic dynamism" and, yet, they may be the centers of illicit activity. Poppy fields in Afghanistan, closed mines in the Democratic Republic of the Congo, and Native American reservations on the border of the US and Canada engaged in cigarette production and distribution are some examples of this latter claim from among the 80 black spots that we have studied. "Indeed, it is often the very conditions that condemn these spaces to the periphery of the licit economy that make them ideal locations for organized criminal activity" (Hall 2012: 376).

In contrast, Hall (2012) also mentions shipping containers that can overwhelm the inspection capability of ports, offshore financial centers, and corruptible public officials that provide spaces for criminal actors within the licit economy. These examples suggest that those involved in transnational criminal enterprises may seek out locations where there is a high volume of legal economic activity in order to mask their own illegal operations. Keefe (2013: 103) writes, "in fact, many of the major hubs in the illicit global economy are also hubs of the licit economy." Consider Naples, Italy as an illustration and, in particular, the Scampia and Secondigliano neighborhoods, which are the home to the Camorra crime groups. Because of the large licit economy that is there, the city can "absorb a high degree of criminality without becoming completely overrun by, or identified with, it" (Keefe 2013: 103). As a number of our black spots demonstrate, illicit activity can be hidden within the legitimate economy and those involved can take advantage of legitimate structures to cover their tracks. Those engaged in illegal operations exploit 'the white noise' of the licit economy.

Illicit actors also appear to seek out areas of legitimate economic activity to gain greater political and infrastructural stability. "Transnational criminal organizations rely for their very existence on some baseline level of infrastructure and services. In fact, many of the dominant hubs in the illicit global economy can be found in ...relatively coherent states" (Keefe 2013: 100). Dubai is one such hub, featuring the intermingling of legitimate and illicit activities. Specifically, Dubai boasts well-established transportation links, a feature reinforcing further agglomeration and the feasible presence of illicit markets. As Fujita and Mori (2005: 398) have observed,

Suppose there are frequent transport services on a given link, ... available on demand. As a result, a large number of shippers are attracted to use the link, which in turn supports even more frequent transport services. This positive feedback mechanism eventually leads to the endogenous formation of trunk lines and transport hubs.

Such a hub and spoke system facilitates those engaged in transnational crime slipping into the system almost unnoticed among the licit actors that predominate.

Other cases of intermingling between the licit and illicit economies involve 'gray markets.' Illicit actors often operate legitimate businesses in a black spot, whether these are fronts for their illegal activities, vehicles for money laundering, or simply another revenue stream with which to finance their principal operations. Consider once again Ciudad del Este in Paraguay on the border with Brazil and Argentina, where all kinds of organizations engaging in transnational criminal activities mix with those engaged in legitimate businesses and with people making purchases tax-free as well as arranging to smuggle and traffic in stolen goods. The benefit of these insights is that they point us to further places where we should be looking for black spots. They also suggest the challenges in separating the licit and illicit economies as each may become involved in using the other.

Other potential causes of agglomeration, beyond those already suggested by NEG, involve knowledge spillovers and innovation. These provide an additional rationale for economic activities to coalesce in particular locations. Although reduction in communication costs facilitates a readier flow of information and operational coordination over long distances, tacit knowledge—that is, know-how that is more effectively communicated and shared through close contact—traverses distances less easily (e.g., Audretsch 1998). The need for tacit knowledge incentivizes firms and individuals to cluster together. Tacit knowledge is important both within a single industry (e.g., computer-based know-how) and among disparate industries which can benefit from new ideas and technologies generated in unrelated sectors by adapting them in innovative ways.

Fear of interdiction, arrests, and incorruptible politicians means that knowledge spillovers are often an important outcome of agglomeration processes for those engaged in illicit activities, if not a catalyst for their initial formation. Such problems can lead to the creation, and instant use, of such things as throwaway cell phones and cryptocurrencies. Particularly in black spots that are occupied by multiple illicit actors, knowledge spillovers lead to the increased usage of such technologies as organizations learn from one another. This knowledge sharing, for example, has been noted within prison systems, an unintended consequence of an institution meant to bring criminals to justice not facilitate the generation of more illicit activity (Shelley 2014).

Moreover, black spots that are located near major agglomerations of legitimate activity can benefit from knowledge and technologies growing out of the legitimate economy. Those involved in transnational crime are quick to adopt new technologies that benefit their operations, for instance, the use of mini-submersibles and drones as well as custom narcotics designed to avoid categorization as drugs. Knowledge spillovers frustrate law enforcement and may spur the development of new black spots as information flows to new areas.

There is, of course, also the desire among certain illicit actors to gain the know-how to build a dirty bomb or to gain the ability to develop chemical or biological weaponry. Among the 80 black spots we have studied so far, 14% have shown some interest in such enterprises. Examples range from areas where there were Soviet nuclear stockpiles and ease of access to parts and know-how to closed uranium mines like the Shinkolobwe Mine in the Democratic Republic of the Congo to A.Q. Khan's black market companies, labs, and expertise found in Pakistan, Malaysia, Dubai, and the Netherlands (see Broad et al. 2004; Collins and Frantz 2018). There is even some suggestion that the laptops captured at a black spot in Ecuador, where a FARC leader was killed in 2008, contained indications that the organization was trying to buy uranium to make so-called dirty bombs (Lyons 2008). Such black spots suggest the emergence of agglomerations based on specialized expertise as well as access to the ingredients necessary to build such weapons. Some have viewed such linkages as representative of a global innovation system (Brown and Levey 2015), while they have been seen by others as examples of the evolving geography of innovation (Primi 2013).

A final potential cause of agglomeration centers around culture and ethnicity. In the previous chapter, we noted that two-thirds of the black spots under study are comprised of heterogeneous ethnic communities. Think about the fact that we find members of Hezbollah and of crime groups from Europe and Asia as well as Latin American transnational criminal organizations such as FARC in Ciudad del Este, Paraguay. This ethnic heterogeneity facilitates the "transnational links that enable global criminal enterprises to flourish" (Keefe 2013: 107). As noted previously, such heterogeneity in Ciudad del Este is the result of decades of immigration from conflict zones in the Middle East and Europe. Shared languages and ways of life, even common business practices, encourage clustering and the social trust needed for effective economic activities. These shared attributes facilitate greater interaction, involving positive externalities for both licit and illicit economic operations. In effect, black spots networks have been built around such diaspora communities, utilizing these shared connections to link their enterprises across the globe.

CONCLUSION

The importance of geographical location in the study of the illicit world cannot be overstated. As this chapter and the previous one have shown, the selection of a black spot involves the interaction of political, economic, and social forces. From the NEG perspective, black spots represent agglomerations of illicit activity. Similar to what NEG argues regarding spatiality within the licit global economy, agglomeration activity occurs at multiple levels within the black spots world too. It starts with a Global North/South divide, proceeds to the regional level, and eventually to the local level, clustering at its most local in specific neighborhoods of cities.

NEG also includes the distinction between locations that facilitate more mobile versus less mobile production capabilities. Black spots focused on more mobile activities tend to be located closer to final markets; those involving less mobile activities are much more land and resource specific. Another insight from NEG is that the illicit global economy arguably approximates a world of monopolistic competition with each illicit operation engaged in providing a quasi-differentiated service/product through illicit supply chains that span and link different black spots, overlapping and competing against one another to produce and supply particular commodities.

A further takeaway from NEG includes the latent potential for the birth of new black spots reflecting the presence of 'multiple equilibria' with different probabilities attached to potential highly differentiated spatial constellations. Such alternative spatial patterning builds on physical features in the landscape, the area's location relative to the availability of transportation and jurisdictional borders, the distance from other black spots, and the efforts of lawmakers to enforce the law. In effect, black spots are often located to defy the traditional notions of borders and legal jurisdictions set by governments. They form in places that facilitate illicit actors exploiting jurisdictional boundaries and, in turn, evading law enforcement.

We concluded this chapter by raising some other plausible causes of agglomeration activity beyond those suggested by NEG. For example, black spots are often located in areas offering a redundancy of alternative transportation possibilities, or where there is close proximity to legitimate, economic activity. Furthermore, there is an indication that, like those in the licit economy, their counterparts in the illicit economy are interested in knowledge spillovers and innovations and seek out black spots where they can readily gain such information or advance their skill sets. Moreover, the formation of black spots often depends on ethnic and cultural ties and the spread of diaspora communities around the globe.

In the previous two chapters, we have emphasized the need to break with convention and examine the world through a fundamentally new spatial lens. We are following in Nordstrom's (2011: 13) footsteps who observed:

> What would the world map look like if extralegal networks ... were charted in addition to the boundaries of formally recognized states? Would the whirls and eddies marking the centers of economic gravity in the world—and the attendant political power—produce a far different constellation of identities, nations, and regions than that familiar from textbooks?

We move next to explore more explicitly the 'whirls and eddies' among black spots as we strive to map and understand the illicit global economy.

REFERENCES

Adelman, Jonathan. 2014. Modeling Insecurity Flow Dynamics in Response to Degradation of Illicit Groups' Safe Havens. Paper Presented at the Annual Meeting of the International Studies Association, Toronto, Canada, March 26–29.

Audretsch, David B. 1998. Agglomeration and the Location of Innovative Activity. *Oxford Review of Economic Policy* 14 (2): 18–29.

Baldwin, Richard. 2016. *The Great Convergence: Information Technology and the New Globalization.* Cambridge, MA: Belknap Press.

Basu, Gautam. 2013. The Role of Transnational Smuggling Operations in Illicit Supply Chains. *Journal of Transportation Security* 6 (4): 315–328.

Broad, William J., David E. Sanger, and Raymond Bonner. 2004. A Tale of Nuclear Proliferation: How Pakistani Built His Network. *New York Times*, February 12.

Brown, Stuart, and David Levey. 2015. The Global Innovation System: A New Phase of Capitalism. *International Journal of Business, Humanities and Technology* 5 (1): 6–10.

Collins, Catherine, and Douglas Frantz. 2018. The Long Shadow A.Q. Khan. *Foreign Affairs*, January 31.

Fujita, Masahisa, and Paul Krugman. 2004. The New Economic Geography: Past, Present and the Future. *Papers in Regional Science* 83: 139–164.

Fujita, Masahisa, and Tomoya Mori. 2005. *Frontiers of the New Economic Geography*. Kyoto: Institute of Economic Research, Kyoto University.

Hall, Tim. 2012. Geographies of the Illicit: Globalization and Organized Crime. *Progress in Human Geography* 37 (3): 366–385.

Insulza, Jose Miguel. 2013. *The OAS Drug Report: 16 Months of Debates and Consensus*. Washington, DC: Organization of American States.

Keefe, Patrick Radden. 2013. The Geography of Badness: Mapping the Hubs of the Illicit Global Economy. In *Convergence: Illicit Networks and National Security in the Age of Globalization*, ed. Michael Miklaucic and Jacqueline Brewer. Washington, DC: National Defense University Press.

Kopp, Pierre. 2004. *The Political Economy of Illicit Drugs*. London: Routledge.

Krugman, Paul. 1991. *Geography and Trade*. Cambridge, MA: MIT Press.

Lyons, John. 2008. Colombia Says FARC Sought to Make "Dirty Bomb". *Wall Street Journal*, March 5.

Nordstrom, Carolyn. 2011. Extra-Legality in the Middle East. *Middle East Review* 41 (Winter): 10–13.

Passas, Nikos. 2001. Globalization and Transnational Crime: Effects of Criminogenic Asymmetries. In *Global Crime Today: The Changing Face of Organized Crime*, ed. M. Galeotti. London: Routledge.

Primi, Annalisa. 2013. The Evolving Geography of Innovation: A Territorial Perspective. In *Global Innovation Index 2013: The Local Dynamics of Innovation*, ed. Soumitra Dutta and Bruno Lanvin. Geneva: Cornell-INSEAD-WIPO.

Rastler, John. 2013. *Don't Forget the Drugs: The Impact of Plan Colombia's Cocaine. Flows on US National Security*. Master's Thesis, Hertie School of Governance, Berlin.

Shelley, Louise I. 2014. *Dirty Entanglements: Corruption, Crime, and Terrorism*. Cambridge: Cambridge University Press.

PART II

Toward Discovering Black Spots
Networks

CHAPTER 4

Activities, Functions, and Linkages

It is time we explored the question that Keefe (2013: 99) has urged those studying the illicit economy to pursue: How do black spots "act as engines and enablers of illicit global commerce"? Ideally, by identifying, mapping, and monitoring black spots, we can begin to link activities, regions, and organizations to supply chains and markets. We can discover where production, transportation, and distribution occur for a variety of activities as well as identify those geopolitical areas that play multiple roles and appear to function as hubs in illicit supply chains. In the process we gain "insights into how territoriality and transnationality are negotiated in everyday illicit practices" and how those engaged in transnational criminal activities "scale the world they live in" (Abraham and van Schendel 2005: 49). We can begin to understand how transnational crime has become "one of the world's most sophisticated and profitable businesses" (Costa 2010: ii). And we can lay the groundwork for discovering linkages among the black spots and the black spots networks necessary for such businesses to be successful.

Several general observations are in order before we begin. They build on what we have learned about the particular places chosen as black spots and notions regarding agglomeration. (1) The 80 black spots that we have studied to date engage in more than one illicit activity. Indeed, only one of these 80 black spots engages in just a single illicit activity. The average number of such activities is 4.4, and 23% are engaged in as many as 5-9 *different* illicit activities. (2) The black spots examined here often perform

© The Author(s) 2020   49
S. S. Brown, M. G. Hermann, *Transnational Crime and Black
Spots*, International Political Economy Series,
https://doi.org/10.1057/978-1-137-49670-6_4

more than one function. Some 63% of the black spots are involved in some combination of production, transportation, and distribution regarding the illicit activities in which they engage. And a little over one-quarter (28%) perform all three functions. (3) Those black spots that perform all three functions appear to act as hubs in the illicit economy—particularly the 17 of these 22 that are also engaged in 5-9 different illicit activities. Each of these observations has implications for learning more about the illicit global economy and will be elaborated as we move through this chapter. In the process we will explore how easy it is to conceive of linkages among the black spots and the development of networks and supply chains.

ILLICIT ACTIVITIES

Much of the literature on transnational crime presents data by a single type of illicit activity, that is, it explores drug trafficking separately from human trafficking separately from the trafficking in natural resources, and so forth. Yet, our black spots case studies suggest that the organizations operating in these areas, in line with what we have just learned from the new economic geography (NEG), have selected places because they offer multiple trafficking and smuggling opportunities. As we have just indicated, the mean number of such illicit activities across the 80 black spots under study is 4.4. To allow for adjustments in market demand, problems in getting a product to market, and confrontations with the law, the organizations governing these black spots seek out locations that provide flexibility. In other words, they diversify. As one US Congressman observed in testimony before Congress in 2014, organizations engaged in transnational criminal activities "do a lot more than drug trafficking—they'll do whatever is profitable. If guns are profitable, they'll traffic guns. If people are profitable, they will traffic people" (Wainwright 2016: 193).

And paralleling the Congressman's comment, 44% of the 80 black spots studied here do, in fact, deal in these three enterprises—trafficking in drugs, weapons, and people—but they do so at the same time. These three illicit activities might be thought of as the standard activities of the black spots that we have examined so far with other activities such as trafficking in natural resources (e.g., timber, cobalt, copper, oil, diamonds, and gold); household goods (e.g., cigarettes, CDs, counterfeit clothes, and art); and counterfeit money and documents as well as money laundering and trading in animals or animal parts being found in particular regions. Some 49% of the 80 black spots are also involved in terrorist or mercenary activities including sea piracy. Table 4.1 shows the percentages of particular illicit

4 ACTIVITIES, FUNCTIONS, AND LINKAGES 51

Table 4.1 Illicit activities in black spots by region of the world

Illicit activity	Africa (N = 14)	Asia (N = 16)	Europe (N = 15)	Latin America (N = 17)	Middle East (N = 13)	North America (N = 5)	Total (N = 80)
Mean number	4.3	4.2	5	4.4	5.3	3.2	4.4
Drugs[a]	43	81	100	94	69	100	80
Weapons[a]	50	75	67	94	85	60	74
People[a]	36	69	87	59	69	20	61
Counterfeit money/documents[a]	43	44	40	41	38	20	40
Money laundering[a]	29	19	60	59	38	20	40
Household goods[a]	29	19	53	24	62	100	40
Natural resources[a]	79	31	27	29	38	0	39
Mercenary/terrorism[a]	36	69	53	29	77	0	49
Animals/animal parts[a]	07	19	0	12	31	0	13

[a]Figures are the percentage of the black spots located in a particular region that engage in the illicit activity as well as the percentage of the total number of black spots examined to date that engage in that illicit activity

activities that were found across the 80 black spots in total as well as by region of the world and the average number of illicit activities by region. As the data indicate, trafficking in drugs, weapons, and people are the activities engaged in most often across the 80 black spots under study—in roughly two-thirds or more of these locations. The other activities were found in around one-third to one-half of the 80 black spots with the exception of the trafficking in animals and animal parts, which was found in only 13% of the 80 black spots.

Table 4.1 also shows that the illicit activities that are the focus of attention in particular regions often differ from these overall data. So, for example, trafficking in natural resources is most prevalent in black spots in Africa. This type of trafficking trumps trafficking in drugs, weapons, or people in this region. Indeed, almost all the 14 African black spots identified so far engage in trafficking in natural resources. The Shinkolobwe Mine in the Katanga Province of the Democratic Republic of the Congo (DRC) is one such black spot. Although the mine is officially closed by order of the government and any mining done there is considered illegal, there is mining activity on the site daily. Large numbers of artisinal miners extract high grades of cobalt, nickel, and uranium as well as low grades of copper from the mine. And some 52 fictitious companies have been involved in the export of minerals out of Shinkolobwe. Then there is the port city of Kismayo in Jubaland, Somalia where the fee charged for exporting locally made charcoal has helped to fund a number of different kinds of traffickers from terrorists to insurgent organizations to corrupt officials. And there is the city of Mbuji-Mayi in the DRC that is rumored to have been constructed on top of diamond deposits and where smugglers and illicit traders can buy diamonds at the dig sites or at the city's night-time diamond bazaars.

Trafficking in drugs, weapons, *and* people as well as engaging in terrorist and mercenary activities are the 4 most prominent illicit activities among the 16 black spots that we have studied in Asia. All four of these activities are found in two-thirds or more of these Asian black spots. An example of such a black spot is Kashgar, a city in Xinjiang Province in the far southwestern area of China near the borders of Pakistan, Tajikistan, and Kyrgyzstan. The city is connected to Islamabad by the Karakoram Highway, the Kulma Pass connects it to Tajikistan, and the Irkeshtam Chinese-Kyrgyz border crossing to Kyrgyzstan. It is on the old Silk Road trading route linking Asia to Europe. As this description suggests, Kashgar is a well-positioned transit point for opiates from

Afghanistan to head toward East and Central China, for heroin precursor chemicals to go from Eastern China to Afghanistan, for weapons from Pakistan to be moved to the Central Asian states, and for migrant workers from Eastern China to be trafficked to Europe. It is also a base for Uighur separatist organizations. In effect, Kashgar is a location involved in the trafficking of drugs, weapons, and people as well as in terrorist activities—all occurring simultaneously, intermingling and using as cover the legal activities ongoing in the city.

The European black spots are engaged in the widest range of illicit activities. All 15 of the black spots studied so far in Europe engage in drug trafficking and almost all (87%) in the trafficking in people. But also around two-thirds add weapons as well as money laundering to the mix. Over half engage in trafficking household goods as well as in mercenary and terrorist activities. This wide range of activities is suggestive of Europe as a major illicit marketplace. Consider the example we have discussed before, the Scampia and Secondigliano neighborhoods in Naples, Italy run by the Camorra crime families. Having access to one of the largest and busiest ports in Western Europe, the Camorra engage in drug trafficking, mainly cocaine, and arms dealing while also producing counterfeit clothing and dealing in stolen art and artifacts as well as in forged documents. Recently, they moved into waste management, gaining contracts through corrupt practices, for hauling and disposing of waste from across Europe. In a similar vein, they have laundered money through investments in concrete supply firms, companies involved in extraction and soil supply, and those involved in land reclamation schemes. These latter activities have been facilitated by securing election to local political offices.

The attention of the 17 Latin American black spots studied here is directed toward drugs and weapons—almost all (94%) were involved in such activities. Close to 60% of the illicit activities of these black spots were focused on trafficking in people as well as money laundering. An example of a Latin American black spot that is involved in these four activities is Manaus, Brazil. It is a free trade zone and port city located on the Amazon River. One of Brazil's busiest ports, the city has become a major transit point for drugs—particularly cocaine—on their way to other areas of Brazil as well as into containers for shipping to West Africa and Europe. Located in the poorest state in Brazil, Manaus is also known for its trafficking in weapons—used to maintain control and in trade for cocaine with smugglers from Peru and Colombia. And it has a reputation for sexual exploitation of minors. Money laundering activities are made easier since Manaus is a free trade zone.

For the 13 black spots that we have examined in the Middle East, the focus is on trafficking in weapons and engagement in mercenary and terrorist activities—85% and 77%, respectively. But roughly two-thirds of these same black spots are also engaged in trafficking drugs, people, and household goods. Consider El Arish, Egypt in the northern Sinai Peninsula, which is in a geostrategic position on the Mediterranean Sea close to the Suez Canal and the border of Israel as well as of Gaza. It is a part of an old trading route known as the Via Maris or 'Route of the Sea' that used to extend all the way from Cairo to Damascus. El Arish is known for its large black market that includes drugs (heroin, opium, and marijuana); weapons (e.g., assault rifles, hand guns, anti-tank weapons, and ammunition); trafficking in people and organs; money laundering; and the smuggling of all kinds of goods (from food to refrigerators to construction materials to small cars) into Gaza. The Bedouins, native to the Sinai, are often the middlemen in the trafficking of people. And Hamas clearly benefits from the movement of goods into Gaza as do Palestinian crime families. The militant group, Islamic State-Sinai Province, has carried out a number of attacks on Egyptian army and police forces located in El Arish.

We have studied the fewest number of black spots in North America— only five—and so the data here are hardly representative. Even so, there is an emphasis on trafficking in drugs, household goods, and weapons. An illustration is Kahnawake, a First Nation Reserve in Canada, located on the southwestern shore of the St. Lawrence River across from Montreal. It has sovereignty and the right of self-governance. With such, it is a tax-free zone with regard to Canadian and provincial government taxes. The latter fact has significance in that Kahnawake is known for trafficking in illicit cigarettes, doing much of the manufacturing of such cigarettes on site using tobacco smuggled from the US. The residents of Kahnawake have also trafficked in firearms and drugs, growing some cannabis on site. There are observed linkages between the smuggling that goes on in the Reserve and organized crime. Organized crime groups help residents in this First Nation community gain access to non-native markets.

FUNCTIONS

In addition to harboring an array of different types of illicit activities, the black spots also serve different functions in illicit supply chains. Some are the source of a particular activity, that is, where it begins—where a particular drug is produced, women and children rounded up, and natural resources mined. Others are involved in the transit of the commodities to a specific market and here there can be many steps—from truck to ship to airplane, from one continent to another, from one organization to another. Storage can also be involved as well as change in the size and form of the commodity as it moves from transit site to transit site. Still other black spots engage in the distribution of the product; they are the end point or destination of the supply chain. Just as we have learned that black spots are involved with more than one illicit activity, they also appear to perform different functions depending on which activity one is observing. In this way, the organizations in charge maintain a diversified portfolio of activities.

Table 4.2 displays the functions of the 80 black spots under study here. An examination of the data indicates that 38% performed only one function. And when they were assuming that role, it generally involved transit of some sort, insuring that goods were moving to a particular destination. As this finding suggests, it then means that around two-thirds of the 80 performed more than one function, often depending on the particular item being trafficked or task being performed. Once again, we see built-in redundancies to provide flexibility. Some 34% of the black spots were involved in two functions. The two functions most likely to be

Table 4.2   Functions that black spots fulfill in illicit supply chains

Function	Number of black spots	Percentage of 80 black spots
Perform single function	*30*	*38*
Source only	4	05
Transit only	23	29
Destination only	3	04
Perform double function	*28*	*34*
Source/transit	18	22
Source/destination	4	05
Transit/destination	6	07
Perform three functions	*22*	*28*
Source/transit/destination		

pursued were acting as both a source and a transit black spot, insuring commodities got to market safely and items needed for production were brought back to the black spot. That leaves 28% of the black spots under study performing all three functions—they were a source, engaged in transit, and were involved in distribution. These particular black spots appear to have functioned as hubs within black spots networks. They are a hive of activity and, we suspect, evidence the widest range of different types of illicit activities. Interestingly, among the 80 black spots studied so far, the destination function seems more likely to occur in conjunction with the source and transit functions rather than on its own. Being a destination suggests that one of the other two functions or both are likely to be present as well.

A perusal of Table 4.2 also suggests that most (86%) of the 80 black spots examined here are involved in the transit function in some form. For those engaged in transnational criminal activities, the transit function is critical to reaching markets and to making things happen. Remember that the transit function can also involve warehousing or storage and an alteration in the commodity involved—smaller portions of drugs, certain types of people, particular household goods being trafficked in particular directions, and so on.

Consider the functions that characterized the black spots' examples we described previously when we were exploring activities. Manaus, Brazil is an example of a black spot that performs a transit function, particularly for cocaine headed to West Africa and Europe. It is a busy port for container ships and a free trade zone with freight of all types moving in and out of its docks. Kahnawake in Canada has two functions. It is both a source of illegal cigarettes and involved in smuggling tobacco from the US for production of the cigarettes. The Shinkolobwe Mine in the DRC also performs both the source and transit functions. Miners dig the minerals out of the mine but they also insure through intermediaries that the minerals are taken to smelting mills nearby for processing and then are put onto trucks to begin the journey to the owners of the 52 fictitious companies that have paid for them to be mined. The Scampia and Secondigliano neighborhoods in Naples, Italy exhibit all three functions. The Camorra crime families governing these neighborhoods are involved in trafficking drugs, playing both transit and destination functions. Moreover, counterfeit clothing is produced there and money laundering is a common occurrence through land reclamation schemes.

Table 4.3   Functions by number of illicit activities

Function	Percentage involved in 1-4 different illicit activities	Percentage involved in 5-9 different illicit activities
Transit (N = 23)	48	52
Source and transit (N = 18)	67	33
Source/transit/ destination(N = 22)	23	77

Table 4.3 lends support to the notion that the function and number of different kinds of illicit activities evident in a black spot are related. As we suggested earlier, it seems likely that those among the 80 black spots that combine the source, transit, and destination functions will engage in the largest number of different types of illicit activities—from 5 to 9 in the 22 studied here. Indeed, 77% of these multifunctional black spots were so involved. Note that the black spots combining the source and transit functions engaged in fewer different illicit activities. In fact, 67% of these black spots were engaged in only 1-4 different illicit activities. These black spots were more focused on specific activities although still leaving room for some flexibility should it be needed. Table 4.3 suggests that the 23 black spots that only pursued the transit function—that is all they did—are about equally likely to be engaged in from five to nine different illicit activities as from one to four such activities. This finding suggests the possibility that location along a traditional trading route may help to enhance the number of different illicit activities engaged in if transit is one's major goal. In fact, all 12 of the 23 black spots that focused primarily on the transit function and were engaged in 5-9 different illicit activities were located on traditional trading routes. Only 4 of the 11 black spots performing the transit function alone and engaged in 4 or less different illicit activities were so located.

A list of the black spots that not only engaged in all three functions but also in five or more different illicit activities is found in Table 4.4. They are listed by region. Among the 80 black spots that we have studied, these 17 appear to be major hubs in the global illicit economy. They seem to play especially important roles in the networks that make up this economy. At the least, they are the most active and involved of the 80 black

Table 4.4   Black spots performing all three functions and involved in five to nine illicit activities by region

---

Africa
Equatorial Guinea (mafia state)
Kismayo, Somalia (black market)
Asia
Rasht Valley, Tajikistan (proto-state)
Azad Kashmir, Pakistan (de facto state)
FATA, Pakistan (de facto state)
Kashgar, China (black market)
Surabaya, Indonesia (black market)
Europe
Gudauta, Abkhazia (black market)
South Ossetia (de facto state)
Urosevac, Kosovo (black market)
Scampia/Secondigliano, Naples (black market)
Latin America
Los Zetas Territory, Mexico (proto-state)
Michoacan State, Mexico (proto-state)
Ciudad del Este, Paraguay (black market)
Middle East
El Arish, Egypt (black market)
Hezbollah Territory, Lebanon (proto-state)
Dubai, United Arab Emirates (black market)

---

spots studied here. An examination of those listed in the table suggests that they are of two types. In addition to being a base of operations for those involved in transnational criminal activities, one type are quasi-autonomous or what have been referred to as 'almost' or 'as if' states while the other type have been black markets for long periods of time, located as they are at geographical crossroads around the globe. Since these black spots appear to play important roles in the illicit economy, let us explore these differences in more detail. In effect, what do we mean by 'almost' or 'as if' states and which black spots fit these criteria? And which have been black markets for long periods of time given their geographic location? In fact, these 17 black spots split almost evenly between these two types. Eight (47%) function as if they were a state and nine (53%) are black markets. These designations are noted in Table 4.4.

HUBS AND THEIR CHARACTERISTICS

Mafia, De Facto, and Proto-States

The eight black spot hubs that exhibit state-like characteristics are often discussed in the literature under labels such as mafia state, de facto state, and proto-state. These terms all get at different notions regarding sovereignty, statehood, and governance. These black spots tend to be governed by a single ethnic group or cartel and to fit most closely the idea of a city-state or pirate island described in Chap. 2. Globalization has facilitated these black spots taking advantage of economic opportunities across the globe, while at the same time enhancing the desire of those involved to be in control and in charge of their own state and/or destiny. Consider some examples from Table 4.4.

Mafia States

Naim (2012: 2) has defined mafia states as states where "government officials enrich themselves and their families and friends while exploiting the money, muscle, political influence, and global connections of criminal syndicates to cement and expand their own power." Equatorial Guinea is a good example of such a mafia state. It functions as a hub of illicit activities with the express intention of increasing the wealth and power of the ruling family and friends and has been alluded to as a criminal state (Wood 2004; Silverstein 2012). Although rich in oil and other natural resources with a GDP per capita larger than any other state in Africa, Equatorial Guinea ranks in the lower quarter of countries on the Human Development Index that measures the quality of life of people in the country. Using foreign bank accounts, shell companies, rigged contracts, monopoly arrangements, expropriation of land, and embezzlement, the ruling family has exploited the natural resources for their own gain. Foreign diplomats have observed that Equatorial Guinea, like the mafia, is a family-run business that just happens to have sovereignty and a seat in the UN (see Blas 2014).

De Facto States

De facto states "are political entities that possess control of territory but lack the international recognition" that Equatorial Guinea has (Mylonas and Ahram 2015: 1). The ruling elites of de facto states have a sense of having achieved 'internal sovereignty' over a portion of the territory of a recognized state while at the same time they lack 'external sovereignty' in the international system (e.g., O'Loughlin et al. 2014; Toal and O'Loughlin 2014). De facto states often reflect 'frozen conflicts' where a piece of an internationally recognized state has broken away; has held territorial control for at least two years; and has demonstrated a desire for sovereignty through a formal declaration of independence, by holding a referendum, by marshaling a militia, by having a flag and governing rules, or similar actions (Caspersen and Stansfield 2011: 3-4; Florea 2014). Unlike the mafia state, however, the de facto state is often forced to engage in illicit activities in order to maintain its economy in the face of blockades, military incursions, and shunning on the part of the state from which it has parted company and/or the international community. Such an example is the South Ossetia black spot.

Assumed to be a part of the Republic of Georgia by most of the world, South Ossetia is officially recognized by Russia which fought a war with Georgia on its behalf to keep it autonomous. Found in the north central part of the territory claimed by Georgia, South Ossetia borders Russia and is separated from the rest of Georgia by the Caucasus Mountains. It is connected to Russia by the Roki Tunnel and to the rest of Georgia by the Trans-Caucasus Highway. Since the dissolution of the Soviet Union in 1991, the South Ossetians have declared and fought for independence from Georgia. And as Fischer (2016) has commented, their severe economic underdevelopment as a result has led to their main sources of revenue being smuggling, black marketeering, and corruption. An original stop on the ancient Silk Road, people still are involved in the trafficking of heroin from Central Asia on its way to Europe. Money from drugs has been used to buy weapons to help the separatist cause. South Ossetia is also known for its illicit timber trade, its trafficking of women and children into the sex trade, and a black market in household goods including major trafficking in cigarettes. Many South Ossetians depend on such trade for their livelihoods. Moreover, there is reputed collusion among the Russian military who are there, South Ossetian businesses, and the separatists, with all benefiting from corruption, extortion, and the illicit flow of counterfeit US dollars.

Other examples of de-facto-like states found in these most active black spots are the Federally Administered Tribal Areas (FATA) and Azad Kashmir, both in Pakistan. Like South Ossetia, these two de-facto-like states have been kept from sovereignty and statehood by Pakistan that, like Russia, is using these areas as a buffer between themselves and an enemy.

In the case of FATA, it is Afghanistan and began back when the British used the Durand Line to seal themselves off from a significant 'other.' In the case of Azad Kashmir, it is a series of wars between India and Pakistan over Kashmiri independence and the so-called Line of Control. In both cases, their semi-autonomous status has led to a dependence on a shadow economy—some have called it a 'coping economy'—with the growth of informal black markets, cross-border trading networks, plunder, misuse of diaspora remittances, drug and arms trafficking as well as the manufacturing of weapons and smuggling of natural resources. And their shadow state system has become involved in tax collection, kidnapping for ransom, extortion, and corruption. As Khan (2012: 115) has observed, "on the one hand these areas are constitutionally part of Pakistan while on the other they are considered 'independent' as per government documents." As a result, they have become a smuggler's paradise and a safe haven for terrorist organizations. And, as we have found, they are engaged in the production, transit, and distribution of illicit activities as well as have become a hub in the illicit economy (Ayaz 2012; Weinbaum 2017).

Proto-States
"A proto-state is a particular type of political unit, one that is organized administratively [within a sovereign state], given some degree of autonomy, and is typically ... constructed around a local ethnic group" (Griffiths 2016: 219). These are "juridically separate communities of people who purportedly have special claims to the jurisdiction as a homeland" (Roeder 2017: 12-13). Four of the black spot hubs listed in Table 4.4 fit this definition: Rasht Valley, Hezbollah Territory, Los Zetas Territory, and the Michoacan State. The organizations governing each of these black spots are focused on gaining control over a particular geographic area that they see as belonging to them. They seek to secure autonomy and political influence in the country in which that area is located. They are not necessarily focused on statehood but on gaining autonomy and control over what happens in their 'territory.'

Take, for example, Hezbollah Territory in southern Lebanon. This is the Shiite region in Lebanon that runs from the Israeli border into South Beirut. It is governed by Hezbollah, a Shi'a Islamist political party and militant group that provides goods and services and protection to the population. But it is—and seeks to remain—an autonomous region in Lebanon with the right to participate in the politics of the country as a separate entity with its own military. Some have described it as a 'state within a state' (Levitt 2007; Assl 2011) having 'foreign' ties to Iran and the administration of Bashar al Assad in Syria as well as its domestic activities. Hezbollah Territory is supported through remittances from its global diaspora communities, charities and front organizations, smuggling of cigarettes, drug trafficking and trafficking in natural resources, selling pirated software and counterfeit goods, extortion, taxation, money laundering, and terror-related activities. Through such activities, it has become a producer, transit zone, and destination for a variety of legal and illegal products. The monies raised are spent to insure the group's agenda of establishing a Shi'a entity in Lebanon and the protection needed to prevent international efforts from keeping such from happening (Levitt 2013; Hubbard et al. 2014).

The Los Zetas Territory is similar in kind to the Hezbollah Territory. Much like Hezbollah, the Los Zetas proto-state is focused on control of territory. "The Zetas have never looked at themselves as a drug trafficking operation. They have always been a military group whose primary goal is to control territory.... The Zetas understood something the other groups did not: they did not need to run criminal activities in order to be profitable, they simply needed to control the territory in which these criminal activities were taking place" (Fitzpatrick 2017: 30). This phenomenon has been referred to as a 'commercial insurgency' (Sullivan and Bunker 2011). The Los Zetas Cartel is focused on maintaining control over the space where their criminal activities occur and, in turn, eliminating the ability of the government to affect what they do. In effect, the cartel leaders view themselves as governing a proto-state where they have territorial control and can administer their own "form of taxation and resource extraction, limit the finances of their enemies, and augment the funding of their military" (Fitzpatrick 2017: 32-33). By being intent on not only controlling the trafficking routes but also the territory through which such routes go, they insure that they can control the political process in their areas and, in turn, the extraction of resources. To them control of territory is important and the maintenance of that control is paramount.

Black Markets

The nine hubs listed as black markets in Table 4.4 have played this role for long stretches of time, many going back to the beginnings of worldwide trade. By black market we mean a market where the goods and services being exchanged are illegal or those doing the purchasing and selling are in non-compliance with government rules and regulations (see Fontinelle 2012). In most places selling drugs or prostitution would be an example of goods and services being exchanged illegally while avoiding paying taxes and/or following regulations such as price controls and rationing are examples of non-compliance. The trade that goes on in a black market is often referred to as comprising the underground or shadow economy. Black markets can exist near borders where goods on one side of the border are legal but illegal on the other side, untaxed on one side but taxed on the other, or just cheaper on one side than the other. They are often found in ports that exist along major international sea routes as well as in prime places along traditional trading routes. As Neuwirth (2011) has observed, black markets and the underground economy provide things that the poorest of the world's population can afford and offer employment where none or little is otherwise available. Of course, black markets also sell goods that reduce the earnings of legitimate businesses; the monies earned can be used for terrorist activities without leaving much of a trace; and those abiding by the law often have to pay higher taxes and obey more regulations as a result. In many ways, these black market hubs are examples of the new economic geography (NEG) and agglomeration detailed in the previous chapter. They often form the economic core in their regions.

It is interesting, then, to note that countries have at times made it easier for such black markets to coexist with legitimate markets by creating free trade zones (or, by other names, free economic zones, free ports, special economic zones, and foreign trade zones). These are areas where regulations allow for "exemptions from duty and taxes, simplified administrative procedures, and the duty free importation of raw minerals, machinery, parts, and equipment" (FATF 2010: 4). Here states make it easy for legal and illegal activities to coexist, particularly given the often inadequate anti-money laundering safeguards in place, lax oversight by authorities, and lack of effective coordination between government officials and those in charge of the free trade zones.

We find an array of different types of black markets in the hubs indicated in Table 4.4. Some are ports on major international sea lanes (Kismayo and Surabaya), others are located in prime places along traditional land-based trading routes (Kashgar, Gudauta, Urosevac, and El Arish), and some are designated as free trade or economic zones (Naples, Ciudad del Este, and Dubai). Let us consider an example of each type.

Seaports
Take, for instance, Surabaya, Indonesia. It is one of the earliest seaports in Southeast Asia, first talked about in the 1400s. It became a major trading port by 1513 on the route between Malacca and the Spice Islands. In the eighteenth and nineteenth centuries, Surabaya became the center of trade for the Dutch East Indies. Currently it is the second busiest seaport in Indonesia. The city is also a financial hub for the archipelago. It is located in northeastern Java along the Madura Strait. With a population of over three million, Surabaya is a commercial center and, as the US Department of State Indonesia 2017 Crime and Safety Report for Surabaya (Overseas Security Advisory Board 2017) reveals, opportunities for illegal activities mix in easily with those occurring in the legal economy. A perusal of this report and that of the United Nations Office on Drugs and Crime in 2017 suggests the following are some of the illicit activities one will find. It is home to one of Asia's largest red-light districts and is central to Indonesia's human trafficking activities. Indeed, many of those involved in Surabaya's brothels have been trafficked both internally and from abroad. This seaport is also believed to have become a hub for drugs from Asia, Europe, and Latin America as well as an important hotspot for the smuggling of timber to China, India, and Australia. The latter smuggling is conducted by organizations that have connections with the port authorities. Moreover, there is evidence of a number of syndicates involved in the drafting of fraudulent documents, important in facilitating the smuggling and trafficking that goes on in and out of the port areas. Furthermore, there are well-known black markets famous for selling endangered animals. And members of the terrorist group Jemaah Islamiyah have had safe houses in the city.

Land-Based Trading Centers
El Arish in Egypt is an example of a land-based black market, even though, as we have already observed, it is located on the Mediterranean Sea. Since the first century, it has been recognized as a trading center, situated in the northern Sinai along the Via Maris or Route of the Sea road that connected Cairo with Damascus and Egypt to the Levant. El Arish served historically as a border town between Palestine and Egypt. Now it is the capital of Egypt's Northern Sinai governorate. As such, it is in a geostrategic position to be involved in the trade as well as smuggling and trafficking activities that move from the Suez Canal and Port Said along the current coastal highway linking the Canal to the northern Sinai and the Egyptian border town of Rafah and the entrance to the Gaza Strip. Indeed, El Arish is 40 miles from Rafah.

As we noted earlier in this chapter, El Arish is known for its large black market that includes trafficking in drugs and weapons as well as money laundering and the arrangements for, and smuggling of, all kinds of goods from food to refrigerators to construction materials to small cars into the Gaza Strip. It is also recognized as a major trafficking hub for African migrants seeking jobs in Israel. Migrants often come to El Arish and seek out smugglers to get them across the border with Israel. Indeed, the Bedouins, native to the Sinai, are often the middlemen in the trafficking of people in this area. Given their chronic unemployment, smuggling has become an important source of employment (Gold 2014). And the Gaza Strip has become dependent on the goods found in the black market in El Arish. Procuring, storing, and transporting smuggled goods into the Gaza Strip has benefited those living in El Arish as has taxing the goods moving into the Gaza Strip benefited Hamas. The resulting money has made Hamas' continued governance and control of Gaza possible. Since the movements unleashed by the Arab Spring, the Sinai and El Arish have become involved in smuggling and trafficking from across Northern Africa and the Bedouin have become even more dependent on smuggling for their economic livelihood. The Bedouin also have increasingly fallen under the influence of salafist foreign fighters seeking refuge in the northern Sinai who, in turn, have taken advantage of the illicit smuggling networks that are in place there (Siboni and Ben-Barak 2014; Herman 2016).

Free Trade Zone
As an illustration of a free trade zone (or special economic zone as it is sometimes called), let's take a look again at Ciudad del Este in Paraguay. Located on the bank of the Parana River at a point where the borders of Paraguay, Brazil, and Argentina meet, Ciudad del Este is joined to Foz do Iguacu, Brazil by the 1,812 foot-long Friendship Bridge. The latter has been known to have up to 30,000 people cross it in a day. Ciudad del Este is part of what is called the Tri-Border Area (or Triple Frontier), given its location at the intersection of the three countries. The city was created to take advantage of this location and in 1962 was designated a free trade zone with duty-free shopping areas located throughout and the creation of over 100 landing strips. Intending for the economic privileges associated with a free trade zone to spur the development of Paraguay, one of the poorer countries in the Americas, the free trade zone also facilitated the creation of a large shadow economy and black market. It is estimated that at one point this informal economy amounted to 75% of Paraguay's GDP (Reyes 2011).

Ciudad del Este thrives on a cash economy, being involved in document and currency fraud, money laundering, selling counterfeit goods, and drug and arms trafficking. It is a place where pirated and counterfeit goods can be imported and then re-exported across borders or sold duty free at a profit. As Lahrichi (2015: 5) has observed: "The city center is a warren of street venders …. There's only one problem. The goods are counterfeit." Indeed, Ciudad del Este is a common member of the 'notorious markets' list put out by the Office of the United States Trade Representative (2017) for trademark counterfeiting and copyright piracy. Although Ciudad del Este as a free trade zone was meant to mitigate Paraguay's lack of ocean access by making it a duty-free distribution center where goods could be packaged and shipped abroad, its money is made by selling cheap and often illegally acquired or counterfeited goods to its neighbors.

The informal economy in Ciudad del Este is heavily dependent on Lebanese and Chinese businessmen who have immigrated into Paraguay, in one instance, because of a civil war and, in the other, because of the money to be made. There are around 30,000 Lebanese Arabs living in the area, many sympathetic to Hezbollah and involved as a diaspora community in sending money 'home' to support the cause. The Chinese are often related to Chinese Triads and involved in overseeing the movement of counterfeit and pirated goods from China into the black market economy in Ciudad del Este. Being a free trade zone makes smuggling goods easier because it provides a marketplace into which to move goods and it facilitates introducing dirty money into the formal economy through a variety of money laundering techniques. Moreover, being located on the border with two other countries, custom documentation and administration varies depending on which border is crossed. With two different political systems, two different countries' borders, and a general lack of oversight, repackaging and relabeling become easy, avoiding paying tax even easier, and smuggling the easiest of all (Reyes 2011; Carless 2014).

LINKS AMONG BLACK SPOTS

Having provided evidence of the multiple products and activities that black spots often engage in and having shown the kinds of functions that they can play, of interest is how they interact to form networks and markets around these activities and functions. To achieve more proactive and effective responses to those engaged in illicit activities, there is a need for a more systematic analysis of illicit "flows, trends, drivers, and impacts," remembering as we go about such study that "organized criminal networks are dynamic, flexible, and opportunistic" (Shaw 2016: 235). And as van Schendel (2005) has observed, we need to do more than put arrows on maps that cross state borders to denote where a flow goes; we need to demonstrate geographically how the black spots are linked. One way to go about building such linkages is to take the hubs we have uncovered and the actions that they are engaged in and explore how neighboring black spots might relate to them. Another way is to study something like the Balkan Route, often talked about as a major smuggling route for moving heroin from Afghanistan into Western Europe. Which of our black spots are found along such a route and how might they operate? Still another way is to explore how we could use the black spots we have studied here to identify a path by which a drug like cocaine found in Latin America might turn up in Naples, Italy. We know that there is a relationship between the cartels in Latin America and the Camorra in Naples. What is at least one way such a linkage might occur?

Connections to Hubs

Since the hubs are responsible for carrying out all functions, it becomes relevant to ask what are they the destination for, the source of, or the transit zone for? As an example, we have already found a link between El Arish and Rafah at the border of the Gaza Strip. El Arish and its black market are the source of a wide range of goods smuggled into the Gaza Strip. Rafah and its tunnel system are a destination for these goods. El Arish, in turn, is the destination for laundering the money raised by such smuggling. There is an interdependence that has developed between the two black spots. Rafah and the Gaza Strip increase the importance of the black market and informal economy that define El Arish. And El Arish—particularly when Egypt has closed its border with the Gaza Strip—becomes the life blood of Gaza.

A second example is the linkage that we discovered between two of our hubs—Ciudad del Este in Paraguay and Hezbollah Territory in Lebanon. The black market in Ciudad del Este provides funds that the Lebanese diaspora located in that city can launder and through front, shell, and charitable organizations send to Hezbollah to help pay for the goods and services necessary to maintain their governance of Southern Lebanon. In this way, a hub known for its gray and black market economies becomes linked with a proto-state on another continent through the actions of a diaspora community. It has been estimated that such an exchange of funds accounts for around $20 million of Hezbollah's budget.

The drugs that are trafficked through the Hezbollah Territory often come from or through the Bekaa Valley which is on the border of Lebanon with Syria. This black spot is well known for its hashish production and trafficking in cocaine. Since the civil war in Syria began, labs for the production of methamphetamine have sprung up in the valley. It is a source of drugs and money for Hezbollah. The Shiite drug trading clans in the Bekaa Valley work closely together with Hezbollah. Not only does Hezbollah profit from the drug trade but it and the clans protect each other. The clans insure Hezbollah's supply lines for their forces fighting in Syria and Hezbollah provides them protection when law enforcement invades the clans' turf (Neumann 2015).

The Balkan Route

An examination of the 80 black spots that we have studied here shows that there are seven located on the Balkan Route, well known as a major trading route for moving heroin and opiates through Turkey and the Balkan countries on their way to Western Europe. Most of these black spots serve a transit function in moving the drugs from one point to another and all engage in the trafficking of drugs. But in the process of transporting the drugs, these black spots are involved in converting opium poppies into heroin, in storage, in repackaging the drugs into smaller amounts for sale, and in arranging where and when to move the drugs. Figure 4.1 illustrates the route.

Two of the seven black spots are located in Turkey at the beginning of the Balkan Route as it moves into that country. One is composed of the Hakkari-Van Provinces and is located near Turkey's borders with Iran and Iraq. This black spot is generally involved in receiving the opium poppies already processed into heroin from labs in Iran. It is home to the Kurdish Workers' Party or PKK who raise funds for their people through smuggling of various types and view this location in Turkey as part of the country of Kurdistan. The PKK are known to control a large portion of the heroin trafficking from Afghanistan, at least that part transiting these two provinces. If the PKK are not involved in moving the drugs going through these provinces, they are engaged in extortion of those who are. The opiates and heroin begin their journey into Southeastern Europe on the

Fig. 4.1   Black spots along the Balkan Route moving heroin to markets in Europe

Balkan Route through the Erzurum/Kars/Igdir Triangle in Turkey, another of our 80 black spots. This triangle of provinces is a little further north from the Hakkari-Van Provinces and it has major rail and road connections to Ankara and then on to Istanbul. Erzurum, in particular, is an important collection and shipment point for drugs as they begin their journey to the Balkan black spots and on to Western Europe.

Another of the seven black spots is Zenica in Bosnia and Herzegovina, an industrial city located in the center of that country. It is a transit point along the Balkan Route for drugs, people, and all kinds of consumer goods. One part of the Balkan Route, to which Zenica belongs, runs through the Gorazde Corridor in Bosnia and Herzegovina into the Sandzak region of Montenegro and Serbia and on to the ports of Durres or Vlore in Albania where goods and people are transported across the Adriatic Sea to Italy. The UN Office on Drugs and Crime (2014) has labeled this the western fork of the central branch of the Balkan Route. The Sandzak region, another of the seven black spots on the route, is noted as having an active drug trade including heroin, cocaine, and hashish. Parts of this region are in Montenegro and parts in Serbia. The major community in this region on the Serb side is Novi Pazar. Roughly 50% of its economy is generated from illegal trade in drugs and people as well as counterfeit clothing. The people being trafficked are thought to come from Moldova through Romania to Zenica and then on to Italy.

Kosovoska Mitrovica, just across the Serbian border in Kosovo, is another of the seven black spots on the Balkan Route. It is also known for its informal economy in cigarettes, alcohol, gasoline, and car parts. With an unemployment rate over 50%, smuggling has become a way of life. Under the control of the Albanian mafia, Kosovoska Mitrovica sits near a major east-west road and along a major railway running from Macedonia through Serbia. In effect, this community provides access for smuggling to the western fork of the central Balkan Route to Italy described above but also to the northern fork of the central route which heads up into Serbia and then into Central Europe. There is evidence that heroin is warehoused in Kosovoska Mitrovica and repackaged into smaller amounts to make transport easier but also to increase the quantity available on which to make a profit.

Near the Macedonian border are two more of our black spots—one in Kosovo and one in Serbia. These two—Urosevac (Ferizaj in Albanian), Kosovo and Presevo Valley, Serbia—are part of the northern fork of the Balkan Route. Here we see some of the redundancy often built into the supply chains of those engaged in transnational criminal activities as these two areas are close to the Macedonian border as well as the border between Kosovo and Serbia. The residents in both are largely ethnic Albanians and influenced by the Albanian mafia. Drugs, especially heroin, are smuggled into Urosevac which is viewed as a storage and repackaging site. They are kept in Urosevac just across the border from Presevo in Presevo Valley. When transportation arrangements are complete, the drugs are sent into Serbia, up to Belgrade, and north out of the Balkans. Western and Central Europe are the target markets for these drugs with consumer expenditures estimated in the billions of dollars. What started in two black spots in Turkey has ended up going into Italy and other markets in Western Europe through Zenica, the Sandzak region, and Novi Pazar *or* up into Central and then Western Europe through Kosovoska Mitrovica, Urosevac, and Presevo in Presevo Valley.

Linking Latin America to Europe

Cocaine from Latin America has been found in Naples, Italy. Indeed, it is well known that the Camorra crime families in Naples have long had ties to groups like the FARC in Colombia; the latter being a major supplier of cocaine to this Italian port city and, in turn, benefiting financially from the arrangement. What if we start in Tabatinga, Brazil which is located in the

'Amazon Trapezoid'—the area where Brazil, Peru, and Colombia meet around the waters of the Amazon River—and see if we can chart a plausible route for cocaine to get to Naples? Tabatinga has a sister city, Leticia, Colombia from which it is divided by a single paved street that forms the international boundary. Together they form one of our 80 black spots. This region has become known as the Tabatinga-Leticia Corridor and the gateway for around 60-70% of the cocaine trafficked into Brazil. Its vast forested areas laced with the Amazon's river network make it ideal terrain for narco-trafficking. It is estimated that 90% of the residents in this corridor have direct links to the drug-trafficking business.

A three-day boat ride down the Amazon River from the Tabatinga-Leticia Corridor is Manaus—a free trade zone and one of Brazil's busiest ports. Indeed, as we noted earlier in this chapter, this black spot has become a major transit hub for drugs—particularly cocaine—on their way to other areas of Brazil as well as into containers for shipping to West Africa and Europe. Located in the poorest state in Brazil, Manaus is also known for its trafficking in weapons—used to maintain control and in trade for cocaine with smugglers from Peru and Colombia. Money laundering activities are made easier because Manaus is a free trade zone. This port is 930 miles by ship down the Amazon River to the Atlantic Ocean and then a five-day journey across the Atlantic Ocean to the Port of Bissau in Guinea-Bissau (another of our 80 black spots).

The Port of Bissau is noted for not having meaningful security so containers routinely enter and leave the country without inspection (Eventon and Bewley-Taylor 2016). Having relative proximity to Latin America (indeed, it is the closest point on the African continent to Latin America), extreme poverty, corrupt military and law enforcement, and porous and poorly controlled borders, Guinea-Bissau has been called a 'narco state' (Loewenstein 2016). It has become a transshipment point for drugs—in particular cocaine—to Europe. There is evidence of the growth of so-called middle men in Guinea-Bissau who play a liaison role between members of the Latin American cartels and those in the Tri-border Area of Algeria, Mali, and Niger—the next stop on the route to Europe and another of our 80 black spots.

This tri-border intersection of southern Algeria, northeast Mali, and northwest Niger resides in a rugged, arid, and desolate stretch of North Africa where the Sahara desert meets the Sahel region. No significant infrastructure separates these three countries from each other and individuals pass freely from one into the others. Moreover, the

Tuareg, who are the predominant ethnic group in this region, are cultur-
ally and historically nomadic and cross all three countries frequently with
total disregard for borders. As a result of these fluid borders, it has also
become a safe haven for terrorist organizations such as al-Qaeda in the
Islamic Maghreb and ISIS affiliates. Bypassing official customs processes,
this area has become the route through which contraband such as cocaine
from Latin America is headed for Europe. In an attempt to keep this
border area stable and from taking up arms against the three governments, the latter have appeared to turn a 'blind eye' to the smuggling—
and/or engaged in collusion with the smugglers.

If one considers that the cocaine arrives in Guinea-Bissau in containers, it is conceivable that the drugs can be easily off-loaded onto pickup
trucks and driven to the Tri-border Area of Algeria/Mali/Niger to be
stockpiled for future shipment to Europe in manageable amounts.
There is evidence of such stockpiling in northern Mali (UNODC 2011).
From Mali, the cocaine can be driven to Tunis and flown to Europe.
But, more likely, it is driven by truck to Tunis and then goes by fast boat
or ferry to Naples and the Camorra located in the Scampia and
Secondigliano neighborhoods who, in turn, see that it is moved further
north into Europe.

We have been able, in the last several paragraphs, to follow cocaine that
originated in Tabatinga, Brazil, and its twin city, Leticia, Colombia, to
Naples, Italy, and in the process have suggested how 5 of our 80 black
spots can function as a global supply chain. We have described only one
route here whereas those involved in trafficking cocaine have a myriad of
routes and, indeed, work hard to change routes to insure their drugs find
a market without interdiction. Consider, for example, that the pickup
trucks from the Tri-border Area of Algeria/Mali/Niger could just as easily
have gone north to Ceuta and Melilla, Spain, and across the Mediterranean
by boat to Marbella, Spain—two more of the 80 black spots. Figure 4.2
displays geographically the route we have described from Latin America
to Europe.

CONCLUSION

Think about what we have learned in examining the geographic locations
that "act as engines and enablers of illicit global commerce" (Keefe 2013:
99). Contrary to the way we usually study, write about, organize our
institutions to deal with, and legislate concerning criminal behavior, we

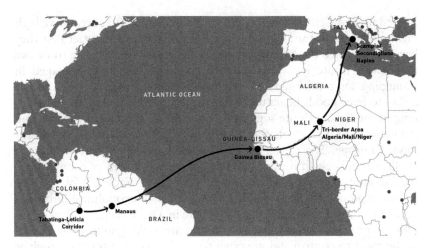

Fig. 4.2 Black spots used to move cocaine from Latin America to European markets

have learned that black spots are generally involved with multiple enter-prises—rarely just one. Such behavior facilitates flexibility based on mar-ket forces. The behavior in the black spots is a lot like the tunnel owner in the Gaza Strip who builds his tunnel big enough to hold a small car to facilitate a wider range of business than is possible when building it small. Or like Ciudad del Este, which has become known as a 'home-away-from-home' for a range of transnational criminal organizations, and, as a result, can engage in a wider range of activities by letting others take advantage of their 'hospitality.' Not only do the black spots feature mul-tiple products, they often play multiple functions in the supply chain. They produce and transport, they process and warehouse for shipment, they transport and distribute, and they do all three but at different times in the process or for different commodities. Those engaged in transna-tional criminal activities seek out locations that facilitate performing more than one function to preserve flexibility and control.

Although with 80 black spots we cannot yet map the illicit global econ-omy, we can theorize about how such links could come into play with the black spots that we have studied in-depth to date. Along the borders of Macedonia, Kosovo, and Serbia as well as the borders of Bosnia and Herzegovina, Montenegro, and Serbia, there are communities that form part of the Balkan Route for the smuggling of drugs, weapons, and people headed toward Central and Western Europe. Most of these areas have high unemployment and smuggling is a way of life. Indeed, the fact that they have been located throughout history along a traditional trading route like the Balkan Route has facilitated and condoned becoming engaged in smuggling and trafficking—it is the easy and normal thing to do. And our ability to trace goods being trafficked into and out of Turkey at the beginning of the Balkan Route suggests the possibility of eventually identifying the network of black spots that a particular commodity follows as it heads toward Europe. The closest we have come here to specifying the links in an illicit supply chain is in elaborating on the movement of cocaine from the Tabatinga-Leticia Corridor in Latin America to Naples, Italy.

In the process we have discovered a number of geopolitical hubs that perform all three functions and participate in a wide range of illicit activities. Some represent ethnic enclaves that are seeking autonomy as well as the right to control and govern a particular piece of territory such as the Hezbollah Territory, South Ossetia, and Azad Kashmir. In order to gain such control, the groups involved in these black spots are often forced to turn to the informal and illicit economies to provide the goods and services needed to govern as well as to build the militias needed to retain control. Such territories are the clearest representatives of our definition of a black spot—areas outside of government control, governed by an alternate social structure, and engaged in transnational criminal activities.

Then there are the black markets that represent a somewhat different kind of hub as they are often found in prime geographic locations for trade and commerce and have usually been engaged in black marketeering for decades, if not centuries. And some have been designated as free trade zones by their governments with a resultant decrease in government oversight by the state in which they are located. Take, for example, Kashgar, China; Ciudad del Este, Paraguay; and Dubai in the United Arab Emirates. In these locations legal and illegal activities mix, corruption is a definite possibility, and the formal government has set these entities up, or enhanced their capabilities, by reducing the taxes, duties, and laws governing interactions. Many of these black market hubs are located in places where a number of different borders, trading routes, or bodies of water meet. Such locations are selected because they facilitate cross-border commerce and the free flow of people as well as goods. They exemplify the primary factors featured in NEG.

Having identified geopolitical and economic characteristics of black spots that can help us elaborate our inventory of such locations, there are two more questions that need asking in understanding how black spots function and why. How do the organizations involved in the governance of black spots affect what happens? And how are black spots financed; in other words, how is illicit money made licit in order to maintain a black spot? It is to these questions that we turn next.

References

Abraham, Itty, and Willem van Schendel. 2005. Introduction. In *Illicit Flows and Criminal Things: States, Borders, and the Other Side of Globalization*, ed. Willem van Schendel and Itty Abraham. Bloomington: Indiana University Press.

Assl, Nima Khorrami. 2011. Hezbollah: A State Above the State. *Foreign Policy Journal*, February 3.

Ayaz, Erum. 2012. Peace and Development in FATA Through Economic Transformation. *TIGAH: A Journal of Peace and Development* 1 (2): 74–95.

Blas, Javier. 2014. Reporting Back: Equatorial Guinea. *Financial Times*, January 23.

Carless, Will. 2014. Welcome to Paraguay's 'Wild West', a Bastion for Bootleggers, Organized Crime, and Maybe Even Islamic Extremists. *GlobalPost*, September 16.

Caspersen, Nina, and Gareth Stansfield, eds. 2011. *Unrecognized States in the International System*. New York: Routledge.

Costa, Antonio Maria. 2010. Preface. In *The Globalization of Crime: A Transnational Organized Crime Threat Assessment*. Vienna: UNODC.

Eventon, Ross, and Dave Bewley-Taylor. 2016. *An Overview of Recent Changes in Cocaine Trafficking Routes into Europe*. Lisbon: European Monitoring Centre for Drugs and Drug Addiction.

FATF. 2010. *Money Laundering Vulnerabilities of Free Trade Zones*. Paris: FATF/OECD.

Fischer, Sabine. 2016. Russian Policy in Unresolved Conflicts. In *Not Frozen*, ed. Sabine Fischer. Berlin: German Institute for International and Security Affairs.

Fitzpatrick, Derek R. 2017. *Greed and Grievance and Drug Cartels: Mexico's Commercial Insurgency*. Fort Leavenworth: US Army Command and General Staff College.

Florea, Adrian. 2014. De Facto States in International Politics (1945–2011): A New Data Set. *International Interactions* 40 (5): 788–811.

Fontinelle, Amy. 2012. *The Mechanics of the Black Market*. Investopedia.com.

Gold, Zack. 2014. *Security in the Sinai: Present and Future*. The Hague: International Centre for Counter-Terrorism, March.

Griffiths, Ryan. 2016. *Age of Secession: The International and Domestic Determinants of State Birth.* Cambridge: Cambridge University Press.

Herman, Lyndall. 2016. Sisi, the Sinai, and Salafis. *Middle East Policy* 23 (2): 95–107.

Hubbard, Ben, Robert F. Worth, and Michael R. Gordon. 2014. Power Vacuum in Middle East Lifts Militants. *New York Times*, January 4.

Keefe, Patrick Radden. 2013. The Geography of Badness: Mapping the Hubs of the Illicit Global Economy. In *Convergence: Illicit Networks and National Security in the Age of Globalization*, ed. Michael Miklaucic and Jacqueline Brewer. Washington, DC: National Defense University Press.

Khan, Raza Rayman. 2012. FATA Political Regime: Changing Legal-Administrative Status of Tribal Areas. *TIGAH: A Journal of Peace and Development* 1 (1): 115–134.

Lahrichi, Kamilia. 2015. Counterfeit Goods Are Big Business in Paraguay. *USA Today*, May 18.

Levitt, Matthew. 2007. Hezbollah Finances: Funding the Party of God. In *Terrorism Financing and State Responses: A Comparative Perspective*, ed. Jeanne Giraldo and Harold Trinkunas. Stanford: Stanford University Press.

———. 2013. *Hezbollah: The Global Footprint of Lebanon's Party of God.* Washington, DC: Georgetown University Press.

Loewenstein, Antony. 2016. How Not to Fix an African Narco-State. *Foreign Policy*, January 6.

Mylonas, Harris, and Ariel I. Abrams. 2015. De Facto States Unbound. PONARS Eurasia, Elliott School of International Affairs, George Washington University.

Naim, Moises. 2012. Mafia States: Organized Crime Takes Office. *Foreign Affairs*, May/June.

Neumann, Jeff. 2015. Wealth and War in Middle East Fuel Appetite for Amphetamines. *Newsweek UK*, November 3.

Neuwirth, Robert. 2011. *Stealth of Nations: The Global Rise of the Informal Economy.* New York: Pantheon Books.

O'Loughlin, John, Vladimir Kolossov, and Gerard Toal. 2014. Inside the Post-Soviet De Facto States: A Comparison of Attitudes in Abkhazia, Nagorny Karabakh, South Ossetia, and Transnistria. *Eurasian Geography and Economics* 55 (3): 423–456.

Office of the United States Trade Representative. 2017. *2017 Out-of-Cycle Review of Notorious Markets.* Washington, DC: Executive Office of The President.

Overseas Security Advisory Council. 2017. *Indonesia 2017 Crime and Safety Report: Surabaya.* Washington, DC: US Department of State.

Reyes, Richard R. 2011. Latin America Special Economic Zones and Their Impacts on Regional Security. Unpublished Doctoral Dissertation, Naval Postgraduate School, Monterey.

Roeder, Phillip G. 2017. National Succession. In *Oxford Encyclopedia of Politics*. Oxford: Oxford University Press.

Shaw, Mark. 2016. "We Pay, You Pay": Protection Economics, Financial Flows, and Violence. In *Beyond Convergence: World Without Order*, ed. Hilary Matfess and Michael Miklaucic. Washington, DC: National Defense University Press.

Siboni, Gabi, and Ram Ben-Barak. 2014. *The Sinai Peninsula Threat Development and Response Concept*. Washington, DC: Brookings Institution, January.

Silverstein, Ken. 2012. Keep the Dictators Out of Malibu. *New York Times*, July 2.

Sullivan, John P., and Robert J. Bunker. 2011. Rethinking Insurgency: Criminality, Spirituality, and Societal Warfare in the Americas. *Small Wars and Insurgences* 22 (5): 742–763.

Toal, Gerard, and John O'Loughlin. 2014. How People in South Ossetia, Abkhazia, and Transnistria Feel About Annexation by Russia. *Washington Post Monkey Cage*, March 20.

United Nations Office on Drugs and Crime (UNODC). 2011. *World Drug Report 2011*. New York: United Nations.

———. 2014. *World Drug Report 2014*. New York: United Nations.

———. 2017. *Country Programme 2017–2020 Indonesia: Making Indonesia Safer from Crime, Drugs, and Terrorism*. Vienna: UNODC.

Van Schendel, Willem. 2005. Spaces of Engagement: How Borderlands, Illicit Flows, and Territorial States Interlock. In *Illicit Flows and Criminal Things: States, Borders, and the Other Side of Globalization*, ed. Willem van Schendel and Itty Abraham. Bloomington: Indiana University Press.

Wainwright, Tom. 2016. *Narconomics: How to Run a Drug Cartel*. New York: Public Affairs.

Weinbaum, Marvin G. 2017. Insurgency and Violent Extremism in Pakistan. *Small Wars and Insurgencies* 28 (1): 34–56.

Wood, Geoffrey. 2004. Business and Politics in a Criminal State: The Case of Equatorial Guinea. *African Affairs* 103: 547–567.

CHAPTER 5

Black Spots, Actors, and Governance

As we discover more about black spots and the linkages among them, we begin to discern that the actors governing these locations have different motivations and goals driving their actions. Such information provides us with hints about where to look for more black spots as well as the directions the flows linking the black spots might take. Consider that the Uighurs in Kashgar, China; the PKK in the Hakkâri-Van Provinces in Turkey; and the Tuareg in the Tri-border Area of Algeria/Mali/Niger have different motivations for the black spots that they choose than do al-Shabaab in Kismayo, Somalia; the Pakistani Taliban in FATA; or the Sinai Province jihadists and, in turn, than do the illegal miners in the Shinkolobwe mine in the DRC; the drug lords in Manaus, Brazil; or the Camorra crime families in the Scampia/Secondigliano neighborhoods in Naples. The Uighurs, PKK, and Tuareg lay claim to a particular territory and are engaged in a dispute with a legitimate government over the rights to that territory—in the cases indicated above with the governments of China, Turkey, and Mali. Al-Shabaab, the Pakistani Taliban, and the Sinai Province jihadists use their geographic bases of operations as the places from which to launch terrorist attacks targeted at inducing fear and increasing their own power in the area. The illegal miners, drug lords, and Camorra crime families are intent on making money and controlling the resources in a region that facilitates these goals.

© The Author(s) 2020
S. S. Brown, M. G. Hermann, *Transnational Crime and Black Spots*, International Political Economy Series,
https://doi.org/10.1057/978-1-137-49670-6_5

The first set of actors listed above—the Uighurs, PKK, and Tuareg—are often referred to as insurgents. They are involved in a protracted struggle with a legitimately constituted government or occupying power with the "objective of gaining control of a population or a particular territory" (Ford 2007: 1). They often have a well-developed identity and history associated with the territory over which they lay claim (Byman 2007). And, generally, such territory is populated by those affiliated with the insurgent group, and its activities are focused on raising the necessary resources to continue the battle.

The second set of actors—al-Shabaab, Taliban, and Sinai jihadists—have been labeled terrorist organizations and appear on a number of governments' watch lists. Such organizations generally engage in premeditated acts of violence that are politically motivated and directed at civilians and non-combatants. The acts usually suggest more violence is to come. Indeed, the acts are intended "to have far-reaching psychological repercussions beyond the immediate victims or targets" (Hoffman 1998: 32). Members of these organizations are inspired by their leaders to engage in acts of violence, even in acts of self-immolation and suicide. Illicit activities serve the purpose of helping the group obtain weapons and the resources needed to carry out acts of terrorism. Moreover, such organizations seek safe havens that provide protection from law enforcement, intelligence services, and the military; they seek what they call 'no go' zones.

The third set of actors—the DRC miners, drug lords, and crime families—is comprised of the transnational criminal organizations that we assumed were the backbone of the black spots. These organizations form the foundation of the illicit global economy and are focused on making such an economy function so that they gain—or, at the least, maintain—their 'businesses' and profits. These are non-state actors who take advantage of difficult geography, impoverished populations, and weak states in establishing their operations (Rabasa et al. 2017). "Corruption, coercion, and white collar collaboration with both the private and public sectors lower risk for these international mafias" while the black spots and their activities provide increased profits (Costa 2010: ii).

In this chapter, we examine what the black spots are like where we find each of these types of organizations separately and then we compare and contrast them. We are interested in exploring the kinds of black spots each type of organization seeks, the activities that it launches from its black spots, interactions with law enforcement, and the major focus of its activities. Some 41% of the 80 black spots studied so far involve insurgents, 31% terrorist organizations, and 28% transnational criminal organizations. We should note that since five of the black spots studied here involved both insurgents and terrorist organizations, the total on which these percentages are based throughout this chapter is 85 rather than 80. We should also note that the 28% indicated here for transnational criminal organizations refers to the black spots that they *oversee on their own*. Transnational criminal organizations were also found in 44% of the black spots involving insurgents and/or terrorist organizations. We will discuss the impact of this overlap after discussing each individual type of actor by itself.

INSURGENT ORGANIZATIONS

The black spots we have studied so far in which insurgent organizations are operating seem to fit several types. They appear to be focused on changing the nature of the political order in a country, to be seeking particular government reforms, or to be working toward the independence for a particular region or area. The geographic areas they often select as sanctuaries or safe havens are the result of a segment of the population being disadvantaged by government policies, the government not having the ability or the will to provide services to that area, and/or events having made the area more vulnerable such as the creation of borders or boundaries that divide a people (e.g., Byman 2007; Staniland 2015; Tollefsen and Buhaug 2015). These organizations generally exploit the resource base in the black spot, intent on using their criminal activities to support the insurgency. Consider some examples.

Examples

South Ossetia
South Ossetia in the South Caucasus region of the state of Georgia is one such place. Called a renegade province by the Georgian government and an independent free zone by the Russians, South Ossetia has all the characteristics of being governed by an insurgent organization. The majority Ossetian population living in this area has long maintained a distinct national identity, like that of their next-door neighbors, the North Ossetians, who exist as a federation within Russia. The two groups are

focused on the development of a semi-autonomous or autonomous repub-lic, which has led the South Ossetians to form a separatist movement. While some members of the separatist movement wish for their own state, others are content to merely rejoin Russia. The dominance of ethnic Ossetians in South Ossetia has ensured that Georgian cultural norms have not taken hold in the region. And these embedded Ossetian norms and rules dictate that the South and North Ossetians are meant to be joined in a common territory.

The development of the illicit economy in South Ossetia has coincided with the separatist conflict, starting with the end of the Cold War until the present. Despite military interventions by the Georgian government and the constant presence of Russian troops, illicit activity continues on a con-sistent and stable basis. In this regard, South Ossetia's main asset is the Roki Tunnel, which passes from North Ossetia (Russia) into South Ossetia. Illicit transactions and bribery of officials are frequent here, with guns, drugs, and counterfeit US dollars exchanging hands almost daily. Other types of corruption are prevalent as well. Indeed, all sides have an economic incentive to maintain the separatist conflict that has led to the cooperation among criminal groups, law enforcement agencies, and the Russian military.

Hezbollah Territory
Then there is the Hezbollah Territory in Lebanon. This black spot is located in southern Lebanon and runs from the Lebanese border with Israel into South Beirut. It is synonymous with where the Shiite popula-tion lives in Lebanon. Sovereignty and freedom from outside intervention have been key components of the cultural narrative of the Southern Lebanese population. Moreover, Hezbollah was created as a way of safe-guarding southern Lebanon from Israeli occupation and military incur-sions and of giving the Shiite population a voice in Lebanese politics commensurate with their size. Over time it has transformed from a small militia into a large organization with both political and military wings.

Hezbollah's illicit activities serve as a source of funding to fulfill its political agenda. In effect, its role as a political party, when combined with its large web of illicit criminal activities, has created a societal dependence on projects financed with 'dirty' money. Hezbollah's numerous social projects, including the construction and administration of infrastructure, have led to communal development, but also to dependence on Hezbollah for goods and services. The Lebanese government is unable to provide the same services and, should Hezbollah be eradicated, could not step in and take its place. Furthermore, the residents of Shiite Lebanon are now beholden to Hezbollah so that they are hesitant to oppose the organization given the immense social benefits brought about by its presence. Indeed, Hezbollah's reliance on its own militia to keep order in this Shiite territory threatens the legitimacy and scope of the Lebanese government while, in turn, insuring it a role in decisions regarding Lebanese politics, even if a disruptive one.

Wa State

And what about the Wa State located in Myanmar (or Burma)? It is in the eastern region of the Shan State on the Myanmar border with the Yunnan Province of China. While there is no recognized Wa State in Myanmar, the United Wa State Party (UWSP) controls a semi-autonomous region (Special Region No. 2) pursuant to a signed agreement with the Government of Myanmar in 1989 and has ever since been seeking further autonomy and its own state. It is serviced by the United Wa State Army (UWSA) composed of around 30,000 soldiers. The UWSA is the military wing of the Party and is financed almost exclusively through criminal activities such as drug trafficking and the manufacture and trafficking of weapons. In engaging in its illicit activities, it has access to China on its border and to the Golden Triangle of South Asia (Myanmar, Thailand, Laos, and Vietnam), a fertile opium-producing area.

When Myanmar was ruled by a military junta, the UWSP was able to bribe or fight its way in maintaining its autonomy. With the move to democracy and an attempt by the newly elected government to achieve unification and a ceasefire among the various militias, the UWSP has been forced to work through political channels to get its autonomous state. In doing so, they always function so as to insure that those with whom they are negotiating recognize that the party has the backing of the UWSA—"the region's largest rebel-led narco-army" (Pagnucco and Peters 2015)—and one of its best armed fighting forces outside of the government's army. Sometimes it is difficult to tell, however, if the organization's focus remains political or its illicit activities have become the primary reason for its existence.

Locations of Black Spots

Some 35 of the black spots examined in this book involve insurgent groups and their activities. In other words, insurgent groups operated in 41% of

Table 5.1   Black spots governed by insurgent organizations by region

Region of the world	% black spots governed by insurgent organizations (N = 35)
Europe	14
Middle East	14
Africa	31
Asia	23
North America	3
Latin America	14

the black spots studied here in a manner exemplified by our discussion of South Ossetia, the Hezbollah Territory, and the Wa State. Table 5.1 displays the percentages of this type of black spot by region of the world. From the data, we observe that this type of black spot is found in every region of the world; however, the largest numbers are found in Africa and Asia. Indeed, roughly one-third of such black spots are in Africa and nearly one-quarter in Asia—or over 50% of the total are found in these two regions of the world. The Wa State, described above, is representative of these black spots in Asia while the Tri-border Area of Algeria/Mali/Niger is representative of those in Africa. This latter black spot is the home of the Tuareg who are a semi-nomadic Muslim people that have openly roamed this tri-border area for centuries.

Geopolitical Conditions

Table 5.2 describes the geopolitical conditions that have helped to create and sustain these particular black spots and the insurgent organizations that govern them. (The figures in the table are the percentages of the 35 black spots overseen by insurgent organizations that fit that particular geopolitical condition.) We note immediately that almost all of these black spots are near international borders. In fact, it is often the borders that are in dispute as these insurgent organizations seek a re-arrangement regarding just where the borders are and/or who has sovereignty over what territory. The fact that over two-thirds of these black spots are located on traditional trading routes, such as the Silk Road or Trans-Saharan trade routes, suggests an assumption of a free flow of trade and people across borders and boundaries and a linkage between trading posts that in some senses may be stronger than traditional notions of sovereignty and statehood. Note that nearly three-quarters of these black spots have been in existence since before the end of the Cold War—often for decades before

Table 5.2 Geopolitical locations of black spots governed by insurgent organizations

Geopolitical location	% black spots governed by insurgent organizations (N = 35)
Near international borders	91
Located on a traditional trading route	69
In existence before 1990	74
Rural	88
Heterogeneous ethnic composition	66
Ethnic composition is conflicted	74
Norms/rules imposed by outside entity	60
Corruption present and visible	83
Located near recent conflict zone	80
Stable as opposed to pulsing	66
Regional/global range of impact	86
Daily/weekly frequency of illicit activity	40
Hub of illicit activities	29

the demise of the Soviet Union. And almost all are in or near more rural and geographically challenging areas such as valleys, gorges, deserts, and mountains. They may have towns and cities within their space but much is hidden from view in terrain that can pose obstacles to the uninitiated.

An examination of life within these black spots, also reported in Table 5.2, indicates that around two-thirds of them have an ethnic composition that is heterogeneous, and in nearly three-quarters, there is conflict among these ethnic groups. Generally, the insurgent organization represents a dominant group within the black spot but it is often in conflict with the 'ruling group' either left behind or being imposed on the area as the Uighurs are by the Han Chinese in Kashgar and the Ossetians are by the Georgians living in South Ossetia. The 60% figure representing the percentage of these insurgent-run black spots where norms and rules are being imposed on them is indicative of what lies behind the conflict. What may save the day is the fact that in almost all these black spots, corruption is a viable alternative to fighting and, as we have observed before, corruption often benefits all and reduces the incentive to resolve the conflict, particularly if that resolution means one side has to give up sovereignty and territory to the other. The fact that 80% of these black spots are near a recent conflict zone lends support to this hypothesis. Maintaining the conflict so that all parties gain something may be better than becoming a part of someone else's conflict where one has less leverage and could lose what one has. Think about the United Wa State Party and Army. They were better able to maintain the semblance of an autonomous territory when they could pay off the junta running Myanmar than when Myanmar became more democratic and that government decided to bring all militias under its control and unite all areas of the country under one leadership even if this meant confrontation with all rebel-held militias.

Illicit Activities

As Table 5.2 also indicates, all but one-third of the black spots led by insurgent organizations are stable and not pulsing (coming and going with efforts at interdiction). As we noted above, these black spots have been in place for well over two decades and have well-established routines, money-making enterprises, often militias, and specific goals. The data in the table suggest that they have a regional and global impact with their activities, although interestingly they are not as focused on engaging in illicit activities on a daily or weekly basis. They appear to be more focused on the long term and insuring their activities have consistent benefits across time. Along this line, a little over one-quarter of these black spots are hubs for illicit activity, that is, these locations are involved in production, transportation, and distribution. Such black spots are intent on insuring their survival through flexibility and opportunism. Two of the examples we began this section with are such hubs—South Ossetia and the Hezbollah Territory in Lebanon. Indeed, there are ten such hubs that are led by insurgent organizations (two in Europe, one in the Middle East, three in Asia, and four in Africa).

On average, these black spots were engaged in 4.3 different illicit activities. As is evident in Table 5.3, the black spots involving insurgent organizations are active nearly 50% or more of the time in six types of illicit activities: trafficking in drugs, weapons, people, natural resources, and household goods as well as engaging in terrorist/mercenary events. Natural resources here include items such as natural gas, chromium, copper, tin, diamonds, ivory, timber, and charcoal. Household goods involve cigarettes, CDs/movies/books, art, artifacts, 'knock-off' clothes, medicines, and computers/cellphones. The insurgents in these black spots pursue a wide range of activities, focused on providing goods and services to their 'territory.'

Table 5.3 Illicit activities flowing from black spots governed by insurgent organizations

Nature of illicit activities	% black spots governed by insurgent organizations (N = 35)
Drugs	71
Weapons	83
People	46
Natural resources	49
Household goods	49
Counterfeit money/documents	37
Money laundering	40
Terrorism	49

Table 5.4 Goals of black spots governed by insurgent organizations

Goals of illicit activity	% black spots governed by insurgent organizations (N = 35)
Military implications	91
Economic implications	74
Political implications	80
Societal implications	74

Goals of Illicit Behavior

What is the intent behind the illicit activity coming out of the black spots governed by insurgent organizations? Does it have military implications, that is, is it focused, for example, on the development of a functioning militia, actual use of military force, protection? Or is it generally related to economic matters, for example, providing goods and services for those in the black spot, employment, money laundering? Or does it have political implications such as infiltration of political institutions, corrupting particular political figures, challenging state authority, undermining elections, assassinations? Or is it intended to undermine society, to create general uncertainty, fear, a challenge to identity and the rules of the game? Table 5.4 indicates which of these four goals holds the attention of the black spots involving insurgent organizations. Almost all (91%) of these black spots are focused on achieving military ends and 80% on gaining political objectives. These two goals are particularly germane to insurgent organizations that have both political and military wings (e.g., Morris 2005; Byman 2007; Metz 2007). We noted these divisions in the Wa State—the United Wa State Party and the United Wa State Army.

But, importantly, close to three-quarters of these black spots are also involved in activities focused on achieving economic and societal goals as well. Indeed, they often seem engaged in illicit activities in order to achieve the economic objectives of providing basic services for those in the organization and residents of the black spot as well as of maintaining a militia. Moreover, such organizations seek to develop a group identity that separates them from their opposition, be it a government or ruling elites, and to create an 'us versus them' atmosphere with those inside the black spot being 'us' and those outside the 'them'—a societal objective (Morris 2005; Tollefsen and Buhaug 2015). All three of our examples of black spots led by insurgent organizations—South Ossetia, the Hezbollah Territory, and the Wa State—are involved in such behavior. In effect, black spots centered around insurgent organizations appear to have all four goals—military, political, economic, and societal—and, as a result, generate insecurity across the board for those whom they oppose.

Government Reactions

Table 5.5 describes the kinds of actions that domestic governments and international coalitions or international organizations have directed at the black spots overseen by insurgent organizations. Domestic peace overtures refer to activities such as negotiation, cooptation, legalization, agreed-upon corruption, and proposed collaboration. At the international level, this can mean foreign aid as well as external advising. Confrontations involve operations conducted by law enforcement, the intelligence services, or the armed forces, including the use of counter-insurgency strategies and tactics. At the international level, such behavior can include a 'shaming campaign,' placing a media spotlight on the area, and/or the use of political/economic leverage.

Table 5.5   State and international government reactions to black spots governed by insurgent organizations

Nature of state and international response to black spot	*% black spots governed by insurgent organizations* (N = 35)
Domestic peace overture	51
Domestic confrontation	77
International peace overture	40
International confrontation	43

The data in Table 5.5 indicate that most of the behavior directed at these black spots occurs at the domestic level and is confrontational in intent. Over three-quarters of the black spots involving insurgent organizations have experienced confrontations from domestic legal, intelligence, and/or military services. Half of these same black spots, however, have also encountered some type of peace overture as well. Given the longevity of many of these black spots (74% have been in existence since the 1970s and 1980s, if not longer), these approaches do not seem to be working for either side. And it is probably why the organizations have turned to having two wings—the political for dealing with the peace overtures and the military for when things get more confrontational. Moreover, we might argue that the insurgent organizations keep their militias in and around the black spots and refuse to disband them because of the lack of trust such inconsistency can generate.

Terrorist Organizations

The black spots studied so far from which terrorist organizations operate are often locations where there are bombings, hostage-takings, kidnappings, assassinations, torture, and murder. The terrorist activities are not targeted at armed forces but usually at civilians and non-combatants. Those victimized, however, are not the ultimate targets. Indeed, terrorism is a "tactic of fear-generating coercive political violence ... performed for its propaganda and psychological effects on audiences and parties to a conflict" (Schmid 2011: 86; see also Hoffman 1998). A major difference between terrorist organizations and the insurgent organizations just discussed is that insurgents generally have "fighting forces orders of magnitude larger than those of terrorist organizations"; they have well-developed militias and generally provide social services in the areas in which they are located and operating (Morris 2005: 5). The following are some examples of black spots from which terrorist organizations are currently operating.

Examples

Ein el-Hilweh

Ein el-Hilweh is a Palestinian refugee camp in southern Lebanon in the midst of Hezbollah Territory, along the coast of the Mediterranean Sea only miles from the Israeli border. Established in 1948 for Palestinians fleeing from northern Israel into Lebanon following the establishment of

Israel, Ein el-Hilweh is the largest such camp in Lebanon and is managed by the UN Relief and Works Agency (UNRWA). It is viewed as a 'state within a state within a state' and called Lebanon's 'zone of unlaw' (Gambill 2003). It is the home of a number of terrorist organizations including several jihadist groups such as Jund al-Sham and Usbat al-Ansar.as well as Fatah al-Islam.

With the spillover of Palestinian refugees and jihadists from the Syrian civil war, this refugee camp has become a hotbed of violence as the jihadists try to assert control over the Fatah authorities who are supposedly in charge. Jund al-Sham, in particular, has used the refugee camp as a place to wage attacks against the Lebanese Army and in Syria as well as in Israel. There is also evidence that Saudi Arabia helps to fund the jihadist groups. And money is known to leave the camp to support instability elsewhere. The dire economic circumstances in the camp—unemployment rates are close to 80%—makes for an environment in which frustration and unrest are endemic.

Sulu Archipelago

Another example is found on the islands of the Sulu Archipelago in the Philippines. Geographically, the archipelago lies in close proximity to the island nations of Malaysia and Indonesia. Given its maritime nature and open waterways, the Sulu Archipelago has become very conducive to terrorist activities. Its population is a mix of migrant populations in communities that are very scattered. Its many small, unofficial ports allow easy entry and exit as the coastlines are lightly guarded. In fact, along with Malaysia and Indonesia, it is considered part of the 'Terrorist Transit Triangle.' Note that the terrorist group Abu Sayyaf has been able to operate relatively freely from the archipelago throughout this region. Focused on gaining more autonomy for the Moro Muslims in the archipelago—in effect, an independent Islamic province—Abu Sayyaf is viewed as only the latest group to respond to Moro political dissatisfaction, though among the most violent. In the summer of 2014, the group pledged its allegiance to ISIS. Abu Sayyaf uses funds gained from kidnappings for ransom and illegal arms dealings to finance its operations and has engaged in bombings, assassinations, drive-by shootings, assaults, and extortion to work toward achieving its goals.

Kismayo

The Kismayo or Jubba Valley area in southeastern Somalia is another black spot from which a terrorist organization operates. Located on the Indian

Ocean, Kismayo is a port city in an area of unrest that is 122 miles from the border of Kenya. The area is home base for the terrorist group al-Shabaab. This group has controlled more and less of the terrain in this black spot at different points in time. Its aim has been to turn Somalia into a fundamentalist Islamic state—or at least some parts of it. Al-Shabaab is formally allied with al-Qaeda but there are factions within the organization that favor changing that allegiance to ISIS. Al-Shabaab has conducted bombings, suicide attacks, assassinations, and attacks on places with congregations of civilians such as malls and university dorms both inside Somalia and across the border in Kenya. The group gains funds through extortion, illegal taxation, and other 'fees' at checkpoints and harbors in the areas it controls. They have also been known to engage in piracy and in the smuggling of weapons, people, household goods, and natural resources between Somalia and Kenya.

Locations of Black Spots

Some 26 of the 80 black spots examined in this book involve terrorist organizations and their activities. In other words, terrorist organizations operated out of 31% of the black spots in a manner exemplified by our description of Ein el-Hilweh, the Sulu Archipelago, and Kismayo. Table 5.6 displays the percentages of this type of black spot by region of the world. As with the insurgent organizations, terrorist organizations are found in black spots in every region. But according to our data, the largest numbers are located in the Middle East and in Asia. Roughly one-third of these black spots are found in the Middle East and close to one-quarter in Asia. In effect, over 50% of the black spots involving terrorist organizations studied to date are located in these two regions. In the Middle East, Rafah in the Gaza Strip is another

Table 5.6   Black spots governed by terrorist organizations by region

Region of the world	% black spots governed by terrorist organizations (N = 26)
Europe	15
Middle East	31
Africa	19
Asia	23
North America	0
Latin America	12

example of such a black spot, and in Asia, other examples are Azad Kashmir and Gilgit Baltistan in the Kashmir region administered by Pakistan.

Geopolitical Conditions

Table 5.7 presents the geopolitical conditions that have helped to create and sustain these particular black spots and the terrorist organizations that govern them. Although not as close to the total for the insurgent organizations, almost all the black spots studied so far in which terrorist organizations provide oversight are near or on international borders. Such places facilitate the ease of movement between legal jurisdictions and make it more difficult to be caught. Moreover, roughly three-quarters of these black spots are found along traditional trading routes where it is as easy to conduct illegal as legal trade. Smuggling is made easier as is extortion and corruption in the movement of people and commodities. Note that in discussing the Sulu Archipelago in the Philippines, we commented on it as a part of the Terrorist Transit Triangle with Malaysia and Indonesia.

Around two-thirds of these black spots are rural and offer geographic challenges to national law enforcement and militaries. This percentage is not as high as that for the black spots inhabited by insurgent organizations but suggests again the availability of hiding places and the ease of

Table 5.7   Geopolitical locations of black spots governed by terrorist organizations

Geopolitical location	% black spots governed by terrorist organizations (N = 26)
Near international borders	88
Located on a traditional trading route	77
In existence before 1990	54
Rural	65
Heterogeneous ethnic composition	62
Ethnic composition is conflicted	54
Norms/rules imposed by outside entity	69
Corruption present and visible	88
Located near recent conflict zone	77
Stable as opposed to pulsing	73
Regional/global range of impact	92
Daily/weekly frequency of illicit activity	65
Hub of illicit activities	12

movement in engaging in either illicit or terrorist activities. Interestingly, black spots inhabited by terrorist organizations are split about 50-50 in whether or not they came into existence before or after the Cold War. Many have morphed from previous terrorist organizations as these factionalized and moved in different directions. Note how the cause of the Moro National Liberation Front in the Sulu Archipelago, whose goal since the 1970s had been to seek a separate state, became that of Abu Sayyaf as the former achieved its objective of an autonomous state. Dissatisfied members of the Moro National Liberation Front decided to push for more—a fundamentalist Islamic state for the Moro.

Examining life within these black spots indicates that around two-thirds of them have an ethnic composition that is heterogeneous but, unlike the black spots inhabited by insurgent organizations, only roughly half of these locations are conflicted. In other words, probably through fear, intimidation, and extortion, the terrorist organizations manage the cleavages in the black spots from which they operate. This hypothesis receives some support from the data that indicate in 69% of these black spots the norms and rules to be followed were imposed. Consider the ruthless attacks and bombings organized by the Jund al-Sham terrorist group in Ein el-Hilweh against the Fatah authorities running this refugee camp in order to gain control. As with the black spots in which the insurgent organizations operated, corruption is rampant in the black spots inhabited by terrorist organizations. Moreover, most (three-quarters) are located not far from a recent conflict—the Syrian and Lebanese civil wars in the case of Ein el-Hilweh, the Moro insurgency in the Sulu Archipelago, and the various periods of civil war and outside intervention in Somalia during the last decades.

Illicit Activities

Table 5.7 also suggests that although law enforcement and national militaries might wish it were not the case, the black spots in our sample out of which the terrorist organizations operate are stable. They are here to stay. However, only 12% are hubs of activity, that is, engage in production, transportation, and distribution in the illicit economy. The Kismayo area is one of *only* three such places. Given the terrorist activities that such organizations engage in, becoming and staying a hub may prove difficult. Extortion, fees/illegal taxation, and intimidation may limit business opportunities. But, surprisingly, the illicit activities in these black spots are more frequent than those occurring in black spots operated

Table 5.8 Illicit activities flowing from black spots governed by terrorist organizations

Nature of illicit activities	% black spots governed by terrorist organizations (N = 26)
Drugs	77
Weapons	69
People	62
Natural resources	23
Household goods	35
Counterfeit money/documents	42
Money laundering	38
Terrorism	65

by insurgent organizations. Roughly two-thirds of these black spots are engaged in daily or weekly activities. Here again, extortion and intimidation may require almost daily reminders to remain viable. Like their insurgent counterparts, terrorist organizations use their locations in order to have a regional, if not a global, impact.

The fact that Table 5.8 shows that around two-thirds of the black spots inhabited by terrorist organizations actually are involved in terrorist activities suggests some validity for our classification of the organizations in this chapter. Indeed, the terrorist activities emanating from these black spots are 1.3 times greater than those from black spots involving insurgent organizations. Engaging in dramatic, violent actions targeted at civilian populations meant to have a long-term psychological effect are characteristic of the organizations found in black spots like the Sulu Archipelago, Kismayo, and Ein el-Hilweh. Three-quarters of these black spots are also places that are involved in smuggling drugs and two-thirds in weapons trafficking—often it is the exchange of drugs for weapons that occurs in the black spot. These activities plus kidnapping for ransom, extortion, intimidation, and illegal taxation or fees provide the basis for how these organizations are funded. On average, the black spots in which terrorist organizations operated engaged in 3.5 different illicit activities.

Goals of Illicit Behavior
Table 5.9 explores the motives of the terrorist organizations located in these black spots. Roughly two-thirds of their activities are focused on the military and the use of force. Interestingly, our examples earlier

Table 5.9   Goals of black spots governed by terrorist organizations

Goals of illicit activity	% black spots governed by terrorist organizations (N = 26)
Military implications	65
Economic implications	54
Political implications	42
Societal implications	50

would suggest that this objective is more to goad law enforcement and the military than to engage them. Al-Shabaab is intent on undermining the Somali Federal Government and the African Union Force sent to try to eradicate it. Similarly, Abu Sayyaf has viewed as one of its goals the taunting of US and Philippine forces sent to eradicate it (Adams 2008). The table indicates that a political objective is less likely for the terrorist organizations' activities than we might have expected given that each of the organizations operating in the black spots in our examples seemed intent on changing the political framework in which they operated. But maybe instead of political, the true objectives are economic and societal. To engage in terrorist activities, these organizations need weapons; to intimidate and extort, these organizations need locales where such is feasible and enough income can be raised to maintain the group and let them pursue what they want to do. And the intention of terrorist activities, as we have noted several times, is to instill fear into a target population—to have a societal-wide impact. The reader should note, however, that none of these goals are at the percentages seen in Table 5.4 for black spots overseen by insurgents.

Government Reactions

Table 5.10 describes the kinds of actions that domestic governments and international coalitions or organizations have directed toward the black spots where terrorist organizations operate. This table suggests that law enforcement at both the domestic and international levels has not coalesced around a type of response to direct at the black spots where terrorist organizations reside. About half the time, the approach is either a domestic confrontation (e.g., operations conducted by law enforcement, intelligence services, or armed forces) *or* an international peace overture (e.g., negotiations, legalization, or cooptation). A lot less emphasis has been put on domestic peace overtures or international confrontation. Interestingly, in the Kismayo area

Table 5.10   State and international government reactions to black spots governed by terrorist organizations

Nature of state and international response to black spot	% black spots governed by terrorist organizations (N = 26)
Domestic peace overture	35
Domestic confrontation	46
International peace overture	46
International confrontation	23

when there was an international confrontation by an African Union Force involving the Kenyan military, al-Shabaab merely co-opted ('corrupted') members of the Kenyan military, insuring that they got a cut of the illegal fees the terrorist organization was receiving for its illicit trafficking in and out of the port and to and from Kenya. International confrontation was turned into a 'peace' overture. It would appear that the terrorist organizations use the black spots to wait out both government and international attempts at intervention.

TRANSNATIONAL CRIMINAL ORGANIZATIONS

Transnational criminal organizations represent the businesses of the illicit economy. They are interested in locating in areas "whose market conditions are favorable and risk of apprehension is low" (Williams 1994: 96). As a result, they are intent on taking advantage of prohibitions. Indeed, as we have previously observed, prohibitions facilitate the creation of illicit markets. Consider prohibitions against drugs, fences at borders, sanctions, treaties regulating development or use of particular items, embargoes, and so forth. Transnational criminal organizations are focused on maximizing profits like any multinational corporation. They are also intent on "safeguarding their trafficking routes and operating areas" which may mean "providing critical social and philanthropic services and employment opportunities to the population in the absence of the state" (Realuyo 2015: 7-8). The following are examples of some black spots from which transnational criminal organizations operate. Remember that here we are only examining the black spots in our sample where transnational criminal organizations *operate on their own.*

Examples

Naples

Consider the Scampia and Secondigliano neighborhoods of Naples, Italy, run by the Camorra crime families, and introduced in previous chapters. Having access to one of the largest ports in Western Europe, the Camorra engage in drug trafficking—cocaine and heroin—and in arms dealing while also producing counterfeit clothing, stealing art, and forging documents. Recently, they have moved into waste management involving hauling and disposing of waste from across Europe, gaining such contracts through corrupt practices. In a similar vein, they have laundered money through investments in cement-supplying firms, companies involved in extraction and soil supply, and those involved in land reclamation schemes as well as gotten themselves elected to local political offices. In effect, having survived for nearly two centuries, the Camorra are deeply imbedded in the society in Naples and have come to be accepted as 'part of life.' Their ability to infiltrate all aspects of local society, from businesses to drug trafficking to services to politics, undermines the Italian state, consistently distorting Rome's actions in the region. Moreover, there is a strong network of family, friends, sympathizers, and affiliates of the Camorra residing in the Scampia and Secondigliano neighborhoods, and it is estimated that over 15% of the population is directly involved in Camorra activities. Their many activities are estimated to earn them around 4.9 billion dollars annually (Schumpeter 2016).

Sinaloa State

A second example is the Sinaloa State in Mexico. This state is located in the northern part of Mexico, some 250 miles from the US-Mexican border. It is bounded by the Pacific Ocean on the west and the Sierra Madre Occidental mountain range on the east. It is the home of the Sinaloa Cartel and has often been referred to as the 'drug capital of Mexico.' While Sinaloa's remote areas are home to drug production and cartel leaders' estates, the state's capital city, Culiacan, is the center of the cartel's drug trading, weapons trafficking, and money laundering operations. In fact, this area in Mexico has long been a center for contraband as well as a base for marijuana and poppy cultivation.

While the illicit economy in Sinaloa is dominated by drug trafficking, the smuggling of weapons and money laundering are used to sustain the Cartel's dominance in the region and to conceal its profits. Cooperating with the drug trade and money laundering operations allows Sinaloans, particularly residents of Culiacan, to enjoy luxuries that are otherwise unattainable. Moreover, Cartel leaders are also a source of affordable loans for small business owners as an alternative to expensive and difficult-to-obtain bank loans. And a deeply entrenched system of informal rules based on this economic dependency has developed that involves turning a blind eye to the Cartel and refusing to cooperate with law enforcement. Indeed, it has been estimated that 20% of the Sinaloa State's economic activities are directly or indirectly due to drug trafficking and one-fifth of the residents of the Sinaloa State are employed by the drug trade.

Chuy Valley

A final example is Chuy Valley that spans the border between Kyrgyzstan to the north and Kazakhstan to the south. The shared border in the Valley between the two countries is very long and porous and affords many opportunities to cross illegally. The economic situation in southern Kazakhstan is poor. There is minimal government infrastructure (paved roads, airports, hospitals, etc.) and few well-paying jobs. Many of the residents are farmers, growing mostly fruits and vegetables. However, the Chuy Valley is the heartland of cannabis production. Indeed, cannabis is found naturally in 10% of the total area of the Valley. The growth of cannabis locally and the smuggling of heroin illegally from Afghanistan represent a growing share of the local economy in southern Kazakhstan. Moreover, it is well understood that government officials and police are corruptible. Indeed, an environment has developed that condones taking bribes and making a living off the drug trade that all parties follow, regardless of ethnic, religious, or political differences. As a result, it is the locals in the Chuy Valley that have set up drug syndicates managed by criminals. Although the Kazak federal government and local law enforcement officials are well aware of the problems, they choose *not* to act aggressively because the organized crime groups involved have little or no political aspirations and only occupy themselves with economic activities that could be viewed as subsidizing the local economy in a way that the federal government cannot.

Locations of Black Spots

Some 24 of the 80 black spots we have studied so far involved *only* transnational criminal organizations. In other words, transnational criminal organizations operated on their own in 28% of the black spots in a manner exemplified by our discussion above about the Scampia/Secondigliano

Table 5.11 Black spots governed by transnational criminal organizations by region

Region of the world	% black spots governed by transnational criminal organizations (N = 24)
Europe	29
Middle East	4
Africa	8
Asia	8
North America	17
Latin America	33

neighborhoods in Naples, the Sinaloa State, and the Chuy Valley. At the end of this discussion, we will look at black spots where the different types of organizations have interacted and operated from the same space.

Table 5.11 shows the percentages of this type of black spot by region of the world. It becomes apparent quickly in the table that the black spots in our sample involving only transnational criminal organizations are located in Europe and Latin America. Almost two-thirds (62%) of them are found in these two regions. The Scampia/Secondigliano neighborhoods in Naples and the Sinaloa State are representative of this type of black spot. Although transnational criminal organizations are found in black spots in other regions, they tend to be involved in governance together with an insurgent and/or terrorist organization. Consider that in Asia, the transnational criminal organizations are involved 33% of the time with an insurgent or terrorist organization; in Africa, 33% of the time, and in the Middle East, 66% of the time. In the Middle East, they are more likely to be involved with a terrorist organization than an insurgent one.

Geopolitical Conditions
Table 5.12 describes the geopolitical conditions that have helped to create and sustain these particular black spots and the transnational criminal organizations that run them. As with the other two types of organizations, almost all these black spots are near international borders. Such placement facilitates easy movement to avoid entanglement with law enforcement as well as access to multiple markets. This type of organization, however, unlike the insurgent and terrorist organizations, is just as likely to choose an urban as a rural area in which to locate. Indeed, they often choose, as we noted with the Sinaloa Cartel earlier, a black spot

Table 5.12   Geopolitical locations of black spots governed by transnational criminal organizations

Geopolitical location	% black spots governed by transnational criminal organizations (N = 24)
Near international borders	83
Located on a traditional trading route	67
In existence before 1990	54
Rural	54
Heterogeneous ethnic composition	63
Ethnic composition is conflicted	29
Norms/rules imposed by outside entity	75
Corruption present and visible	92
Located near recent conflict zone	46
Stable as opposed to pulsing	79
Regional/global range of impact	96
Daily/weekly frequency of illicit activity	50
Hub of illicit activities	29

that includes both, again to provide flexibility and to facilitate production, warehousing, and distribution. Like the insurgent and terrorist organizations, the black spots chosen by transnational criminal organizations generally are found along traditional trading routes. Naples, for example, has been a port for centuries welcoming legal and illegal freight. And, as we noted earlier, the Sinaloa State has long been a center for contraband and cross-border trade. The black spots selected by transnational criminal organizations are about 50% as likely to have become operational since the end of the Cold War as before it.

An examination of life within the black spots run by transnational criminal organizations indicates that their ethnic composition is likely to be heterogeneous. See Table 5.12. However, unlike the black spots in which insurgent and terrorist organizations are found, they tend to be less conflicted. Indeed, only roughly one-third of these black spots provide evidence of conflict. This may be because the transnational criminal organizations exercise control and engage in intimidation to get it—or, as our examples suggest, these organizations may offer opportunities to a poor community that lead to indebtedness and loyalty. Regardless, in 75% of these black spots, norms and rules are imposed by the transnational criminal organizations. Add to these data that in almost all (92%) of the

black spots from which transnational criminal organizations operate corruption is rampant and we have even more evidence to support their intent
on exercising control over their locations and the populations in them.
Unlike the black spots inhabited by insurgent and terrorist organizations,
the black spots chosen by transnational criminal organizations are less
likely to be located near a recent conflict zone. They are interested in a
place without interference from refugees, asylum seekers, and 'others'
who might disrupt business. In effect, transnational criminal organizations
select places that they can invest in and make 'home.' We note that the
Sinaloa Cartel has operations in 50 countries and 17 other Mexican states
but they 'live' in the mountains and cities of the Sinaloa State.

Illicit Activities
Table 5.12 also indicates that just like the insurgent organizations, roughly
one-third of the black spots inhabited by transnational criminal organizations were hubs, that is, spaces where these groups are engaged in all the
functions necessary for making their businesses profitable and for keeping
the monies 'in house' so to speak. The two Naples neighborhoods in
which the Camorra operate are such a hub as is the Sinaloa State for the
Sinaloa Cartel. Interestingly, the data suggest that transnational criminal
organizations do not necessarily put pressure on their black spots to be
engaged all the time in illicit activities, that is, daily or weekly. Only 50%
of these black spots evidenced such behavior. For example, the marijuana
in the Chuy Valley is seasonal so it is difficult to have daily or weekly activity. But almost all (96%) are intent on having a regional or global impact.
The 'transnational' in their name is important. Moreover, to have relevance in global illicit supply chains, they have to participate at least at the
regional level.

   On average, these black spots were involved in 3.5 different illicit activities. As is evident in Table 5.13, trafficking in drugs was the most frequent
activity emanating from these black spots controlled by transnational criminal organizations. Drugs of all kinds are part of their repertoire and often
the major focus of attention. Unless, or until, such usage is legalized, trafficking in drugs is a stable business and there are always other markets when
some are disrupted as well as different chemicals to add to make new drugs.
The second most frequent activity was money laundering. Almost two-thirds
of these black spots evidenced such behavior which far exceeded similar

Table 5.13   Illicit activities flowing from black spots governed by transnational criminal organizations

Nature of illicit activities	% black spots governed by transnational criminal organizations (N = 24)
Drugs	88
Weapons	58
People	50
Natural resources	17
Household goods	20
Counterfeit money/documents	50
Money laundering	63
Terrorism	13

Table 5.14   Goals of black spots governed by transnational criminal organizations

Goals of illicit activity	% black spots governed by transnational criminal organizations (N = 24)
Military implications	33
Economic implications	100
Political implications	63
Societal implications	75

behavior on the part of black spots operated by insurgent and terrorist organizations. Note that the black spots from which transnational criminal organizations operate only engage in terrorist activities 13% of the time.

Goals of Illicit Behavior
Table 5.14 indicates the emphasis that transnational criminal organizations place on their economic agenda. All (100%) of the black spots from which these organizations operated focused on their businesses and choosing an environment that was conducive to doing well in such businesses or creating such an environment in places where state government was lax, not present, unable to provide services, or corruptible. These organizations showed little interest in military kinds of issues. However, a societal focus was important in three-quarters of these black spots, suggesting an intent on the part of the transnational criminal organizations on building an identity within the area in which they operate—on becoming the 'Robin Hoods' to the population or insuring through intimidation that

Table 5.15 State and international government reactions to black spots governed by transnational criminal organizations

Nature of state and international response to black spot	% black spots governed by transnational criminal organizations (N = 24)
Domestic peace overture	25
Domestic confrontation	71
International peace overture	67
International confrontation	29

there is a distinctive 'us' to be a part of and a 'them' to be avoided. As we noted in discussing the Chuy Valley black spot, there is also an interest in inducing the police and law enforcement officers to transition from being 'one of them' to becoming a 'part of us' in shaping the politics of the area.

Government Reactions

The data in Table 5.15 show that most of the reactions to what transnational criminal organizations are doing in the black spots they oversee involves either domestic confrontations or international peace overtures, that is, either operations conducted by law enforcement, intelligence services, or armed forces in the country in which they are located *or* an international peace initiative. It is interesting that these reactions occur at both the domestic and international levels. One wonders if they happen at the same time in a kind of 'good cop, bad cop' manner or at the same time and cancel each other out. Or do they allow the transnational criminal organizations to play one level off against the other? Both the Camorra in the neighborhoods in Naples and the Sinaloa Cartel in Sinaloa State have insured through the use of bribes, corruption, cooptation, intimidation, extortion, and assassination that the federal government will have little impact in their terrain. They have created what could be called narco-black spots. These black spots have become much like 'company towns' where all are dependent on the transnational criminal organizations and they are in charge.

COALITIONS

At the beginning of this chapter, we indicated that there are some black spots among those that we have studied that are home to combinations of the three types of organizations we have been discussing. That is, insurgent organizations are co-located with terrorists, and transnational criminal organizations are living in arrangements with insurgent and/or terrorist organizations. These arrangements become important because they suggest that governance in these black spots might mirror what happens in coalition governments. Who is in charge? How is power shared if there are differences in influence? Is there an impact on the types of activities that flow from these black spots? Combinations of these different types of organizations are found in roughly one-third (27) of the black spots we have examined.

Two of these 27 black spots are home to all three types of organizations: Hezbollah Territory in Lebanon and the Abu Kamal area that lies near the border of Syria with Iraq. We have talked about the Hezbollah Territory earlier in this chapter but not about Abu Kamal. The latter is the place on all maps of the original Islamic State (ISIS) caliphate that is the border crossing between the organization's holdings in Syria and those in Iraq. This crossing is where the Euphrates River narrows and it has been a major smuggling route for thousands of years. It became particularly useful to Iraq when the United Nations imposed sanctions on that country during the rule of Saddam Hussein, as a way for foreign fighters to join al-Qaeda in Iraq during the US invasion, and a means for ISIS to maintain control of its Caliphate. This black spot is home to an insurgent organization, terrorists that prey on Iraq, and criminal syndicates that use it, as one member of the US military put it, as "a general supply point for everything" (Al-Tamimi 2013).

Surprisingly, these are the only 2 black spots of the 80 studied here that contain all 3 types of organizations. It is more common for there to be two types of organization located together in a black spot. There are five black spots (6%) occupied by both insurgent and terrorist organizations. (Note it is these five black spots that increase our total number of black spots under investigation in this chapter from 80 to 85.) Some 37% (13/35) of the black spots that are home to insurgent organizations are also home to transnational criminal organizations. This percentage is over half (54% or 14/26) for terrorist and transnational criminal organizations.

The major finding with regard to where we find insurgent and transnational criminal organizations together revolves around hubs—that is, the black spots that engage in production, transport, and distribution. It would appear that insurgent organization hubs are often co-located with those of transnational criminal organizations. Almost half (46%) of those black spots that are hubs for insurgent organizations—think Kashgar, China and Gudauta, Abkhasia—are places where transnational criminal organizations have set up flourishing smuggling operations and where they are generally engaged in money laundering as well. There appears to be a symbiotic relationship between these two types of organizations. Insurgents need resources to maintain militias and to provide the services necessary to keep control over a particular area. Transnational criminal organizations can exploit such needs through their business enterprises. And because the insurgent organizations are likely to be resident in the area for the long haul, the transnational criminal organizations are insured a fairly safe haven for their operations.

The more interesting set of findings occurs for the black spots in which terrorist and transnational criminal organizations are co-located. We find transnational criminal and terrorist organizations operating together in black spots in the Middle East (43%) and terrorist organizations operating more on their own in Asia (33%) and Africa (33%). (In the other regions, there are only one or two black spots in which the two types of organizations work together). Consider Rafah at the border of the Gaza Strip and the Bekaa Valley in Lebanon; these are black spots where terrorist and transnational criminal organizations operate in consort. Then look at FATA in Pakistan and Kismayo (Jubbaland) in Somalia, where terrorist organizations seem to operate more on their own. Part of what allows the coalition of organizations to operate in the Middle East is the general heterogeneity of the areas (71%) in which the black spots are located and the attention paid to economic issues (79%) in these spaces. The black spots in which the terrorist organizations operate alone are more homogeneous (56%) and a little less focused on economic concerns (67%). The transnational criminal organizations appear interested in co-locating with other organizations where there is heterogeneity so that their businesses can flourish without them being the center of attention.

Also of interest are the differences in illicit behavior going on in these two types of black spots. Three-quarters of the black spots in which terrorist organizations operate on their own engage in terrorist activities on a regular basis. This figure is only 57% for the black spots that terrorist and transnational criminal organizations co-inhabit—or 18% less when the two are in the same location. The focus on trafficking in weapons is exactly the opposite between the two types of black spots. Some 83% of the black spots where terrorist organizations operate alone traffick in weapons, whereas only 57% of the black spots where transnational criminal organizations are also present traffick in weapons. The black spots where both terrorists and transnational criminals are active are more likely to emphasize smuggling drugs (86%) and trafficking in people (64%). These figures are 66% and 50% when the terrorist organizations operate alone. Again, we see the emphasis on heterogeneity in both inhabitants and behavior when the transnational criminal organizations join in and a more defined focus on terrorism and the tools to facilitate such activity when terrorist organizations are found alone. One can wonder if having a transnational criminal organization located in a black spot with them shifts the focus of the terrorist organization toward the business end of governance. And, in turn, does having a terrorist organization present allow the transnational criminal organization to hide in plain sight and conduct its business?

CONCLUSION

This examination of the organizations controlling the black spots studied to date suggests that there are certain characteristics all three types of organizations—insurgent, terrorist, and transnational criminal—look for in a place to use as a base of operations. They are intent on locating around international borders and on taking advantage of traditional trading routes. They prefer areas where the population is ethnically heterogeneous and where corruption is endemic. Often these places appear to be areas where they can impose control over the norms and rules governing the space probably as a result of the corruption potential. We are encouraged by these findings as the factors that fit all types of organizations can be used in developing algorithms to assist us in identifying further black spots. Such a process can help us fill in the blanks that we noted in the previous chapter and facilitate us in building the networks described in that chapter.

But we also learned that these three types of organizations exhibit differences in the locations that they choose as well. Indeed, one size does not fit all much of the time. Thus, the different types of organizations appear to be found in black spots in different regions of the world. Insurgent organizations are more common in the black spots in Africa and Asia (54%), terrorist organizations in the Middle East and Asia (54%), and transnational criminal organizations in Europe and Latin America (63%). And they look for different types of terrain in which to locate. The black spots inhabited by insurgent organizations are more rural than those overseen by the other two types and the black spots inhabited by the transnational criminal organizations are more urban. Moreover, insurgent and terrorist organizations are found in areas not too far away from conflict zones whereas transnational criminal organizations steer clear of such locations. Furthermore, the black spots have different functional emphases: insurgents focus on insuring that they have weapons, terrorist organizations on trafficking drugs to support their terrorist activities, and transnational criminal organizations are interested in having facilities for money laundering and black market operations. And they have different types of effects that they hope to perpetrate: insurgents are focused on military, economic, political, and societal goals; terrorist organizations on military, economic, and societal goals, and transnational criminal organizations on economic goals—indeed, at 100%. Once again, this examination provides us with grist for identifying further black spots. This time the algorithms would be more organization and flow specific.

We also examined how state governments and international entities have tended to react to the different types of black spots that we have studied. Black spots inhabited by insurgent organizations have experienced governments alternating between domestic peace overtures and confrontation. It is almost as if the governments do not recognize—or refuse to recognize—that the whole point of an insurgency is to gain legitimacy and sovereignty, or at the least autonomy, over one's own land. With transnational criminal organizations, governments have engaged in domestic confrontations or have brought in international entities with peace overtures. Again, we see an inconsistency in the approach. And we see the willingness of the criminal organization to play one level of authority off against the other. Or, as we noted in discussing the US's Plan Colombia earlier in this book, these organizations merely re-locate for a while until things cool down in the black spot and they can return. Terrorist organizations receive the most ambiguous treatment—a little bit of domestic confrontation as well as a few domestic peace overtures along with a little bit of international confrontation and the extension of an olive branch. With terrorist organizations, government behavior seems to be context specific and targeted at particular black spots and organizations. There is an appearance of trial and error in these actions with not much long-term effect.

We will return to the implications of these findings in the last chapter of the book and the challenges that they raise to those studying these different types of organizations and those involved in their interdiction. But, first, let us explore how these organizations finance their activities and the operations within their black spots. What are the methods they use to finance this illicit economy?

REFERENCES

Adams, Jonathan. 2008. In Basilan, Philippines, a US Counterterrorism Model Frays. *Christian Science Monitor*, December 11.

Al-Tamimi, Aymenn Jawad. 2013. The Factions of Aba Kamal. *Middle East Forum*, December 18.

Byman, Daniel. 2007. *Understanding Proto-Insurgencies*. Santa Monica: RAND Corporation.

Costa, Antonio Maria. 2010. Preface. In *The Globalization of Crime: A Transnational Organized Crime Threat Assessment*. Vienna: UNODC.

Ford, Christopher M. 2007. Of Shoes and Sites: Globalization and Insurgency. *Military Review* 83 (3): 85–91.

Gambill, Gary C. 2003. Ain al-Hilweh: Lebanon's "Zone of Unlaw". *Middle East Intelligence Bulletin* 5 (6), June.

Hoffman, Bruce. 1998. *Inside Terrorism*. New York: Columbia University Press.

Metz, Steven. 2007. *Rethinking Insurgency*. Carlisle: Strategic Studies Institute, US Army War College.

Morris, Michael. 2005. *Al Qaeda as Insurgency*. Fort Belvoir: Defense Technical Information Center.

Pagnucco, Ray, and Jennifer Peters. 2015. Backed by China, a Massive Narco-Army Angles for More Power in Myanmar. *Vice News*, June 12.

Rabasa, Angel, Christopher M. Schnaubelt, Peter Chalk, Douglas Farah, Gregory Midgette, and Howard J. Shatz. 2017. *Counternetwork: Countering the Expansion of Transnational Criminal Networks*. Santa Monica: RAND Corporation.

Realuyo, Celina. 2015. The Future Evolution of Transnational Criminal Organizations and the Threat to US National Security. Defense and Technology Paper 107, National Defense University Press.

Schmid, Alex P. 2011. Academic Consensus Definition of Terrorism. In *Handbook of Terrorism Research*, ed. Alex P. Schmid. London: Routledge.

Schumpeter. 2016 The Crime Families of Naples Are Remarkably Good at Business. *The Economist*, August 27.

Staniland, Paul. 2015. Every Insurgency Is Different. *New York Times*, February 15.

Tollefsen, Andreas F., and Halvard Buhaug. 2015. Insurgency and Inaccessibility. *International Studies Review* 17 (1): 6–25.

Williams, Phil. 1994. Transnational Criminal Networks. In *Networks and Netwars: The Future of Terror, Crime, and Militancy*, ed. John Arquilla and David Ronfeldt. Santa Monica: RAND Corporation.

CHAPTER 6

Financing the Illicit Economy

As with the legal economy, finance furnishes the lifeblood for illicit activity. With the exception of pure barter—for example, the direct exchange of drugs for weapons—there must be a reliable means of transferring value for transnational criminal, insurgent, and terrorist organizations to function as ongoing concerns and to maintain their infrastructure. Like the production, transport, and distribution of illicit commodities via a network of black spots, illicit financial flows inhabit a spatial mosaic of their own. In some cases, the mapping of illicit financial flows mirrors the geographic journey of trafficked goods and people. In other cases, illicit finance becomes its own network. Rough estimates of the amount of money in this illicit economy a year suggest that it accounts for around 3.6% of global GDP or 2.1 trillion US dollars (Schneider et al. 2015).

Just as traffickers flexibly alter their routes in response to official crackdowns, the purveyors of illicit finance also adapt to avoid detection and arrest. Illicit financial actors are talented improvisers, exploiting both traditional and cutting-edge techniques for moving money around the globe. In so doing, they accomplish a variety of objectives. They minimize transaction costs, lower the risk of detection, store value securely, and maintain liquidity. There is also the need to 'clean' the money that has been obtained illicitly—to disguise its origins and make it appear legitimate in order to allow for its use in the licit global economy without drawing the attention of enforcement officials. This objective requires laundering the money, an act that often involves illicit funds being placed in businesses or financial institutions, layered (moved through transactions numerous times to mask their origins), and then integrated with legally generated funds. Naylor (2004: 137) has referred to this three-step process as involving "dissociation, obfuscation, and legitimation" with the intent of making the money "appear sufficiently legitimate that it can be used openly."

This chapter focuses on the methods used to finance the illicit economy, particularly its honed techniques for laundering money. Such methods include recourse to the international banking system, traditional remittance vehicles known as hawala (from the Arabic word 'to transfer'), cash couriers, non-bank money exchange institutions, creation of untraceable or impenetrable shell and front companies, and prepaid access devices as well as the use of free trade zones (FTZs) and offshore financial centers. As suggested by this list of methods, the spectrum of financial transmission activities ranges from cash smuggled in person or in containers moving by rail, road, sea, or air to the sophisticated structuring of financial packages utilizing the latest internet-based payment systems. The purchase and export of vehicles and other trade-based methods of transferring value transnationally provide still another means of underwriting illicit activities. And all are willing to finance themselves via ostensibly licit sources such as through deep-pocket donors to charities and non-profit organizations or through small money remitters who inadvertently get caught up in 'their causes.' Moreover, fraudulent finance, such as the circulation of counterfeit money and the corruption of state and local officials, provides still another source of funding. In sum, these organizations utilize every feasible means of gaining and keeping access to their funds.

Since no single method of money laundering or transfer is fool-proof, we note where the underwriters of criminal activities have improvised in response to state efforts to clamp down on their customary channels. Our black spots case studies provide us with important clues regarding the particular paths chosen for the movement of funds. Since black spots are geographic areas, they tend to be the places where one looks first for evidence of financial flows (e.g., for cash or 'hard currency' or the exchange of commodities and services for such monies). And 39 of the 80 black spots (49%) examined in this book offer indications of how illicit actors in that particular geographic location are approaching the task of transforming illegally acquired funds so that they are regarded as legal. We will build on information learned from our investigation of these particular black spots in the discussion that follows. Let us start by examining the use of the international banking system.

The International Banking System

Banks offer major advantages for the transmission of resources. In particular, they provide a degree of security that cannot be replicated through cash transactions. Banks can, in principle, transfer funds of any amount to any financial center with the stroke of a key. Transmission is virtually instantaneous in the case of wire transfers involving cash deposits and withdrawals. In fact, money can move among a whole succession of banks in jurisdictions around the world within minutes.

Cash can be accessed anywhere ATM machines are located, and such can be done utilizing stolen identities. The chances of detection can be lowered by luring third parties, including ostensibly innocent 'money mules,' to make cash withdrawals or to accept deposits into their accounts and wire the funds elsewhere as well as by using money orders. Banking regulations notwithstanding, that such illicit transfers take place within a global system involving huge sums of daily transactions, financial products, and counterparties serves to complicate monitoring and supervision. According to surveys done by the Financial Action Task Force (FATF), financing of criminal activities typically involves utilizing banking services "as a part of a train of transactions, with funds … moving in and then directly out of their countries" (FATF/OECD 2010a: 24). Consider, for example, the Neuva Loja black spot in Ecuador. Since Ecuador dollarized its economy, Nueva Loja, located on the border between Ecuador and Colombia, has become a place that the Revolutionary Armed Forces of Colombia (FARC) and other transnational criminal organizations can use to launder money through its various financial institutions. Estimates are that the FARC moved between 500 million and 1 billion dollars through Neuva Loja and on into the international banking system after dollarization occurred (World Bank Group 2016). It does not hurt that this community is located near the Lago Agrio oil fields. Both their personnel and the company regularly use these financial institutions, providing some cover for those involved in money laundering.

The key disadvantage today for transnational criminal, insurgent, and terrorist organizations and those funding them in using the international banking system is the enhanced potential for detection. The freezing of assets, blocking of accounts, and the shuttering of financial pipelines appear to pose a greater risk for such groups today. Unusually large, one-off deposits or rapid withdrawals, in particular, often arouse suspicions about the possibility of illicit activity. Efforts to avoid detection have encouraged the wider practice of structuring—or at times called 'smurfing' by the banking industry—where larger bundles of cash are broken down into smaller deposits or withdrawals which circumvent anti-money laundering reporting requirements (Internal Revenue Service 2006; Dunn 2014). In the US, such requirements come into play when the amount reaches $10,000 a day. The Sinaloa State black spot, home of the Mexican Sinaloa Cartel, is well known for structuring. Drug profits are smuggled across the US border with Mexico in the form of cash, run through Mexican currency exchange houses, and deposited into Mexican bank accounts which then can be wired to banks in the US or internationally. To get around reporting requirements at both currency houses and banks, the Cartel employs "legions of individuals—including relatives, maids, and gardeners—to convert small amounts of dollars into pesos or to make deposits into local banks.... They can use an army of people like Smurfs and go through $1 million before lunchtime" (Smith 2010). We note in this regard that the Sinaloa State often ranks among Mexico's top six states in total bank deposits but only around 17th in economic production (Roig-Franzia 2008).

In addition, we know from press reports that otherwise legitimate global banks like HSBC with branches located in the Sinaloa State have facilitated money laundering by terrorist organizations and drug cartels. And sometimes this behavior has been blatant such as the report of members of the Sinaloa Cartel depositing "hundreds of thousands of dollars in cash in a single day using boxes designed to fit the exact dimensions of the teller's window at HSBC branches in Mexico" (Burnett 2014). Standard Chartered Bank branches in the Wa State black spot in Myanmar were also alleged to have allowed hundreds of millions of dollars in illicit transactions within the region (see, e.g., *The Economist* 2012). Although neither bank admitted purposeful engagement in illicit activities, both UK banks agreed to pay fines. Having failed to comply fully with regulations, other European institutions such as UBS and BNP Paribas have also been penalized by US authorities. In addition to incurring significant fines, such banks risk an even more onerous outcome, effective isolation from the US dollar transaction clearing market.

Distinguishable from global players whose banking activity remains overwhelmingly legitimate are banking institutions that operate regularly on the edge of legality or conduct unambiguously illicit activities. Such banks provide a range of services to shady actors while shielding them from the purview of financial regulators and law enforcement officials. Consider, for example, two banks in Myanmar designated as primary money laundering concerns by the

US Treasury in November 2003—the Myanmar Mayflower Bank and the Asia Wealth Bank. These banks were used by the United Wa State Army and the United Wa State Party to legitimize their drug trafficking funds. Also, consider the millions that Wachovia Bank (now part of Wells Fargo) had to pay in a settlement for laundering drug profits from black spots like the Sinaloa State that came to the bank via Mexican currency exchanges. A classic example is the Bank of Credit and Commerce International (BCCI), informally known as the 'Bank of Crooks and Criminals International.' BCCI "was an all-purpose illicit financial hub, providing banking services for drug trafficking, arms trafficking, and money from the Middle East, Europe, and South America. It was the quintessential bad bank" (Zarate 2013: 61).

Note that it is branches of these members of the international banking system that are engaged in the initial money laundering—branches located within the black spots that maintain the accounts of local residents as well as accounts for the leadership of the transnational criminal, terrorist, or insurgent organizations involved in the governance of the black spot. These branches are operated by residents of the black spot. In testifying before the US Senate about Hezbollah finances, Levitt (2005) observed the use of local Hezbollah operatives in Western Union offices in southern Lebanon. It is believed that in some cases "Hezbollah gets a cut of the 7% service fee charge split between Western Union and the local agent," while "in other cases, Hezbollah simply uses the money wiring company to launder and transfer funds" (Levitt 2005: 12). Employees loyal to the organizations controlling the black spot facilitate making illicitly earned money licit by moving it into the global financial system. The branch banks, currency exchanges, and money-wiring services operated and/or controlled by those engaged in transnational criminal activities provide alternative ways for these organizations to do business with the international banking system which sooner or later they will do through layering and integrating the illegal funds with those obtained legally. Consider that the bulk of the funds for the terrorist attacks on September 11, 2001 (9/11) were "passed through Sun Trust Bank accounts in Venice, Florida" (Bowers 2009: 386). And Dubai, a black spot studied here, was a key financial transit route for the funds going to Florida and then to the attackers.

Non-Bank Methods of Value Transfer

But what about ways that have been used to transfer sums of money efficiently and securely without using the banking system? An original reason for the development of non-bank transfers was to be able to have funds reach individuals and groups in locations where few transnationally linked banks existed or where individual recipients lacked bank accounts. For transnational criminal, terrorist, and insurgent organizations, a key factor for non-bank transfers is to circumvent the banking anti-money laundering regulations and currency controls increasingly being put into place as symbolized by the 'internationally endorsed global standards' in the Financial Action Task Force's (FATF) recommendations regarding money laundering and the financing of terrorism and proliferation (FATF 2012). The rationale for non-bank forms of money laundering is to distance the funds from the predicate crime via an intricate process of placement, layering, and integration with legally generated funds, much like we have already observed happens with regular banking. With terrorist and insurgent finance, the idea is also how best to channel the funds—be they legally or illegally derived—to the organizations involved in these activities. More often than not, such transfers are closely co-mingled with legally derived funds. This behavior underscores a theme highlighted throughout this volume—how difficult it often is to distinguish between the illicit and licit economies. These non-banking methods are called informal value transfer systems or IVTS. Among those we have found being used in the black spots studied here are hawala transactions, trade-based money laundering, cash couriers, creation of shell or front companies, exploitation of charities and non-profits, and recourse to digital currencies and alternative payment systems. Let us explore each of these in more detail.

Hawala

One classic IVTS practice is the hawala system, "an informal money transfer system popular in the Middle East, North Africa, and South Asia that dates back to the Middle Ages" (Mayyasi 2014: I). The hawala system goes by a number of different names across these regions from fei-ch'ien in China to padala in the Philippines, hul kuan in Hong Kong, and hundi in India (O'Brien 2007). In its beginning, hawala facilitated trade along transnational routes like the Silk Road. In its most basic form, hawala involves "money transfer without money movement" (Jost and Sandhu 2006: 5). In effect, hawala is a means of transferring value transnationally without the actual or even virtual movement of money. It facilitates people sending "money internationally via an informal network of money lenders and businessmen who rely on their reputation rather than formal contracts" (Mayyasi 2014: 1). This form of transfer largely circumvents the generally more costly bank transmissions and money-wiring services like Western Union. The typical arrangement involves party 'A' who deposits cash with a local establishment 'X.' Establishment X then alerts a counterpart 'Y' in another country that an individual 'B' in their locale, using a specific code for the transfer, will be collecting a certain amount of local currency from Y. The direction of the transfer can also be reversed using this same setup.

The hawaladars involved in conducting the hawala arrangement are often located in a local ethnic market or travel agency but they also are found in convenience stores, import/export businesses, places engaged in foreign exchange, car rental establishments, and casinos—places that can deal in cash. More recently, those involved in hawala banking have become embedded in "economic rather than ethnic communities... evolving into brokers between different actors in the informal economy, perpetrators of organized crime, and businessmen with 'black money'"(van de Bunt 2008: 700). Indeed, these latter actors are often called 'money remitters' and are useful as launderers because they can skirt regulatory scrutiny, generally undercut charges of banks and wire services, guarantee the anonymity of the parties involved, are not involved with a bureaucracy and so can facilitate a rapid transfer, and are versatile (Bowers 2009).

These hawaladars—money remitters or brokers—located as they are in various parts of the globe settle their accounts in a variety of ways. If they are business partners, they may engage in 'under' or 'over-invoicing.' That is, an invoice that is sent accounts for the amount owed and is either over or under what is needed to cover the money transferred via the hawala transaction. In this way, hawala fees become a side-business, supplementing the principal business' cash flow or working capital. With the funds from the main and remittance businesses co-mingled, it can be unclear how much of the overall revenue flow is attributable to each activity. In this way, the depositing of remittance-related cash and checks in local banks can be masked, just part of the normal banking practice for most small businesses. These hawaladars may also travel overseas regularly and, as part of this travel, settle with the broker. Alternatively, the balance may be eliminated via the physical transfer of currency or by the smuggling of precious metals and other high-value goods. This versatility makes identifying and regulating what has become known as the 'black hawala' (that involved in money laundering) more difficult, ensuring its usefulness in the illegal economy (Jost and Sandhu 2006).

All roads seem to lead to Dubai when the subject of the hawala system and money laundering is discussed. Some (Duaij 2009) have called Dubai the 'washing machine' for smugglers, traffickers, pirates, terrorists, and transnational criminals. Others (Jost and Sandhu 2006) have observed that when hawala financial centers are being considered, Dubai is high on the list if not at the top. As one of the black spots among the 80 investigated here, Dubai provides us with an example of how the hawala system can work in the finances of the illicit economy. Indeed, "Dubai, unlike many other South Asian nations, allows essentially unregulated financial dealings" (Jost and Sandhu 2006: 11). As the Tax Justice Network's (2018: 1) report on Dubai indicates, it is "unquestionably one of the world's best known tax havens or secrecy jurisdictions" built around its identification as a free trade or economic zone and its "ask-no questions, see-no-evil approach to commercial or financial regulation." This same Network notes that much of the money coming into Dubai is in the form of gold or cash. Davidson (2008) describes how Dubai's hawala money laundering system has evolved into a hybrid system that involves mixing the informal banking system with the formal. As our discussion of the ways in which hawaladars work the system indicates, this practice makes it even more difficult to distinguish what is legitimate from what is illicit money. Some (Glenny 2009; Tax Justice Network 2018) have argued that if Dubai did not already exist for insurgents, terrorists, and transnational criminals, it would be invented.

Consider the following example involving Dubai. Naresh Kumar Jain, the so-called hawala king, has been arrested and freed a number of times on money laundering charges and for doing so for drug dealers. The original charges occurred in Dubai where he spent 20 years building his hawala network of businesses and contacts. "From Dubai, he allegedly provided customers with funds in a country of their choice" growing out of a network "so extensive and lucrative that he often did not have to physically move money" (Laville 2009). Among his customers were heroin dealers who worked the Balkan Route, drug cartels in the Americas, the Russian mafia, diamond smugglers in Africa, the Taliban, and Osama Bin Laden. He is reported to have used places like a beauty parlor in Italy to assist him in laundering around $4 million a day and his network is rumored to have involved the hybrid hawala system described above to launder around $2.2 billion a year. He used banks and exchange houses located in Dubai to allow him to layer the money, turning what was 'dirty' money into 'clean.' Always the emphasis was on making the money trail difficult to follow and legitimate as soon as possible. As one Dubai businessman put it, money laundering built the place, it and the "region's long-established informal money-transfer network known as hawala" (Mathiason 2010).

Trade-Based Money Laundering

Another classic form of IVTS involves the exploitation of the global trading system. Called trade-based money laundering or TBML, this process "uses trade to conceal the origins of (often illegally obtained) funds" (Sullivan and Smith 2011: 1). This form of money laundering has grown exponentially with the growth of international trade and the increased regulation of the banking system worldwide. If, as some have observed, the banking system is the 'front door' for money launderers, then TBML could be considered 'the back door' and it is currently 'wide open' (Zdanowicz 2009; Cassara 2015). Indeed, TBML has become a major method for integrating dirty money into the legal economy. International trade has a number of attractive qualities for illicit actors: the large volume renders individual transactions insignificant; trade crosses international borders and, thus, regulatory jurisdictions; it is easy to make the transactions complex and to co-mingle illegitimately acquired monies with legitimate funds; and customs agencies generally have limited resources with little sharing of data between countries (see FATF 2006). In effect, it is easy to manipulate the system.

Generally, TBML involves the use of one or more of the following methods: over- and under-invoicing of goods and services, multiple invoicing, over- and under-shipment of goods and services, and falsely described goods and services (Sullivan and Smith 2011). These techniques are fairly self-explanatory. But TBML also often employs the banking system and it can involve money remitters or hawaladars as described in the previous section. Indeed, one TBML technique involving a number of these methods has achieved some fame among illicit actors and law enforcement as being a rather effective way of laundering money through trade. Called the 'black market peso exchange,' it was originally designed to help drug cartels in Latin America 'repatriate' the monies they earned upon selling their smuggled drugs in the US (FATF 2006; Becerra 2015). It involved these cartels buying goods in the US with illicit dollars and then shipping the goods back home where they were sold in the currency of that country and the proceeds were re-acquired by the cartel. Such TBML could involve a broker on both sides who made the purchase and shipping arrangements or a front company of the cartel in the US could purchase the goods and send them to a front company in Latin America. At some point in time, such a process uses the international banking system. TBML usually involves collusion among the parties involved in the transactions and, importantly, crosses international borders with the intention of complicating detection (Becerra 2015).

Most of the black spots studied here have used TBML. Two examples are instructive. The first was divulged as the result of something called Operation White Whale under the aegis of both Interpol and Europol. This operation was centered around the black spot of Marbella, Spain (BBC News 2005; Crawford, 2005; Walker 2005). It involved a broker who was a corporate lawyer; a building boom in this seaside location on the Costa del Sol; a Dutch company and its subsidiary; money from the Yukos petrochemical giant in Russia, assumed to be ill-gotten gains; and drug money resulting from the sale of drugs throughout Europe. Seized documents suggested that "large sums of money were diverted from Yukos, the Russian oil group, to a Dutch company and then reinvested in a Spanish unit" in the Marbella area (Crawford 2005). It was observed that criminal networks in the area had become the driving force behind the construction industry. Roughly 500 million euros were estimated to have been laundered through "phantom companies and property deals along the Costa del Sol" (Walker 2005).

A second illustration involves the Sinaloa State black spot in Mexico and the Sinaloa Cartel that governs it. The Sinaloa Cartel had ransom money that was to be paid to them in dollars and they needed to get it home as pesos (Mozingo et al. 2014; Taxin 2014). So they turned to a fashion wholesaler in Los Angeles and had the ransom money delivered to this business which acted as a broker and paid for clothing that had been shipped by 17 other businesses to an importer in the Sinaloa State. In other words, the fashion wholesaler used the ransom money to cover the debts of an importer in the Sinaloa State. Then that importer used pesos to pay the Sinaloa Cartel the original ransom. In effect, the money never crossed the border but companies on both sides were paid and the Cartel received its money in domestic currency. As was noted on CNN, "the city of Los Angeles is now the nation's epicenter for money laundering by international drug cartels" (Martinez et al. 2014).

Cash Couriers

"Physical transportation of cash across an international border is one of the oldest and most basic forms of money laundering" (MENA FATF 2015). When one has moved cash across a border, the rules and regulations change as the state jurisdiction changes. This basic fact is probably one significant reason why the majority of the black spots studied in this project are found along international borders. And, as the Europol Financial Intelligence Group (EFIG) (2015) has observed, law enforcement faces a problem when cash couriers are involved in moving money across a border in linking the cash that they are carrying to illicit activities. Moreover, for law enforcement "the movement of cash via freight and mail remains a blind spot" (EFIG 2015: 7). Since cash moves across the world on a daily basis, it is anonymous and leaves no audit trail. Moreover, the illicit economy itself is largely cash-based. It is easy to see how cash couriers have come to play an important role in illicit financing. The use of such couriers facilitates illicit actors moving their monies to places where they have easier access to its placement and where "they may have greater influence in the economic and political establishment" (EFIG 2015: 18)—in other words, to such places as black spots.

There are myriad ways of carrying cash across a border and insurgents, terrorists, and transnational criminals have become creative in their use of such services (see, e.g., MENA FATF 2015). It can be carried by individuals often hired specifically for this purpose. On individuals, the cash can be concealed in clothing, in luggage, or even swallowed internally. It can be driven over in some kind of motor vehicle—for example, stashed in "spare tires, engine transmissions, and truckloads of baby diapers" (Booth and Miroff 2010). It can go in a cargo container or other type of cargo consignment. Cash can go by mail or fast parcel service. It can cross borders on air passengers, as air cargo, or by small aircraft. Then there are go-fast boats. And with forged documents and a lot of cash to carry, the same person can have multiple identities or multiple persons can have the same identity. There can be spotters to check when and how the flow is going on a given day and to estimate what seems the most propitious time to cross the border. Furthermore, larger banknotes such as the US $100 bill, the 500 euro bill, and the Swiss 1000 franc note facilitate cash couriers carrying large sums of cash in less space and bulk. In fact, illicit actors will pay more than "face value for high-value notes because of how convenient they are to transport" (*The Economist* 2016: 87–88). There has been a push by governments and law enforcement to eliminate these large banknotes because of their use by cash couriers but it has been hard to do.

As an example, consider the *New York Times* piece entitled "Along the US Mexico Border: A Torrent of Illicit Cash" (McKinley and Lacey 2009). The authors describe how cash flows "South over the Mexican border daily like a motorized river." In our case studies of three black spots along this border—Nogales; Ciudad Juarez, and the Tohono O'odham Reservation—we have observed the use of cash couriers to transport money from the US into Mexico. They have found ingenious hiding places like placing cash under the floor in a Mexican passenger bus and in duffle bags balanced on the heads of people as they waded across the Rio Grande. "There is an entire cottage industry devoted to building secret compartments in vehicles" (McKinley and Lacey 2009). Indeed, as a chief of financial operations for the US Drug Enforcement Association once observed, "they have multiple, multiple options. They can hide a million dollars in a tractor-trailer or they can carry it across the border in a handbag" (Booth and Miroff 2010). And for the cartels getting caught is just the price of doing business as it is generally a small percentage of what actually flows into their coffers. Given the success of cash couriers, there are now persons and businesses on both sides of the border who specialize in the cross-border movement of cash; they manage the flow, arrange for couriers, and generally assist in the smuggling operations such as paying off border guards and customs officials.

One of the black spots studied here uses couriers to move gold—"a universally accepted currency" that "acts as a medium for exchange in criminal transactions" (FATF/APG 2015: 6, 11). That black spot is Goma in the Democratic Republic of Congo (DRC). Often involving a broker, gold coming out of this eastern area of the Congo is estimated to annually yield profits in the range of 30–120 million dollars for transnational criminal activities (UNEP-MONUSCO-OSESG 2015). The gold is generally couriered out of Goma into Rwanda, Burundi, or Uganda. Typically, it is transported by air, using helicopters or fixed-wing small aircraft. It is assumed that there is a courier onboard the aircraft as well as one at the landing site across the border who sees to it that the smuggled gold is mixed at this intermediate stop with legitimate product. Its final destination, once more by air, is Dubai–again accompanied by a courier and perhaps even carried in luggage since it has become legitimate. As has been observed, often "gold's faint paper trail disappears as soon as it arrives in Dubai" and it can go anywhere from there (Bariyo 2013).

Shell Companies, Front Companies, and Other 'Creative' Corporate Structures

Corporate structures like shell and front companies are used by insurgent, terrorist, and transnational criminal organizations to facilitate hiding the proceeds of their illicit activities and in the process lend these funds legitimacy. In addition to concealing the source of this money, consider that these corporate structures also conceal the ownership of the funds. This process allows organizations to maintain control over their assets while severing the link with the activities that originally generated the funds. (see FATF 2006; Morrisey n.d.'). Shell companies are intentionally set up to "obfuscate ownership" whether "the purpose is criminal or not" (Duhaime 2016). And they are often set up in offshore financial centers to ensure that the funds have crossed an international border as well as to reduce inevitable regulation and information that is releasable to the public.

Front companies are 'actual' businesses. They have employees and carry out activities intended to be profitable. But when owned by insurgent, terrorist, and transnational criminal organizations, they can also conceal illegal activities or the proceeds of illegal activities. They can be a subsidiary of a shell company or of a larger company. Such companies protect the 'true owner' from scrutiny and liability and facilitate the laundering of monies raised illicitly. By allowing for the co-mingling of funds, these companies make monies resulting from illegal activities appear legal (Reuter and Truman 2004). Front companies often are companies that are themselves cash-based such as restaurants, bars, casinos, used car dealerships, and other types of storefront businesses. They may also be companies that are useful in carrying out the illegal activity, for example, a trucking company, an importer or exporter, a tourist agency. Front companies are often involved in the trade-based money laundering described earlier.

In addition to facilitating the integration of illicit funds into the licit economy, shell and front companies are used to hide or obfuscate the 'true identity' of the beneficiary of the monies changing hands. To facilitate this endeavor, insurgent, terrorist, and transnational criminal organizations often use what are called "specialized financial intermediaries" (FATF

2006: 5). These intermediaries are generally lawyers and accountants. The law firm of Mossack Fonseca which was implicated in the release of the 'Panama Papers' is a case in point (see The International Consortium of Investigative Journalists website). This release of documents indicated how the law firm assisted in setting up shell corporations, some of which were judged to be engaged in illegal activities. These intermediaries may not know the reason for which the illicit organization is using the shell or front company. But even if they do, their interaction is protected by the lawyer–client privilege if the intermediary is a lawyer and the banking secrecy laws of the state in which they are incorporated if an accountant.

Such intermediaries are also useful in the creation of trusts which separate the illicit proceeds from the organization or individual responsible and, in effect, make the monies legal. And such trusts can be set up for specific periods of time. These intermediaries also can be engaged in the purchase of real estate which, in turn, converts the dirty money into something legal. Moreover, intermediaries can be involved in the buying of insurance policies, purchased in lump sum and then redeemed with a so-called sanitized check paid by the insurance company (Reuter and Truman 2004). Consider how difficult tracking illicit funds becomes if a shell company sets up a trust, provides the funds to purchase real estate, pays to incorporate a front company, and/or buys insurance.

The Camorra clans that oversee the Scampia and Secondigliano neighborhoods in Naples, Italy have linked a number of these strategies together. Known for using front companies to sell original and counterfeit clothing, they also have used private businesses as a front to facilitate them bidding for and negotiating lucrative contracts for waste removal. The Euro-zone crisis provided a strategic opportunity for these clans to play the specialized financial intermediary role described above. The crisis made it difficult for many legitimate small businesses to gain immediate access to short-term bank credit. By providing such loans, the clans could launder their illegally gained money as well as earn interest and assume ownership of another front company should the business default on the loan. Moreover, such usury served to eliminate competition for their own businesses. In effect, it allowed the clans to increasingly "assert their sovereignty over the territory they control"—their black spot (Di Natala 2012: 1).

Also consider the behavior of the transnational Irish-led drug cartel that emanated from Marbella, Spain, a favored black spot "given its proximity to Morocco, a major drug exporter, and to Gibraltar, a center for the movement of capital of all types of origin" and "a real-estate market on the Costa del Sol that provides a range of money-laundering opportunities" (Guell 2016). This particular group started its operation by opening several front businesses that imported inexpensive foods from Spain to Ireland. Once established and with a record of exporting such products on vehicles associated with their companies into their own warehouses in Ireland, they began smuggling drugs in these shipments. Note how this process facilitated the monies earned from drugs being co-mingled with the funds earned from food shipments. In effect, the cartel became a wholesaler for drugs to various gangs throughout Ireland. This operation was repeated in the UK. As the overall business grew, the front companies were tied to a parent front company in Spain where the cartel was based. The monies from the co-mingled funds were also used to purchase real estate—residential and small retail businesses—in Marbella as well as in places like Dubai. These purchases involved a web of lawyers and accountants worldwide. We know about this cartel and its intricate use of front companies and intermediaries from police files as part of Operation Shovel. The monies were so intricately layered and integrated into the legal economy that investigators were "unable to find enough direct evidence to link the key men to specific crimes with which they could be charged" (Lally 2016: 5).

Charities and Non-Profits

A different type of IVTS involves charities and non-profits or, as they are often referred to, non-governmental organizations (NGOs). Such organizations mask or disguise the flow of financing to support criminal, terrorist, and insurgent organizations. Think about the flow of cash from donors to the on-the-ground activities of most charities. A donor gives money to a charity; the charity mixes the money from a variety of donors and transfers it to a grass-roots organization or aid group in another country; this organization then puts the money to use in a particular project. In effect, to achieve their ends, donors pass their money through a series of intermediaries. Often this money trail crosses international borders. The benefits of using such NGOs are four-fold: (1) the missions of these organizations are generally intended to "make the world a better place" and thus they enjoy the public's confidence; (2) the offices of the grass-roots organizations and activities are often located in or near conflict zones where the black spots discussed in this volume are found; (3)

such organizations focus on raising money from a variety of donors to carry out activities in far-flung comers of the world and are involved in integrating these funds and transferring their sums to such places; and (4) this mixing and transferring of funds shield "the ultimate end-users from scrutiny" (Levitt 2004: 3). As an illustration, consider the case of a Russian national who "gave money to a charity, a company (receiving money from other charities) also gave money to that same charity, that charity then gave money to other charities (both legitimate and illegitimate), and one of those recipient charities finally distributed the money to individuals in cash, wire transfer, courier, and goods form" (Bowers 2009: 212).

As this example suggests, the charities themselves, as well as the donors, may be legitimate or illegitimate. There are 'sham' or shell-like charities just like there are such corporations. Such NGOs become a pass-through for money to illicit organizations. And some act as front organizations for such illicit groups. The Goodwill Charitable Organization is a case in point. It was located in Dearborn, Michigan and indicated on its incorporation forms that it "provided assistance to poor people" and, yet, its pamphlets indicated that the funds raised by the organization went to Hezbollah and its Lebanon-based Martyrs Foundation (Litvin 2011: 22). This latter foundation supports the widows and orphans of suicide bombers. In effect, the Goodwill Charitable Organization operated as a fundraising arm for Hezbollah. Indeed, Hezbollah is known to have established the Goodwill Charitable Organization as a front organization to help it in raising and laundering money to assist in the governance of its territory back in Lebanon (Glaser 2010). This particular charity is only one of many such organizations worldwide used to funnel monies to Hezbollah (Levitt 2007).

The charities put in place by illicit organizations often build on particular characteristics that are found in the black spot where they reside or in the diaspora communities that are related to them. The Hezbollah Territory and organization just mentioned depend on charitable donations pulled together by networks of Lebanese nationals living in Africa, Europe, Latin America, and the US—for example, cells in Charlotte, North Carolina; Ciudad del Este, Paraguay; and Cotonou, Benin (Levitt 2007). Indeed, the German government is funding a Hezbollah-operated Refugee Club Impulse directed at the large Middle Eastern refugee population in that country (Emerson 2016). In the Zenica black spot in Bosnia and Herzegovina, money from Islamic countries is laundered through humanitarian organizations to finance religious education in Wahhabi Islam for young Bosnian Muslims. In addition, there are courses in computer and internet skills as well as marksmanship, explosives, and martial arts (Michaletos 2010). And in the Muzaffarabad black spot in Pakistan, the various insurgent and terrorist organizations rely on donations from diaspora communities across the Middle East, Islamic NGOs, and Pakistani and Kashmiri businesses. As has been observed, these groups receive "witting or unwitting contributions from mosques, NGOs, internet users, wealthy donors, and charitable foundations" (Smith 2009: 67).

Prepaid Access Devices

Sometimes referred to as new payment products and services (NPPS), we are referring here to the use of electronic transactions that "offer an alternative to traditional financial services" (FATF 2013: 4). Introduced in the late 1990s, these prepaid access devices include such products and services as prepaid cards, mobile payment services through phones and wallets, and internet-based payment services. We are going to focus here on prepaid cards and will deal with the other types of devices in the next chapter when we explore black spots as they are related to the internet and cyberspace.

Prepaid cards are an alternative to credit and debit cards and have a number of characteristics that facilitate their use for laundering money. They involve paying up front for the card, whereas with credit cards the cardholder pays after the purchase or service is performed and with debit cards the cardholder pays for the product or service at the time of purchase. For prepaid cards, there is a certain degree of anonymity to the process as there is no need to set up a traditional bank account nor manage a payment account. The most versatile of the prepaid cards are reloadable, can be used at ATM machines, and are transferable. That prepaid cards have become a big business is evident in the fact that more than 623 billion dollars were loaded onto them in 2015 alone (Rosenberg and Wolf 2016). As has been noted about prepaid cards, they offer "convenience, accessibility, immediate liquidity, anonymity, transferability, and transportability" (King 2013: 1). And as has been noted about insurgent, terrorist, and transnational criminal organizations, they can be "ingenious when it comes to exploiting vulnerabilities in payment systems" (Sienkiewicz 2007: 9).

There are two types of prepaid cards (see ICE 2006; Sienkiewicz 2007). The first are closed system cards in the form of gift cards or phone cards. These are usually sold in preset amounts and are generally linked to a particular retailer and the goods and services that it offers. They are neither reloadable nor redeemable for cash but they are transferable—thus the use of gift in its name. The second type are called open system cards; they are generally network branded like credit cards with a logo on the front. They can be initialized at the beginning with large dollar amounts, they are reloadable, and many can be used at an ATM to withdraw cash without having a bank account. For illicit actors, they have a number of exploitable vulnerabilities. These general purpose reloadable (GPR) prepaid cards can be reloaded anywhere in the world with access to that particular network; in many parts of the world there is no maximum load limit; they can be used at ATMs for cash, activated online, and taken across borders without a declaration requirement. With the sharing of PIN numbers, these GPR prepaid cards become transferable.

Just like many of the financial arrangements we have discussed in this chapter, prepaid cards often involve intermediaries between a buyer and a bank or electronic financial institution. For both types of prepaid cards, there has only recently been a move for banks to create direct links to the prepaid cards. Instead, for most of these cards, intermediaries involve a program manager, a distributor, and load/reload sites and networks (King 2013). The program managers are the third-party firms that design, produce, market, and service the prepaid cards as well as maintain records regarding the cards. Examples of such managers are American Express, Visa, H & R Block, and GE Capital who are under contract to a financial institution. The distributors are the firms that sell the prepaid cards such as grocery and drug store chains, big box retailers, and internet retailers, The load/reload networks are generally money-service businesses that provide services to the buyers of cards via physical or virtual sites.

Although in the US there are limits to the amounts allowed on these prepaid cards similar to what one can deposit in a bank account at one time ($10,000), that is not the case in other countries. Regardless, as several illicit actors were heard to argue: "Forget bulk cash; it's heavy and hard to hide, and not convenient for crossing borders. A safer alternative is electronic cash loaded on prepaid cards. They are barely distinguishable from credit or debit cards but much more versatile" (Associated Press 2011). With high-limit prepaid cards, it does not take many to smuggle bulk cash across a border. And such is becoming the case between the US and its southern border where there is no current mandatory declaration of the amount of money that one is carrying on such cards (Stiles 2013; Rosenberg and Wolf 2016). "A drug trafficking foot soldier simply loads up a prepaid card with dollars and walks across the border without having to declare sums over the usual $10,000 reporting requirement, thus carrying a car trunk's worth of cargo in his wallet" (Ellingwood and Wilkinson 2011).

Consider some ways that insurgent, terrorist, and transnational criminal organizations could use prepaid cards in a money laundering scheme. Take gift cards, for instance. The illicit actor could purchase gift cards at the highest levels allowable in the US from retailers also found in other countries. These gift cards could be sent to an accomplice in another country who sells the cards in the local currency which then ends up in the insurgent, terrorist, or transnational criminal organization's hands (Sienkiewicz 2007: 12). With the reloadable prepaid cards, a scenario might be as follows: prepaid cards are purchased using 'dirty' money with the purchased cards being used to buy additional prepaid cards. The second set of purchased prepaid cards are used at an ATM for cash. "The last step could be to place the laundered money onto prepaid cards which are then used either to purchase retail goods or to pay another criminal" (Sienkiewicz 2007: 7). It has been reported that one of the men involved in the Paris terrorist attacks in November of 2015 traveled throughout Europe before those attacks on an Italian prepaid card linked to the Camorra and their black spot home base in Naples (Nadeau 2015).

GEOGRAPHICALLY ORIENTED METHODS OF VALUE TRANSFER

The previous discussion suggests the complexity of the ways in which insurgent, terrorist, and transnational criminal organizations obtain the financing necessary to continue their activities and gain access to their profits. These illicit actors cross borders to take advantage of changes in rules and regulations as well as use intermediaries to make tracking what they are doing more difficult. They are involved in building the cross-border networks that facilitate the placement, layering, and integration of their illicit funds into the legal economy. We turn now to a set of geographic spaces that have become critical links in such networks across the last several decades, namely, free trade zones and offshore financial centers.

Free Trade Zones

Free trade zones (FTZs) are "designated areas within a country in which incentives are offered to support the development of exports, foreign direct investment, and local employment" (FATF 2010b: 4). As we noted in Chap. 4, other names for such areas are special economic zones, foreign trade zones, and export processing zones. These areas have proliferated in the last four decades from 79 in 1975 to roughly 3,000 now in 135 countries accounting for around "68 million direct jobs and over 500 billion dollars of direct trade-related value" (International Chamber of Commerce 2013: 9). These FTZs are located on borders or ports of entry into countries and offer the following kinds of incentives: no duties or fees are charged on re-export of items; customs duties and excise taxes are deferred on imports until they leave the FTZ and enter the country proper, and customs procedures are streamlined. Moreover, many offer the possibility of private ownership to companies located on the property; indeed, in 2010 some 62% of the companies in these zones were privately owned, up from 25% in the 1980s (FATF 2010b).

Illicit actors have taken advantage of "relaxed oversight, softened customs controls, and the lack of transparency in these zones" (International Chamber of Commerce 2013: 1). Consider that goods can be shipped through FTZs around the world and not be subject to export control. Insurgent, terrorist, and transnational criminal organizations can create legal entities in these areas and have access to the international financial system. They can manufacture and repackage goods for export and use the FTZ for their smuggling operations. Some have been known to send their goods to multiple and geographically dispersed FTZs to disguise the illicit nature of the products. It should come as no surprise that a number of these FTZs are among the 80 black spots studied here and as such tend to be regional hubs for illicit activity. Among these are Ciudad del Este in Paraguay and Dubai in the United Arab Emirates. A number of the black spots have easy access to such zones like the Hezbollah Territory has to the Port of Beirut and the Darien Jungle to the Panama Pacific Special Economic Zone. These FTZs facilitate the operation of front companies, trade-based money laundering, currency exchange, access to banking and financial intermediaries, and the purchase and shipment of goods to other FTZs as well as the use of cash couriers and prepaid cards.

Take the example of Dubai and its Jebel Ali Free Trade Zone. This FTZ includes the largest man-made harbor in the world, the biggest Middle Eastern port, and the ninth top container port in the world. Though 22 miles south of the city of Dubai, the port is linked to the airport and offers trucking service. It contributes roughly one-fifth of the Dubai economy, providing services for over 5000 companies from 120 countries. Indeed, companies can be 100% privately owned with registration procedures being rather simple. Given its location in the Persian Gulf, this FTZ serves markets in the Gulf countries as well as Africa, Europe, and the Indian subcontinent. Businesses are exempt from taxes and duties as well as are guaranteed the ability to transfer capital and profits. Moreover, there is a possibility to conduct trades online. And there is access to hawaladars and a range of financial intermediaries. In sum, this FTZ, meant to appeal to legitimate business, has proven attractive to illicit actors as well. As has been noted by the Financial Action Task Force (FATF 2014: 20): "Dubai seems uniquely important for the Afghan opiate trade. It is not only a place to make deals, arrange shipments, and establish criminal networks but also a global financial centre for cash movement, informal value transfer transactions, the accumulation of criminal proceeds in bank accounts, and the investment of criminal assets."

Offshore Financial Centers

An offshore financial center is viewed as "a jurisdiction that provides financial services to nonresidents on a scale that is disproportionate with the size and the financing of its resident economy" (Calvery 2012: 5). The offshore in the title refers to residents from one jurisdiction holding their assets in the financial institutions that are located in a different jurisdiction. Persons have moved their money out of their home jurisdiction—from being onshore—to the financial institutions of another jurisdiction—to offshore. Such a movement can be beneficial if the financial institutions in the other jurisdiction face stricter banking secrecy laws and offer a low tax or tax-exempt environment. These centers also help to conceal the identities of the actual owners of the assets. They are good places in which to park monies derived from illegal activities.

Generally, such offshore financial centers offer subsidiaries or branches of home (onshore) banks which, in turn, are found in other offshore financial centers around the world. Such jurisdictions offer a variety of financial services ranging from setting up shell and front companies to facilitating money exchanges as well as the services of brokerage houses and trust companies. A range of different types of intermediaries are available to help those interested in trade-based money laundering, cash couriers, and appropriate documentation for goods and services. It is useful if the offshore financial center is located in an economy that facilitates cash transactions and informal banking operators like hawaladars. Moreover, offshore financial centers are often found geographically close to their target audience but with linkages to other such centers around the world. Offshore financial centers help "money trails disappear, connections become obscure, and investigations encounter so many obstacles that they are often abandoned" (Blum et al. 1998: 56).

Peshawar, Pakistan, the administrative center for one of the black spots studied here—the Federally Administered Tribal Areas (FATA)—is an offshore financial center for the drug trafficking enterprise and terrorism in Afghanistan. Located near the eastern end of the Kyhber Pass linking Pakistan and Afghanistan, this city, dating back to 539 BC, has long been a center for trade between South and Central Asia. Peshawar is where both illicit and licit monies intended for Afghanistan and, in particular, its capitol area enter from the outside world. It provides a connection to the banking system that hawaladars in Pakistan use in transferring money to their counterparts in Afghanistan. Indeed, over 50% of "all transactions inside Afghanistan and across its borders are being conducted via the informal banking system"; it is low cost, convenient, and accessible and they have been transferring money this way since the eighth century (FATF 2014: 15). As an added benefit, the Afghan Transit Trade Agreement with Pakistan that governs this well-used trading route through the Khyber Pass between Peshawar and Torkham (Afghanistan) eliminates customs duties, taxes, dues, or charges of any kind on traffic in transit across the border between these two locations.

The money market at Chowk Yadgar in Peshawar is heavily populated by hawaladars, currency exchange houses, and gold dealers. These money-service providers or financial entrepreneurs operate as part of the informal economy. "Discussions with formal bankers in Peshawar have confirmed reports that money arrives electronically into Pakistani banks" (Thompson 2006: 178). Hawaladars, in turn, make frequent visits to the major banks in Peshawar. The routine from there goes something like this: a drug payment comes into a Peshawar bank through a wire transfer from the UK; it is fragmented into parts; part is transferred via a hawaladar to a counterpart in the Helmand province in Afghanistan who uses the money to finance imports from Dubai through the informal banking system and either uses or sells the goods; any profits go back by cash courier to a hawaladar in Peshawar who puts them into a bank account until the monies need to be used again. In effect, the formal and informal banking systems are intertwined with the 'offshore' financial system rendering it difficult to separate what is illegal from what is legal.

CONCLUSION

A number of observations emerge from our exploration of the methods insurgent, terrorist, and transnational criminal organizations use to finance their activities and black spots. To start with, cash and borders are important to the illicit economy. Cash is what such organizations generally receive as they move to market or engage in their operations. Unless they are bartering one item for another, they are being paid in cash. If that cash is in US dollars, euros, or British pounds, it is recognizable in all corners of the globe. Cash is also convertible into different currencies and, as such, becomes difficult to track. Borders are important because they facilitate movement from one jurisdiction to another and the change in regulations and law enforcement that occurs with such movement. It is no accident that a large percentage of the black spots examined in this book are found near borders. Such geographic placement makes following illicit money more difficult as it is not necessarily illegal when moved to a new jurisdiction.

In making their earnings fungible and legitimate, illicit actors engage in a complex of money laundering techniques. Transnational criminal, insurgent, and terrorist organizations take seriously the notion of layering in the money laundering process. As a result, "it is widely recognized that nearly 95% of money laundering goes undetected" (Miklaucic and Brewer 2013: xx). But it is also equally true that the particular money laundering techniques used are related to the geography and level of development in the particular black spot that is involved. For example, we note the heavy use of hawala in our discussion above of Peshawar and the FATA black spot in contrast to the reliance on front companies and trade-based money laundering by organizations based in the Marbella, Spain black spot. And recall the use of gold instead of cash in the Goma, DRC black spot, a readily available resource mined in the area, in contrast to the cash couriers going across the US-Mexico border to the Sinaloa State with prepaid cash cards. Transnational criminal, insurgent, and terrorist organizations use what is readily available.

Such geographic spaces as free trade zones and offshore financial centers allow illicit actors to become more innovative. Indeed, two requirements for success in these locations are the availability of a wide range of financial services and an informal economy. Dubai has had success in part because it can provide hawaladars as well as front companies and prepaid cards. Given that a number of the black spots that we have studied here are free trade zones or qualify as offshore financial centers, we are interested in examining other such places to see if they fit the definition of a black spot. Indeed, these locations may turn out to be the centers of the illicit economy, linking the other black spots in their region and globally. As we noted with Dubai, it has serviced black spots from Africa (e.g., Goma), the Middle East (e.g., Hezbollah Territory), and Central Asia (e.g., FATA).

The methods of money laundering that we have discussed have involved a number of intermediaries. In effect, money laundering provides jobs and business for individuals who are not necessarily a part of an illicit organization. Hawaladars, cash couriers, lawyers, accountants, real estate brokers, small business owners, prepaid card program managers and distributors, import/export businesses, to name a few, are part of the process. These people and organizations depend on illicit activity for their livelihoods and work to insure that the money laundering, the illicit organization, and the black spot succeed financially. We have observed how even charities can get caught up in the money laundering enterprise.

The end products of money laundering are legitimacy and profit. But this complex process also engages others for whom those controlling a black spot are responsible if they are to be effective. These transnational criminals, insurgent, and terrorist organizations become vested in the network of black spots that are critical to conducting their business. But unlike a legitimate corporation, most of what such organizations do is shadowy in nature and outside the law. The challenge these organizations face is laundering their profits within the legal economy while maintaining themselves and the black spots that they have built, operate, and govern. As a result, they are continuously on the lookout for new ways to launder money, for intermediaries that offer innovative services, and for black spots that they can control or work through.

In this and the previous two chapters, we have explored the activities and functions of the black spots studied in this book as well as the actors operating from and controlling these black spots and how they managed their businesses financially. Now we want to examine some challenges arising out of what we have discovered about black spots. In particular, do they exist in cyberspace, a 'virtual' rather than a spatial reality?

REFERENCES

Associated Press. 2011. Prepaid Cards Attract Money Launderers. *Post Standard*, May 20.

Bariyo, Nicholas. 2013. Inside Congo's Link in the Gold Chain. *Wall Street Journal*, April 14.

BBC News. 2005. Spain Cracks $300m Money Racket, March 13.

Becerra, Robert J. 2015. The Black Market Peso Exchange and the Small Exporter. *International Law Quarterly* 32 (3): 10–11, 34–37.

Blum, Jack A., Michael Levi, R. Thomas Naylor, and Phil Williams. 1998. *Financial Havens, Banking Secrecy, and Money Laundering*. New York: United Nations.

Booth, William and Nick Miroff. 2010. Cartels' Cash Flows Across Border. *Washington Post*, August 26.

Bowers, Charles B. 2009. Hawala, Money Laundering, and Terrorism Finance: Micro-Lending as an End to Illicit Remittance. *Denver Journal of International Law and Policy* 37: 379–419.

Burnett, John. 2014. A Wash in Cash, Drug Cartels Rely on Big Banks to Launder Profits. *NPR*, March 20.

Calvery, Jennifer Shasky. 2012. Combating Transnational Organized Crime: International Money Laundering as a Threat to Our Financial System. Statement before the Subcommittee on Crime, Terrorism, and Homeland Security, Committee on the Judiciary, United States House of Representatives, February 8.

Cassara, John A. 2015. *Trade-Based Money Laundering*. Hoboken: John Wiley & Sons.

Crawford, Leslie. 2005. Hot Money in Spain's Costa del Crime. *House Price Crash Forum*, March 22.

Davidson, Christopher. 2008. *Dubai: The Vulnerability of Success*. London: Hurst & Co.

Di Natala, Leandro. 2012. *Usury: The Bank System of Camorra.* Brussels: European Strategic Intelligence and Security Center Briefing.

Duaij, Abdulrahman. 2009. Hawala: The Main Facilitator for Middle Eastern Organized Crime Groups. Unpublished Paper, George Mason University.

Duhaime, Christine. 2016. The Anti-Money Laundering Lawyer's Primer on Beneficial Ownership and Numbered, Shelf and Shell Companies. *AML Law in Canada,* April 24.

Dunn, Stephen J. 2014. Bank Deposits, Structuring, and Asset Forfeitures. *Forbes Magazine,* April 19.

Ellingwood, Ken and Tracy Wilkinson. 2011. Mexico Sets Its Sights on Cartels' Cash. *Los Angeles Times,* November 27.

Emerson, Steven. 2016. Report: German Refugee Program Money Given to Hezbollah Operatives. *Algemeiner,* April 21.

Europol Financial Intelligence Group (EFIG). 2015. *Why Is Cash Still King?* The Hague: European Police Office.

FATF. 2006. *The Misuse of Corporate Vehicles Including Trust and Company Service Providers.* Paris: FATF/OECD.

———. 2010a. *Financial Action Task Force Annual Report 2009–2010.* Paris: FATF/OECD.

———. 2010b. *Money Laundering Vulnerabilities of Free Trade Zones.* Paris: FATF/OECD.

———. 2012. *International Standards on Combating Money Laundering and the Financing of Terrorism and Proliferation.* Paris: FATF.

———. 2013. *Guidance for a Risk-Based Approach: Prepaid Cards, Mobile Payments and Internet-Based Payment Services.* Paris: FATF.

———. 2014. *Financial Flows Linked to the Production and Trafficking of Afghan Opiates.* Paris: FATF/OECD.

FATF/APG. 2015. *Money Laundering and Terrorist Financing Risks and Vulnerabilities Associated with Gold.* Paris/Sydney: FATF/APG.

Glaser, Daniel L. 2010. Testimony on Charities. Testimony Before Subcommittee on Oversight and Investigations, Committee on Financial Services, US House of Representatives May 26.

Glenny, Misha. 2009. *McMafia: A Journey Through the Global Criminal Underworld.* New York: Vintage Books.

Guell, Oriol. 2016. Turf War Between Irish Mafias Spills over into Marbella. *El Pais,* March 10.

ICE. 2006. Prepaid Cards an Emerging Threat. *The Cornerstone Report* 3 (1): 4.

Internal Revenue Service. 2006. *Internal Revenue Manual.* Washington, DC: Treasury Department.

International Chamber of Commerce. 2013. *Controlling the Zone: Balancing Facilitation and Control to Combat Illicit Trade in World's Free Trade Zones.* Paris: International Chamber of Commerce.

Jost, Patrick M., and Harjit Singh Sandhu. 2006. The Hawala Alternative Remittance System and Its Role in Money Laundering. Financial Crimes Enforcement Network, US Department of the Treasury and INTERPOL/FOPAC.

King, Douglas. 2013. *Have Anti-Money Laundering Measures Kept Pace with the Rapid Growth of GPR Prepaid Cards?* Retail Payments Risk Forum Working Paper, Federal Reserve Bank of Atlanta, January.

Lally, Conor. 2016. Who Is the Kingpin Behind Irish-Led Cartel Based in Spain? *Irish Times*, February 7.

Laville, Sandra. 2009. India Arrests Hawala Money Laundering Suspect Naresh Jain. *The Guardian*, December 8.

Levitt, Matthew. 2004. Charitable Organizations and Terrorist Financing: A War on Terror Status Check, Stein Program on Counterterrorism and Intelligence. Washington Institute for Near East Policy, Washington, DC, March.

———. 2005. Hezbollah: Financing Terror through Criminal Enterprises. Testimony Before Committee on Homeland Security and Government Affairs, US Senate, May 25.

———. 2007. Hezbollah Finances: Funding the Party of God. In *Terrorism Financing and State Responses: A Comparative Perspective*, ed. Jeanne Giraldo and Harold Trinkunas. Stanford: Stanford University Press.

Litvin, Kate. 2011. *Does Charitable Aid Fund Social Services or Suicide Bombers? Exploring Hezbollah's and Hamas' Involvement in US Charities.* University Honors in International Studies, American University, Spring

Martinez, Michael, Priscilla Riojas, and Jacqueline Hurtado. 2014. Los Angeles "Epicenter" of Cartel Money Laundering, Feds Say. *CNN*, September 12.

Mathiason, Nick. 2010. Dubai's Dark Side Targeted by International Finance Police. *The Guardian*, January 23.

Mayyasi, Alex. 2014. Hawala: The Working Man's Bitcoin. *Priceonomics*, February 7.

McKinley, James C., Jr., and Marc Lacey. 2009. Along the US-Mexico Border a Torrent of Illicit Cash. *New York Times*, December 25.

MENA FATF. 2015. *Money Laundering through the Physical Transportation of Cash*. Paris: FATF and MENAFATF.

Michaletos, Ioannis. 2010. An Outlook of Radical Islamism in Bosnia. *Serbianna*, September 25.

Miklaucic, Michael, and Jacqueline Brewer, eds. 2013. *Convergence: Illicit Networks and National Security in the Age of Globalization*. Washington, DC: National Defense University Press.

Morrisey, Deborah. n.d. *Shells, Trusts, and Similar Entities in International Money Laundering*. Miami: ICE.

Mozingo, Joe, Tiffany Hsu, and Victoria Kim. 2014. LA Fashion District Firms Raided in Cartel Money Laundering Probe. *Los Angeles Times*, September 10.

Nadeau, Barbie Letza. 2015. Is the Mafia Saving Italy from ISIS or Just Profiting from Them? *Daily Beast*, December 11.

Naylor, R.T. 2004. *Hot Money and the Politics of Debt*. Montreal: McGill-Queen's University Press.

O'Brien, Craig. 2007. Hawala and Western Business Principles. Master's Thesis, National Intelligence College.

Reuter, Peter, and Edwin M. Truman. 2004. *Chasing Dirty Money*. Washington, DC: Peterson Institute of International Economics.

Roig-Franzia, Manuel. 2008. Mexico's Drug Cartels Take Barbarous Turn: Targeting Bystanders in Sinaloa Brings Widespread Carnage and Terror. *Washington Post*, July 30.

Rosenberg, Mica and Brett Wolf. 2016. Money Laundering Rule on Prepaid Cards Stalled After Industry Pushback. *Reuters*, August 10.

Schneider, Friedrich, Konrad Raczkowski, and Bogdan Mroz. 2015. Shadow Economy and Tax Evasion in the EU. *Journal of Money Laundering Control* 18 (1): 34–51.

Sienkiewicz, S.J. 2007. *Prepaid Cards: Vulnerable in Money Laundering?* Payment Cards Center Discussion Paper 07–02, Federal Reserve Bank of Philadelphia.

Smith, Jack D. 2009. Disrupting Terrorist Financing with Civil Litigation. *Case Western Reserve Journal of International Law* 41: 67.

Smith, Michael. 2010. Banks Financing Mexican Drug Gangs Admitted in Wells Fargo Deal. *Bloomberg News*, June 29.

Stiles, Nicole. 2013. Theft and Money Laundering: The Dark Side of Prepaid Cards. *NW3C News*, August 8.

Sullivan, Clare, and Evan Smith. 2011. Trade-Based Money Laundering: Risks and Regulatory Responses. Research and Public Policy Series 115, AIC Reports, Australian Institute of Criminology.

Tax Justice Network. 2018. *Financial Secrecy Index 2018: Narrative Report on the United Arab Emirates (Dubai)*. Chesham: Tax Justice Network.

Taxin, Amy. 2014. Fashion District Raid Funds $100 Million of Laundered Mexican Cartel Ransom Money. *The Christian Science Monitor*, September.

The Economist. 2012. An Unsettling Settlement—Standard Chartered v New York, August 18.

———. 2016. Getting Rid of Big Banknotes Is Not As Easy as It Looks, March 3.

Thompson, Edwina A. 2006. The Nexus of Drug Trafficking and Hawala in Afghanistan. In *Afghanistan Drug Industry*, ed. Doris Buddemberg and William A. Byra. Vienna: UNODC/World Bank.

UNEP-MONUSCO-OSESG. 2015. *Experts' Background Report on Illegal Exploration and Trade in Natural Resources Benefiting Organized Criminal Groups in Eastern DR Congo:. Final Report*. Nairobi: UN Environment Programme.

Van de Bunt, Henk. 2008. A Case Study on the Misuse of Hawala Banking. *International Journal of Social Economics* 35 (9): 691–702.
Walker, Jane. 2005. Police Crack Huge Racket in South of Spain. *Irish Times*, March 14.
World Bank Group. 2016. *Responses to Illicit Financial Flows: A Stocktaking.* Washington, DC: World Bank.
Zarate, Juan. 2013. *Treasury's War: The Unleashing of a New Era of Financial Warfare.* New York: Public Affairs.
Zdanowicz, John S. 2009. Mitigating the Risks of International Trade Transactions Through Effective Monitoring. Paper Presented at the 2009 Mid-Atlantic Anti-Money Laundering Conference, September 22–24.

PART III

Extensions and Implications

CHAPTER 7

Black Spots in Cyberspace?

Central themes of this book have revolved around rethinking sovereignty and the global economy. What happens when we introduce the notion of cyberspace, a domain that appears to eliminate political jurisdictions and to move globalization to a new level? Do black spots become less relevant to the study of illicit activities as criminals, insurgents, and terrorists increasingly adopt cyber-technology? Or are black spots just as likely to be found in this so-called virtual world in ways similar to the physical world of states? This chapter explores if there are black spots in cyberspace.

We will start by introducing the concept of cyberspace and exploring how it relates to the illicit world. Of interest are the various ways criminal actors use cyber-technology to enhance their operations. In other words, are illicit activities changing in response to the evolution of cyberspace? Building on this discussion, we will show the relevance of the notion of black spots to cyberspace and provide examples of their impact.

CYBERSPACE AND THE ILLICIT WORLD

Some 48% of the world's population were linked into the internet by the end of 2017 (ITU 2017). Around 81% of the population in the developed world had access to the use of devices connected to the internet at this point in time, with 41% of those living in developing countries having such access. In effect, people are doing more and more online, from banking to making purchases to seeking information to keeping in

© The Author(s) 2020
S. S. Brown, M. G. Hermann, *Transnational Crime and Black Spots*, International Political Economy Series,
https://doi.org/10.1057/978-1-137-49670-6_7

contact. It is becoming a giant marketplace that spans the globe. Moreover, transactions take only seconds. As Choo and Grabosky (2013: 1) have observed, one "person acting alone can communicate with millions of people, instantly, and at negligible cost." And this cyberspace, as it is often referred to, falls outside the governance of any one country. Instead, a multitude of private infrastructure owners and operators cooperate through networked governance. Consider the infrastructure of fiber-optic cables, cell towers, personal computers, servers, browsers, the domain naming system, and software that is necessary to provide the access for users. The non-state actors involved in providing this infrastructure work with one another while remaining free to define their own policies and make decisions about access to their portion of the cyberspace network (Mueller et al. 2013). In effect, sovereignty is challenged—maybe more than ever before—by the power that cyberspace affords to these non-state actors. This non-governmental approach to governance renders cyberspace relatively borderless and hard for states to regulate. Indeed, cyberspace poses a 'jurisdictional dilemma for states' (Adams and Albakajai 2016). Its users live in between a Westphalian state system where established borders define sovereignty and the rule of law and a virtual transnational world that lacks notions of sovereignty while emphasizing shared governance among state and non-state actors. In response to this dilemma, a corporate leader was overheard saying: "OK, whose laws do I follow? We have many countries and many laws but just one Internet" (Cohen-Almagor 2012: 355).

Former US Attorney General Janet Reno observed that while cyberspace has brought many benefits to society, it has also brought with it new opportunities for criminal activities (Chawki 2006). "Computer-mediated crimes are more convenient, and profitable, and less expensive and risky than crimes not mediated by the Internet" (Cardenas et al. 2009: 1). Cyberspace offers transnational criminals, insurgents, and terrorists an environment that is essentially borderless and provides them with transnational access to large numbers of users where contact is instantaneous and there is often confusion as to just who is in charge (Adams and Albakajai 2016). Indeed, it is these very characteristics that have led criminals to cyberspace and that have led them also to create black spots. As the data in previous chapters have suggested, black spots are areas outside effective government control, governed by alternative social structures, and that facilitate engaging in illicit activities. Moreover, if we include in our discussion the so-called deep web and darknet, then cyberspace also provides

anonymity—being invisible and off law enforcement and media radars—
another characteristic of black spots noted in previous chapters.
The deep web is a term used to describe that part of the web that is not
retrievable using standard search engines such as Google. It is essentially
information 'hidden in plain sight' as those involved with the deep web
have begun using more 'dynamic database-centric design' instead of the
more static page design that is the focus of standard search engines
(BrightPlanet 2012). The deep web contains private internet and pass-
word protected sites as well as the internet of things which link machines
to machines. Then there is the darknet (also referred to as the black web
or black net) which should not be confused with the deep web. "The
darknet is a small part of the deep web that is kept hidden on purpose"
(Bischoff 2016). The focus here is on anonymity, on remaining unknown
and deliberately free from the "prying eyes of the searchable web" (Chacos
2013). It takes a special tool to access the darknet. Among the most commonly used currently is Tor which is short for The Onion Router. Tor sites
generally are followed by the word 'onion' instead of 'com,' 'edu,' or
'org.' To keep a user's identity anonymous, Tor employs a network of
volunteer relays that circle the world. A user's internet connection is
encrypted and routed through this network before arriving at its destination, albeit more slowly but anonymously.

The darknet raises a dilemma for the shared governance of cyberspace.
It "provides the means to perpetrate wide-spread criminal activities with
little chance of apprehension" (Chawki 2006: 2). Think markets in drugs
and weapons, hacker havens, pornography forums, gambling sites, and
credit card scammers. But it also has become a bastion for free speech—a
refuge for dissidents from events like the Arab Spring, blogs in countries
where free and open speech is frowned upon, a place for whistleblowers
and journalists to exchange information, somewhere for libraries con-
taining radical political literature to exist, a place that enables free and
open online chat rooms or forums, and a site where companies can share
information without giving such knowledge to their competitors. At
issue is how one regulates the criminal without also targeting the free
speech and freedom of expression that the darknet facilitates. In effect,
to protect online free speech for one set of actors, the darknet facilitates
another set of actors using the technology for illegal activities without
fear of detection—or, at the least, the ability to "complicate the task of
the police in identifying and apprehending the person responsible"
(Chawki 2006: 6). Regulation becomes even more difficult because

those online activities that use something like Tor can involve a number of countries along the way. Whose jurisdiction is responsible?

Transnational criminal organizations, insurgents, and terrorists have taken advantage of these various facets of cyberspace. And they have tended to do so in three ways (see, e.g., Choo and Grabosky 2013). The first is like many legitimate organizations. They use the tools in cyberspace to support their on-the-ground global operations. Cyber-technology becomes the tool through which they gather information and coordinate with one another across black spots while maintaining degrees of anonymity. These tools are also used to connect with potential buyers of illicit goods, recruit new members, solicit funds to support their organizations, and provide 'know-how' and training related to their illegal activities. This way of using cyberspace is a combination of offline and online activities but the online endeavors reinforce what is happening offline and on-the-ground geographically and logistically. Cyberspace merely facilitates and speeds up 'normal' behavior.

Then there are criminals, insurgents, and terrorists who do just the opposite. Their offline activities support the illegal activities that the organizations are engaged in online. Consider cyrptomarkets like the Silk Road. This online black market was involved in the buying and selling of drugs via the darknet. But like Amazon and other such e-commerce sites, the drugs were mailed offline to purchasers. Given the international reach of such operations, shipments are made across borders and care is taken to camouflage the packages and places of origin. Indeed, these markets have gained the name of the 'Amazons of the Darknet' (*The Economist* 2014) and, as we shall discuss later, represent one way of thinking about black spots in cyberspace.

Lastly, there are the criminals, insurgents, and terrorists who do all their activity in cyberspace. These are the hackers, the phishers, the scammers, and those engaged in denial of service attacks as well as those running the command and control centers for botnets. Their operations center around exploiting what cyberspace has to offer—its scale, its relative anonymity, its timeliness, and its jurisdictional complexity. Those involved in these online endeavors are malware specialists and highly adaptable. When the shared governance of cyberspace or individual jurisdictions agree to cooperate in closing down one type of pursuit, these online criminals innovate to meet the challenge. For example, in spring 2016, the US Supreme Court amended Rule 41 of the Federal Rules of Criminal Procedure to allow judges to issue warrants giving permission to the FBI "to remotely access" and "seize information from an infinite number" of computers in "multiple jurisdictions anywhere in the country" if their locations had been concealed by technical means (Adams 2017: 727). Almost immediately among online cybercriminals ways were proposed and implemented for evading such a hack (e.g., Bischoff 2016).

CYBERCRIME

We have suggested why criminals are drawn to cyberspace. But what are they doing and how? Just what is involved in cybercrime, the term often used to indicate the criminal activity that takes place in cyberspace? Defined in a number of ways, definitions usually refer to criminal activities carried out using networked computers or related technologies that involve such devices as the object of the crime or as a tool with which to commit the crime (see, e.g., UNODC 2013; Gaspareniene and Remeikiene 2015). McAfee (2018: 1) has estimated that such cybercrimes annually cost the global economy around $600 billion and represent 0.8% of global GDP— "as crimes they rank third behind government corruption and narcotics as a global economic problem." Wall (2005) has developed a framework for examining cybercrime that covers the wide range of criminal activities that have been identified in cyberspace. He identifies four types of cybercrime: cybertrespass, cyberdeception/theft, cyberporn, and cyberviolence. Moreover, he suggests how these are used in the three ways described above that criminals, insurgents, and terrorists tend to engage with cyberspace. That is, cybercrime augments what criminals are already doing, it provides new opportunities for them to carry out their criminal activities, or it becomes the focus of such activities. Let's explore each of these types of cybercrime in more detail.

Cybertrespass

Cybertrespass involves the "crossing of invisible boundaries in online spaces" (Holt and Bossler 2014: 2). As Wall (2005) suggested, this category involves hacking and cracking, but it also includes the development of malware, trojan horses, viruses, and worms. In effect, hacking and cracking and these software tools represent an automated way to engage in trespassing and to acquire information from users without their knowledge. These activities make it possible to build what are called botnets which are computers linked together under the guidance of a botherder and a command and control center with those owning the computers having no knowledge that their particular computer is involved and being used. Some argue that hackers focus on the networked systems themselves while crackers focus on software programs (Negi 2011). Regardless, we are interested here in hackers and crackers bent on using their skills for illegal purposes—so-called malicious hackers and crackers. Consider the use of spam as a way of infecting computers. Spam involves the release of a large volume of unwanted messages which, if opened, enable malware to infect computers that are unlikely to have effective countermeasures in place. This infection usually occurs in one of two ways: (1) When the attachment to the message is opened, the virus/trojan horse/worm inside is installed in the recipient's computer or (2) there is a hyperlink to a web page that when accessed downloads the malware onto the unsuspecting victim's computer.

An example is the Mariposa 'Butterfly' Botnet (Correll 2010; Broadhurst et al. 2013). The malware used to infect computers was created by a Slovenian with the intention of infiltrating large numbers of computers that could then be controlled by cybercriminals. The malware was made to self-propagate to computers that were not yet infected but in the same network. The infected computers were used to gather bank account information and passwords. As often happens, this malware was then sold to a Spanish group (Nightmare Day Team) that linked together 12 million computers into a worldwide botnet that, like before, stole login data from various businesses such as banks. Although the team's leader and several other members, plus the malware creator, were arrested in 2010, the Butterfly Bot reappeared in 2012 with that particular transnational cybercrime group earning over $850 million before they, too, were arrested.

Cyberdeception/Theft

While cybertrespass types of cybercrime target the computer—indeed, the integrity of the computer is central to the crime—cyberdeception and theft use the computer as a tool in committing crimes. This type of cybercrime involves "various forms of fraud that are facilitated through technology" (Holt and Bossler 2014: 3). Whereas spam and botnets are used to reach a wide audience, the emphasis here is on phishing and a variety of advance-fee fraud schemes. Phishing involves seeking sensitive information such as usernames, credit card data, and passwords by using an electronic communication in which a sender presents him or herself as a trustworthy person/entity. A neologism on the word 'fishing,' the intent is to use bait to catch a fish. The advance-fee fraud is a setup where the electronic communication presents recipients with a problem: they owe overdue tax money to the Internal Revenue Service; they can gain money by helping the emailer transfer a rather large sum of money between accounts; or a work at home scheme is provided that requires a down payment. Advanced-fee fraud has become known as the Nigerian email scheme as many perpetrators claim to reside there.

Cyberdeception also contains 'online piracy.' This criminal activity involves creating or obtaining copies of TV shows, films, books, games, music, and/or software without the permission of the entity holding the copyright or license. Cyberpiracy cost the television industry around $31.8 billion in 2017, the music industry 71,060 jobs, and US federal, state, and local governments around $422 million in lost tax revenue (Bevir 2017; Global RADAR 2017). Online piracy is often tricky to contain because "pirate sites and services tend to operate in multiple jurisdictions and are purposefully set up to evade law enforcement" (Van der Sar 2017).

Consider the case of the RUS 13 Extortion (UNODC 2012; Broadhurst et al. 2013). This use of cyberdeception involved British bookmakers. In effect, the cybercriminals held the bookmakers hostage while extorting funds from them. The bookmaking companies in this case were vulnerable because bets were made online and the companies needed to remain attached to the internet for their business to occur. A Russian cybercriminal group used anonymous mail servers, virtual private networks, and proxy servers to launch a distributed denial of service (DDoS) attack on the bookmaking companies' servers. DDoS attacks are generally meant to overwhelm a company's website and take it offline. This DDoS attack "flooded the target company's server with approximately 425 unique IP addresses establishing over 600,000 simultaneous connections with the company's web server, sending requests for information at over 70 MB per second (the web server would normally receive requests at 2 MB per second)" (UNODC 2012: 111–112). In effect, the attack severed the company's website from the internet. The cybercriminals made a demand for $40,000 or the attack would be continued and the company put out of business.

Cyberpornography/Obscenity

This type of cybercrime, like the one that follows, focuses on content-related online criminal activities. This category centers around the ease with which persons can create and share explicit content and pornographic materials on the internet and web (Holt and Bossler 2014). Here is another place where online activity has expanded dramatically what is possible offline. Indeed, it has facilitated the porn industry becoming a multibillion dollar industry. This type of online behavior is not, however, illegal in all cultures and for all ages, presenting some difficulties for law enforcement and freeing the hand of the cybercriminal. Note that in the US at 18 it is legal to participate in and view pornographic material. Online subcultures have arisen in the form of web forums and internet chat rooms around topics related to pornography. Cyberspace has also had an impact on the sex trade and sex workers in facilitating connections between customer and client as well as in sex tourism (Holt et al. 2013). But probably where online technology has had its greatest impact in this area is with regard to pedophilia. Cyberspace increases the feasibility of making, sharing, and distributing child pornography as well as solicitation of minors. Data suggest that 70% of child sex trafficking victims are sold online (Couch 2014).

There are indications that this category of cybercrime might effectively be elaborated into cybertrafficking. There is growing evidence that "online technologies give traffickers the unprecedented ability to exploit a greater number of victims and advertise their services across geographic boundaries" (Latonero 2011: iv). Online classified websites have become targets for such use as have social networking sites. Such sites allow traffickers to seek out victims and to advertise their sexual services. Consider the case of the Erotic Services section of Craigslist. From 2001 through 2010 when Craigslist's Erotic Services section was under fire, the percentage of American adults using such online classified websites grew from 32% to 53% (Zickuhr 2010). Such "online classified ads make it possible to pimp kids to prospective customers with little risk" (Allen 2010). Craigslist first changed its Erotic Services section to Adult Services to meet the growing criticism and number of legal cases as well as began to charge a small credit card fee that had to be accompanied by a phone number to help reduce the anonymity of posting an ad. Even with this change, 28 state attorneys general wrote a letter to Craigslist demanding that it remove this Adult Services section due to continued use of the site for sex trafficking

(Latonero 2011). At a Congressional hearing in 2010, the leadership of Craigslist announced it was closing its Adult Services section in the US and followed soon after by closing it worldwide. And, indeed, after the US Congress passed the Stop Enabling Sex Trafficking Act in spring 2018, Craigslist eliminated personal ads as well (Fielding 2018). Even so, cyber-traffickers still post ads in other parts of this online site using coded or fake material.

Cyberviolence

This type of cybercrime refers to activities online that involve "injurious, hurtful, or dangerous materials with the intent of producing physical or emotional harm" (Holt and Bossler 2014: 4). Such activities include bullying, stalking, or harassing others as well as forums, chat rooms, and newsgroups that circulate materials for making weapons or engaging in terrorist actions. This type of cybercrime is also associated with what is called hactivism or using cyberspace to promote political movements and particular ideologies. Moreover, it is where the development of malware that can interfere with others' security and well-being falls. Cyberspace allows these kinds of messages to spread across vast distances and countries instantaneously as well as facilitates targeted attacks with specific people, groups, and institutions in mind. Cybercriminals involved in cyberviolence have used distributed denial of service to accomplish their aims as well as counter-hacking and forms of vigilantism to prove their points.

Lulz Security, known by the nickname LulzSec, represents an example of cybercriminals that fits into the hactivist tradition (Broadhurst et al. 2014). The 'lulz' in the name is a neologism for 'lol' or 'laugh out loud' and the intent in their hacking attacks was to draw attention to insecurities built into online systems while having fun and showing off their skills. LulzSec is responsible for the 2011 attack on Sony Pictures that compromised a million user accounts. They used an SQL injection to attack the website and release the information from the user accounts onto the internet. LulzSec is also known for engaging in a distributed denial of service attack on the US Central Intelligence Agency that took its website offline for roughly three hours. And in retribution for a Frontline story they thought unfair to WikiLeaks and Private Manning's role in its leaks of US classified material, LulzSec hacked into the Public Broadcasting Service (PBS) who ran the program, stealing user information as well as inserting their own fake story indicating that Tupac Shakur and Biggie Smalls were alive and well and living in New Zealand. Throughout, those involved in LulzSec have indicated that by releasing hacked users' names or letting organizations know that they were hacked, it has given users and organizations notice that their security is inadequate and needs upgrading (Anderson 2011).

CYBERCRIME AND BLACK SPOTS

A lot of the previous discussion has focused on cybercriminals and their activities—so-called cybercrime. What about black spots? Are there similar kinds of areas in cyberspace or is all of cyberspace a black spot? Our discussion to this point would seem to suggest the latter. And, yet, there is a certain geographical grounding to cyberspace, given the infrastructure necessary to keep it going. We would like to propose that there are four types of black spots in cyberspace. Two types are much like the more traditional black spots covered already in this book. They are areas in countries that are outside of government control, governed by alternative illicit social structures, capable of breeding and exporting insecurity, and doing so under the radar of law enforcement. For these two types, what occurs offline is as important to their success as what occurs online. The other two types do all of their illegal activities online but are still dependent on a location in the cyberspace infrastructure to insure that they can do what they want to do. And in that space, the characteristics of a black spot remain intact. In what follows, we will explore some examples of these four types.

Offline/Online Black Spots

Hackerville

In some circles this town of a little over 100,000 in Romania is also known as Cybercrime Central, given how many hackers, scammers, and phishers live within its boundaries (Franceschi-Bicchierai 2015). Ramnicu Valcea is the community's name and it is located roughly three hours away from Bucharest, Romania's capitol, in the foothills of the Transylvanian Alps. It is not uncommon for visitors to the area to be told by cab drivers that many of its inhabitants "steal money on the internet" (Bhattacharjee 2011: 1). Expensive cars are visible on the streets in the bustling city center as are new shopping centers, nightclubs, and apartment buildings. But it was not always this way. As with much of Romania, after the 1989 revolution that saw the overthrow of Ceausescu and the end of communist rule, young people struggled to find jobs. Cybercafes changed this outlook, offering cheap internet service, and young males in particular took advantage of this easy access to the internet. They "got busy posting fake ads on eBay and other auction sites to lure victims into remitting payments by wire transfer" (Bhattacharjee 2011: 3). Indeed, at one time, there were two dozen Western Union offices within a four block area in the center city.

As their scams have run into problems, those involved have adapted, setting up fake websites to sell bogus products and swipe credit card information. Americans are a favorite target given their growing preference for buying things online. As one of those involved indicated, "stealing on the internet is easy." They "bamboozle four or five users per week....and in the end are left a few hundred thousand dollars richer" (Bran 2013: 3). In addition to those involved in these scams and phishing exploits, there are hackers who have breached NASA's and the Pentagon's servers, the emails of such personages as George W. Bush, Hilary Clinton, Colin Powell, and others ostensibly to show the flaws in their security systems. Still others hack for hire and the targets are unlimited, from the search engine giant, Google, to social networks and governments.

Ramnicu Valcea resembles the black spots discussed in other places in this book. Its form of insecurity happens to involve cyberspace but the hackers, scammers, and phishers are found in a particular geographic location. Law enforcement from a variety of countries are working to limit what those involved in cybercrime are doing but as one police officer commented, "you arrest two of them and 20 new ones take their place" (Bhattacharjee 2011: 6). The crew involved in these cybercrimes are the life blood of the community. And as is known throughout the town, the crime is directed at foreigners, not their own countrymen. In many respects, Ramnicu Valcea is suggestive of agglomeration as it has become a haven for cybercriminals with particular skills and interests.

Underground/Darknet Markets
The Silk Road is probably the most infamous of these darknet markets but these are online black markets that "mirror the offline black markets they were meant to replace" (Greenberg 2016: 4). Earlier in this book, we talked about such places as Ciudad del Este, Dubai, and the Scampia/Secondigliano neighborhoods in Naples as examples of such offline or geographically located black markets and black spots. The online darknet

markets are "online anonymous marketplaces where buyers and sellers can meet and conduct electronic illicit commerce transactions" just like is done legally on Amazon or eBay (Soska and Christin 2015: 33). The emphasis here is on anonymity where names remain unknown. To facilitate anonymity, these marketplaces are often located on the Tor network and use the bitcoin electronic payment system. But in a manner like Amazon, the items that are bought are sent by mail or some kind of express system to the buyer. To avoid scams and being shut down by law enforcement, these markets have employed escrow systems and a variety of online maneuvers to insure buyers get their product and the sellers their money. Data suggest that even with scams and takedowns by law enforcement, these darknet markets average a total daily volume between 300,000 and 500,000 customers (Soska and Christin 2015: 47). Popular darknet markets in 2018 were Dream Market, Wall Street, and Point Marketplace selling drugs, counterfeit items, and digital goods (Sedgwick 2018). Indeed, in 2018, 25% of people using drugs in the UK accessed them through darknet markets as did 30% of Norwegians, and 46% of Finns—the top three in overall use of darknet markets according to the Global Drug Survey (Winstock et al. 2018).

Drugs bought on these darknet markets often cost more than those on the street (remember mailing costs to get from seller to buyer) but they have been found to be of higher quality. In effect, sellers on the darknet markets receive reviews, and it is easier to learn who has a positive as opposed to a negative reputation. Such markets also help cut down on the violence that the street dealer and buyer can face, and both are less likely to be arrested (Soska and Christin 2015). But there can still be rivalry among markets as well as sellers and buyers that can result in distributed denial of service attacks targeted at a market and blackmail or exposure of personal information for sellers and buyers (*The Economist* 2016). Overall, though, these darknet markets have shown surprising resilience to adverse events. When one is taken down or its managers abscond with sellers' earnings, another rises to take its place. In fact, there have been several iterations of the Silk Road marketplace. Moreover, there is growing stability in the product being sold and the price over time as the markets become the competition for street dealers (Soska and Christin 2015). In the parlance of black spots in this book, these darknet markets have become an important distribution site in the global drug trade. But unlike the on-the-ground black market, these markets can ship quality products globally, reliably, and anonymously.

Online Only Black Spots

Botnets

Another potential black spot in cyberspace is what is called a botnet. More than the botnet itself, it is the command and control center which is in charge of the botnet that is the black spot. "A botnet is essentially a mass hack"—it involves a network of victim computers and/or mobile devices that have been surreptitiously infected with malware and are controlled remotely by criminals (Caldwell 2016: 1). Botnets make these machines act like robots, thus the name. Botnets are used in denial of service attacks, stealing and using sensitive personal information, spam attacks, phishing, mining digital currency, and ransomware attacks where a user's computer is held hostage until a ransom is paid. Botnets range from hundreds to millions of infected devices. In effect, once infected, the information on the device is no longer completely under the 'legitimate' user's control.

Infected machines receive commands from command and control centers which provide the instructions that launch the network into action to achieve a particular illicit purpose. Those in charge of the botnet—the botherders—also rent out their botnets as well as sell the malware to be used in organizing another network. The infrastructure of botnets has adapted as law enforcement and others have been able to take down command and control centers located in particular servers. In effect, the cybercriminals have adapted and now use a peer-to-peer (P2P) organization where commands are transmitted through 'neighbor' bots. Command and control is embedded in the botnet rather than in a separate, stand-alone server. And operators often overlay their network on a legitimate infrastructure such as Tor and use public key encryption in addition to P2P networking systems.

An example of a botnet that continues to be resilient in the face of attempts to take it down is Koobface—an anagram for Facebook. It is a computer worm that can affect Microsoft, Mac, and Linux operating systems. The worm focuses on social networks such as Facebook, Skype, Twitter, and Myspace. Indeed, it is spread through such networks, banking on the trust that develops between friends interacting on these sites. The malware collects login information from the victim's social networking sites and sends messages to his/her 'friends' with a request to view a video. Messages run something like the following: "I saw your silly face in that movie, check it"; "my friend caught you on a hidden cam"; "you look awesome in this new movie" (Kiguolis 2017: 3). Responders are told that they need to update their Flash to see the pictures and once the 'friend' clicks to install the update, Koobface's infection files are installed. Once in a victim's computer or mobile device, Koobface has access to all kinds of information like credit cards and bank account information and can continue to push the victim to install anti-virus programs such as an anti-Koobface program. By controlling the victim's search engine, it directs "the user to affiliated illicit websites offering various scams such as false investments, fake AV programs, fake dating services" (Broadhurst et al. 2014: 14). Money is made through pay-per-install and pay-per-click.

The Koobface command and control server is known as the 'mothership' which "acts as an intermediary between the pay-per-click and rogue security software affiliates and the compromised victims" (Prince 2010). Five of the botherders directing Koobface have been identified. Referred to as 'Ali Baba & 4,' they are Russian nationals residing in the St Petersburg area (Leyden 2012: 1). Those in charge have been very resilient and adaptive, changing the overall structure of the botnet to respond to successful takedowns and attempted ones (Broadhurst et al. 2014). Focused on financial gain, these botherders have been estimated to earn around $2 million annually. Indeed, those involved with the mothership have been known to brag about the money they are making daily through Koobface (Kiguolis 2017). These botherders and their botnet are most active in the US, Canada, the UK, Italy, and Germany.

Rogue ISPs and 'Bad Neighborhoods'
In order for cybercriminals to engage in any of the activities that we have been describing in cyberspace, they need "hosting services and good bandwidth" (Freed 2010: 6). And we can guess some of the characteristics that the hosting services must also have. They should allow for anonymity, not be too choosy about their customers, be in an area with few cybercrime laws or lax enforcement, and allow for interaction, if possible, with other cybercriminals. They are looking for Internet Service Providers (ISPs) that either are already "under the influence of criminal organizations or knowingly tolerate their activities" (Stein-Gross et al. 2009: 1). ISPs are companies or organizations that for a fee provide clients with equipment and connectivity to the internet and to the web as well as online storage. Of interest to cybercriminals are those ISPs that offer 'bullet-proof hosting' where they are guaranteed continued service even when the clients are engaged in malicious or illegal activities. Such ISPs are often

called rogue networks or cybercriminal 'havens.' These ISPs are likely to be hosting a number of malicious activities in their networks and have garnered the name 'bad neighborhoods' (Moura 2013; Moura et al. 2014). Or, as Krebs (2010) in his blog has noted, they resemble the "red light district of the web."

These rogue ISPs and so-called bad neighborhoods have a geographic location and act much like black spots even though all the activity takes place in cyberspace. They operate a domain of Internet Protocol (IP) addresses that are distributed to those who subscribe to their internet/web service. And according to a number of studies (e.g., Stone-Gross et al. 2009; Van Eeten et al. 2010; Moura 2013; Moura et al. 2014), these ISPs are often small and regional and, in turn, have contracts with upstream and transit ISPs for actual connections with the internet and web. The particular ISPs selected by cybercriminals are generally those that have few contractual requirements; inadequate or lax fraud checking; allow for integration with anonymity services such as Tor and paying by Bitcoin; and are located in a jurisdiction, province, or country lacking in resources, the predisposition to investigate, or laws permitting such actions. In effect, cybercriminals seek ISPs that have demonstrated a history of turning a blind eye to malicious or illegal activities and allow for such behavior even when there are complaints about abuse.

These same studies have found differences in the rogue ISPs that cybercriminals use to engage in cybertrespass and cyberdeception/theft crime—or, in cyberspace vernacular, spam and phishing activities. Examining the blacklists for spam and phishing (e.g., Composite Black List, Passive Spam Blocking List, and Phishtank), it was noted that the ISPs who engaged in lots of spamming were found in developing countries and in areas where they could build extensive botnets to carry out their campaigns. In fact, the top 20 ISPs on the spamming blacklists accounted for almost 50% of all spamming observed in the data. But the ISPs involved with phishing were found in the US and more developed countries as this illegal activity relies on stable hosts that can be counted on to be online all the time so that whenever users accept the email or web opportunity directed at them, the cybercriminals are ready to steal their personal information. Of interest in a discussion of black spots is the fact that these different business models lead to the involvement of different ISPs in cyberspace and different geographic locations on the ground.

Consider the following examples of rogue ISPs. One that has been designated by a number of security firms as among "the baddest of the bad" (Krebs 2007a, b; Vernetti 2010) is the Russian Business Network or RBN which registered as an ISP in 2006 and was originally located in St Petersburg. Organizations operating through its internet and web hosting services have engaged in spam, child pornography, online casinos, phishing scams for identity theft, piracy, and internet pharmacies. RBN specializes in bullet-proof hosting, insuring that its websites are reachable regardless of attempts by law enforcement to take them down. Indeed, the network has had no 'official' website. To sign up, a potential client has had to use instant-messaging services or visit specific online forums as well as prove that they are not law enforcement officers. Known to charge ten times the going monthly rate for their services, RBN has made its money off its internet and web hosting and, in this way, protected itself from prosecution. It is the clients who carry out the illegal activities, not RBN. RBN just insures that they can engage in such activities. Moreover, if clients do not target Russian companies and consumers, it is less likely that there will be complaints lodged against the ISP from Russian law enforcement. In 2006, the groups operating through RBN's hosting services accounted for about one-half of all phishing or ID identity theft scams (Krebs 2007a). As more upstream ISPs began walling their customers off from the internet/web or, more particularly, walling off specific problematic sites, RBN shut down its Russian servers and with its 406 web addresses and 2,090 domain names fragmented into smaller, more mini-ISPs in China, Turkey, Ukraine, Panama, and the US. Instead of one RBN, there were now ten (Vernetti 2010). As a chief research officer at a security services firm observed, "blocking problematic networks typically means they merely go to a new place on the Internet" and resume offering clients their services as before (Krebs 2007b). They adapt.

In a ten-story building in downtown San Jose, California, we find another example of a rogue ISP—the McColo Corporation. This relatively small firm was home to servers that for a time were involved in distributing a significant portion of the world's spam. McColo's servers were legendary for their consistent speeds and for being 'bulletproof' or immune from shutdown requests lodged by other ISPs or foreign law enforcement (Krebs 2008, 2014). This ISP hosted the command and control centers for six major botnets that managed millions of compromised computers engaged in the sale of counterfeit pharmaceuticals, designer goods, fake security products, and child pornography via email (Clayton 2009). McColo's services, mainly hosted in the US, were cheap, reliable, and fast. It was observed that one of the hosted botnets, Mega-D, could send out ten billion email messages a day. When complaints were lodged against particular clients hosted by McColo, those responsible would indicate that they were looking into it and would do so by moving that particular client to a different section of the network with new identifying information. After more than three million complaints to the US Federal Trade Commission, the McColo ISP was finally taken offline by its upstream hosts in early November 2008. In the weeks following the takedown, observers noted that spam was reduced by as much as 75% worldwide as infected computers across the globe were disconnected from their command and control centers (Clayton 2009; Krebs 2014). Although across time spam recovered as these command and control centers were moved to other rogue ISPs, spam filters used by upstream and downstream ISPs became less effective because they were built around the blacklists of ISPs generally available and an important member of those lists—McColo— had been removed (Clayton 2009).

A final example is CyberBunker, a rogue ISP whose leadership has called it the Republic of CyberBunker and its head the Minister of Telecommunications and Foreign Affairs (Pfanner and O'Brien 2013). CyberBunker is an ISP that, according to its website, is a leader in anonymous service hosting and will support any client except those engaged in child pornography or "anything related to terrorism." Among its clients have been The Pirate Bay and WikiLeaks. It derives its name from its original headquarters in a former NATO bunker built in 1955 and located in The Netherlands. CyberBunker is perhaps best known in the rogue ISP world for its dispute with Spamhaus that resulted in one of the largest ever reported distributed denial of service (DDoS) attacks (Jenkins 2011; CyberBunker 2016). The attack peaked at 300 gigabits per second and its effects lasted a week. It was the result of Spamhaus adding CyberBunker to its spamming blacklist for a second time, it having been dropped by one upstream ISP roughly two years earlier. We have already observed that such blacklists are used by 'legitimate' ISPs in their spam filters. The leadership of CyberBunker complained that by adding them to the Spamhaus blacklist, the latter was acting as judge, jury, and executioner and was, in effect, censoring the internet. The leadership of CyberBunker appears to have instigated the DDoS attack with a post on Facebook asking, "Yo anons, we could use a little help in shutting down the illegal slander and blackmail censorship project 'spamhaus.org'" (Pfanner and O'Brien 2013). This call to arms brought out other rogue ISPs unhappy with Spamhaus that organized themselves into the 'Stophaus' movement and pursued the DDoS attack. The attack was directed at upstream ISPs linked to spamhaus.org as well as regional internet exchanges in Europe and "disrupted Internet service for millions of users in Europe." It has been referred to as the attack that almost broke the back of the internet (Prince 2013; Krebs 2016).

CONCLUSION

Although we have provided only a few examples of darknet markets, botnet command and control centers, and rogue ISPs, those we have suggest that there are, indeed, some 'bad neighborhoods' in cyberspace that facilitate cybercrime of a variety of kinds. Research indicates that we can identify and study these entities using the blacklists that are relatively commonplace regarding who is misbehaving. We note that these lists are called blacklists because such a title suggests that there are black spots in the cyberspace structure. But as our examples suggest, things in cyberspace appear to be ever changing as markets, botnets, and rogue ISPs come and go and as they fragment and move to more hospitable locations geographically as well as on the internet and web. And just like their on-the-ground counterparts, cybercriminals are always adapting and on the lookout for areas where they can be in charge that facilitate what they want to do without legal interference, that help them make money, and that maintain their anonymity. Cyberspace appears to add to this list of requirements the characteristics of worldwide access and instantaneous communication which increase the effect that criminal organizations can have and the range of possible locations from which they can operate. At the same time, cyberspace increases the problems for governments and law enforcement. The networked governance system in cyberspace means that non-state actors carry as much weight as state actors do. And they have limitless space in which to maneuver even if shut down in one place. Moreover, there is the problem of whose laws count and if one must be physically in a place to be shut down.

REFERENCES

Adams, Devin M. 2017. The 2016 Amendment to Criminal Rule 41: National Search Warrants to Seize Cyberspace, "Particularly" Speaking. *University of Richmond Law Review* 51: 721–773.

Adams, Jackson, and Mohamad Albakajai. 2016. Cyberspace: A New Threat to the Sovereignty of the State. *Management Studies* 4 (6): 256–265.

Allen, Ernie. 2010. Domestic Minor Sex Trafficking. Testimony before the Subcommittee on Crime, Terrorism, and Homeland Security, Committee on the Judiciary, US House of Representatives, September 15.

Anderson, Nate. 2011. LulzSec Manifesto: "We Screw Each Other Over for a Jolt of Satisfaction." *Ars Technica*, May 17.

Bevir, George. 2017. Cost of Online Piracy to Hit $52bn. *IBC 365*, October 30.

Bhattacharjee, Yudhijit. 2011. Welcome to Hackerville: The Romanian Cybercriminal Hotspot. *Wired*, March.

Bischoff, Paul. 2016. Guide: How to Access the Deep Web and Darknet. *VPN & Privacy*, May 31.

Bran, Mirel. 2013. In Romania, a Quiet City Has Become the Global Hub for Hackers and Online Crooks. *Le Monde* (English Edition), January 7.

BrightPlanet. 2012. *Deep Web: A Primer*. brightplanet.com, June 4.

Broadhurst, Roderic, Peter Grabosky, Mamoun Alazab, and Steve Chon. 2014. Organizations and Cybercrime: An Analysis of the Nature of Groups Engaged in Cybercrime. *International Journal of Cyber Criminology* 8 (1): 1–20.

Broadhurst, Roderic, Peter Grabosky, Mamoun Alazab, Brigitte Bohours, Steve Chon, and Chen Da. 2013. Crime in Cyberspace: Offenders and the Role of Organized Crime Groups. Working Paper, Australian National University Cybercrime Observatory, May 15.

Caldwell, Leslie R. 2016. Highlighting Cybercrime Enforcement. Speech at Center for Strategic and International Studies, December 7.

Cardenas, Alvarao A., Svetlana Radosavac, Jens Grossklags, John Chuang, and Chris Hoofnagle. 2009. An Economic Map of Cybercrime. Paper Presented at the 37th Research Conference on Communication Information, and Internet Policy, George Mason University.

Chacos, Brad. 2013. Meet Darknet: The Hidden Anonymous Underbelly of the Searchable Web. *PC World*, August 12.

Chawki, Mohamed. 2006. Anonymity in Cyberspace: Finding the Balance. Computer Crime Research Center, July 9.

Choo, Raymond, and Peter Grabosky. 2013. Cyber Crime. In *Oxford Handbook of Organized Crime*, ed. Letizia Paoli. Oxford: Oxford University Press.

Clayton, Richard. 2009. *How Much Did Shutting Down McColo Help?* Cambridge: Cambridge Computer Laboratory, Cambridge University.

Cohen-Almagor, Raphael. 2012. Freedom of Expression, Internet Responsibility, and Business Ethics: The Yahoo Saga and Its Implications. *Journal of Business Ethics* 106 (3): 353–365.

Correll, Sean-Paul. 2010. Inside Mariposa—The Largest Botnet Takedown in History. *ISSA Magazine*, May.

Couch, Robbie. 2014. 70 Percent of Child Sex Trafficking Victims Are Sold Online: Study. *The Huffington Post*, July 25.

CyberBunker. 2016. Spamhaus Blackmail War. http://cyberbunker.com/web/spamhaus.php. Accessed 24 July 2018.

Fielding, Sarah. 2018. Craigslist Has Banned Personal Ads Thanks to a New Trafficking Law—Here's How Sex Workers Say It Could Put Them in Huge Danger. *INSIDER*, March 20.

Franceschi-Bicchierai, Lorenzo. 2015. Inside "Hackerville," Romania's Infamous Cyber Crime Hub. *Motherboard*, June 17.

Freed, Anthony M. 2010. An Interview with UN Cybersecurity Expert Raoul Chiesa. *The Huffington Post*, April 15.

Gaspareniene, Ligita, and Rita Remeikiene. 2015. Digital Shadow Economy: A Critical Review of the Literature. *Mediterranean Journal of Social Sciences* 6 (6): 402–409.

Global RADAR. 2017. US Government Stopping Piracy Across the Globe. *Global RADAR*, December 25.

Greenberg, Andy. 2016. The Silk Road's Dark Web Dream Is Dead. *Wired*, January 14.

Holt, Thomas J. and Adam M. Bossler. 2014. Cybercrime. *Oxford Handbooks Online*. Oxford University Press, June.

Holt, Thomas J., April M. Zeoli, and Kathleen Bohner. 2013. Examining the Decision-Making Processes of Sex Tourists Using Online Data. *Journal of Qualitative Criminal Justice and Criminology* 1: 122–155.

International Telecommunications Union (ITU). 2017. *ICT Facts and Figures 2017*. Geneva: ITU.

Jenkins, Quentin. 2011. Dutch ISP Attempts False Police Report. *Spamhaus News*, October 14.

Kiguolis, Ugnius. 2017. Koobface Worm Proliferates and Makes Astounding Profit for Its Owners. *2SpyWare*, February 7.

Krebs, Brian. 2007a. Shadowy Russian Firm Seen as Conduit for Cybercrime. *Washington Post*, October 13.

———. 2007b. Russian Business Network: Down, But Not Out. *Washington Post*, November 7

———. 2008. Host of Internet Spam Groups Is Cut Off. *Washington Post*, November 12.

———. 2010. Naming and Shaming 'Bad' ISPs. *Krebs on Security*, March 19.

———. 2014. How a Car Wreck in a Moscow Square Affected the Spam We Receive Everyday. *Krebs on Security*, December 29.

———. 2016. Inside "The Attack that Almost Broke the Internet." *Krebs on Security*, August 26.

Latonero, Mark. 2011. *Human Trafficking Online: The Role of Social Networking Sites and Online Classifieds*. Los Angeles: Center on Communication Leadership and Policy, Annenberg School for Communications and Journalism, University of Southern California, September.

Leyden, John. 2012. Five Koobface Botnet Suspects Named by New York Times. *The Register*, January 18.

McAfee. 2018. *The Economic Impact of Cybercrime—No Slowing Down*. Washington, DC: McAfee and Center for Strategic and International Studies.

Moura, Giovane C.M. 2013. Internet Bad Neighborhoods. The Netherlands Center for Telematrics and Information Technology, University of Twente.

Moura, Giovane C.M., Ramin Sadre, and Aiko Pras. 2014. Bad Neighborhoods on the Internet. *IEEE Communications Magazine* 52 (7). preprint.

Mueller, Milton, Andreas Schmidt, and Brenden Kuerbis. 2013. Internet Security and Networked Governance in International Relations. *International Studies Review* 15 (1): 86–104.

Negi, Yogita. 2011. Pragmatic Overview of Hacking & Its Counter Measures. Proceedings of the 5th National Conference, INDIACom, New Delhi, March 10–11.

Pfanner, Eric and Kevin J. O'Brien. 2013. Provocateur Comes into View after Cyberattack. *New York Times*. March 29.

Prince, Brian. 2010. How The Koobface Botnet Made $2 Million in a Year. *eWeek*, November 13.

Prince, Matthew. 2013. The DDoS that Almost Broke the Internet. *The Cloudflare Blog*, March 27.

Sedgwick, Kai. 2018. These Are the Most Popular Darknet Marketplaces Right Now. *Bitcoin News*, May 1.

Soska, Kyle and Nicolas Christin. 2015. Measuring the Longitudinal Evolution of the Online Anonymous Marketplace Ecosystem. Proceedings of the 24th USENIX Security Symposium, Washington, DC, August 12–14.

Stone-Gross, Brett, Christopher Kruegel, Kevin Almeroth, Andreas Moser, and Engin Kirda. 2009. FIRE: Finding Rogue Networks. Paper Presented at the 25th Annual Conference on Computer Security Applications, Honolulu, December 7–9.

The Economist. 2014. The Amazons of the Darknet, November 1.

———. 2016. Shedding Light on the Dark Web, July 16.

United Nations Office on Drugs and Crime (UNODC). 2012. *Transnational Organized Crime in Central America and the Caribbean: A Threat Assessment*. Vienna: UNODC.

———. 2013. *Comprehensive Study on Cybercrime*. Vienna: UNODC.

Van der Sar, Ernesto. 2017. US Government Teaches Anti-Piracy Skills Around the Globe. *Torrent Freak*, December 17.

Van Eeten, Michel, Johannes M. Bauer, Hadi Asghari, Shirin Tabatabaie, and Dave Rand. 2010. *The Role of Internet Service Providers in Botnet Mitigation: An Empirical Analysis Based on Spam Data*. Paper Presented at the Ninth Workshop on the Economics of Information Security, George Mason University, June 7–8.

Vernetti, Gianmaria. 2010. *The Power of Networking: An Insight of the Russian Business Network*. United Nations Interregional Crime and Justice Research Institute, July.

Wall, David S. 2005. *Cybercrime, Deviance, and the Internet*. Cambridge, UK: Polity.

Winstock, Adam R., Monica I. Barratt, Larissa J. Maier, and Jason A. Ferris. 2018. *Global Drug Survey 2018: Key Findings Report*. London: Global Drug Survey.

Zickuhr, Kathryn. 2010. *Generations 2010*. Pew Internet & American Life Project, December 16.

CHAPTER 8

Discoveries and Challenges

With this book, we have brought a novel approach to the study of transnational crime. Instead of examining an individual criminal organization, a particular type of illicit criminal activity, or what goes on in a specific region as is usually the case, we have focused on the safe havens that those engaged in transnational crime use as locations for their operations. What is it about these geographic spaces that renders them conducive to illicit activities, and how are such locations interlinked within the illicit global economy? Do these safe havens challenge the Westphalian state system much like the black holes in the universe challenge Newtonian physics and do they exhibit characteristics of the new economic geography (NEG)? Can we develop a map of these locations as viewed through the eyes of those engaged in transnational criminality? These are the basic questions with which we began this book.

Our study started with the discovery of how important illicit activities were to the community of Ciudad del Este, located at the corner of Paraguay as it meets Argentina and Brazil. A brief residency there suggested that the community was controlled and essentially governed by those engaged in illicit activities. Was Ciudad del Este a fluke or were there other such locations—parts of countries—that fell outside effective state government control; where an insurgent, terrorist, or transnational criminal organization (TCO) appeared to govern instead; that depended on illicit activities to finance what went on in the locale; and that were interested in remaining invisible to law enforcement and the media? This book

© The Author(s) 2020
S. S. Brown, M. G. Hermann, *Transnational Crime and Black Spots*, International Political Economy Series,
https://doi.org/10.1057/978-1-137-49670-6_8

focuses on 80 such places including Ciudad del Este. Table 1.1 in Chap. 1 listed these 80 black spots as we call them.

We learned that it is possible to use open source materials to answer a common set of questions about each black spot, allowing us to create a database across the 80 black spots while also facilitating the writing of in-depth case studies about each. As a result, we could examine a particular black spot in depth or tally the answers to specific questions across the set of black spots. The data that we have presented in this book come from this latter data analysis. The descriptions of particular black spots illustrative of these data come from the in-depth case studies. The last question in our coding manual (see Appendix A) asks those writing an in-depth case study to indicate other potential black spots that they found in doing their case. We have identified a range of potential black spots in the process but, perhaps more importantly, validated the original 80 as they continued to be named as well. So what did we discover? In particular, what do these 80 black spots tell us about sovereignty and the illicit economy?

DISCOVERIES

Those involved in transnational criminal activities look for certain types of places from which to operate. They tend to focus on international borders and the ease with which such borders can be traversed as well as access to traditional trading routes where economic activity is constant. These safe havens are generally found in the borderlands of weakly governed states where the citizenry is not well served by the official government and can be incentivized to cede authority to actors other than the government. Such locations often present some challenges terrain-wise reducing law enforcement's effectiveness. The black spots also seem to be located in places with heterogeneous ethnic populations, facilitating the mingling of different types of people with no one group necessarily standing out. And such communities often bring with them a degree of conflict, begging for some group or organization to arbitrate and control it and in the process create and impose rules and regulations necessary for governance. The places chosen provide redundancies in both illegal activities and ways of ensuring commodities get to market. All but one of the black spots facilitated access to multiple illicit activities and most provided alternative transit routes to markets via road, air, and water for added flexibility.

The black spots appear located so as to exploit the tensions that often exist between sovereignty and globalization. Globalization has made it more difficult to control what crosses borders. With improvements in transportation, access to transnational capital, and distance-spanning technologies, sovereignty no longer provides a sanctuary for states. As a result, borderlands have increased relevance to those engaged in transnational criminal activities. Because laws and regulations vary at country borders, locating black spots near borders allows those involved in illicit activities to move easily between legal jurisdictions and to continue unabated with their activities. Like the city states, pirate islands, and feudal castles of old, black spots reside in these borderlands overseen by those engaged in illicit operations. Such places effectively become sovereign spaces of their own with borders, rules, and the provision of security as well as employment and services for residents.

How do black spots act as enablers and engines of the illicit global economy? Here we have discovered the relevance of the new economic geography (NEG) literature in helping us understand the role that black spots play. NEG focuses on the spatial patterning of economic activity, notably the forces driving the concentration of such activity versus its dispersion. With black spots, we have learned the importance of international borders and traditional trading routes to the selection of a location—what NEG would call first-order effects. National borders arguably are the initial catalyst that draws the transnational criminal element to a particular location. But it is the second-order effects—the availability of roads, rivers, and airports as well as multiple illicit activities—that focus their attention. These second-order effects attach mobility, flexibility, and redundancy to a particular choice of location. Also relevant are the specific immobile factors of production that are tied to a location such as the skills of the residents, the nature of transportation costs, the availability of natural resources and other materials, and the relative effectiveness of law enforcement in that area (e.g., the prevalence of corruption and the probability of interdiction). Care and thought are put into the selection of a black spot and such rumination is reflective of NEG.

Not only do the selected black spots facilitate engaging in multiple illicit activities, they also provide opportunities to perform more than one function. Around two-thirds of the 80 black spots studied here provided those engaged in transnational criminal activities with the possibility of engaging in two or more functions from production to transit to distribution. The 17 of the 80 black spots that allowed those pursuing transnational criminal activities to perform all three functions as well as engage in from five to nine different illicit activities add complexity to our notion of what a black spot is. These appear to be *hubs* in the global illicit economy. Found in all parts of the globe, eight of these were the locations where particular ethnic groups resided who were seeking autonomy in or from the state in which the space was found. The leadership governing these areas was forced to become involved in illicit activities because recognition, goods and services, and/or protection were not being offered or were being deliberately withheld by the state. Often these areas are located where the borders accepted by the international community split particular ethnic groups, tribes, and peoples, providing them with little hope for re-connection. The nine other hubs were the black markets that have generally played this role for long stretches of time, many back to the beginnings of world-wide trade. In these areas, legal and illegal activities co-exist and those engaged in transnational criminal activities seek them out because they can get 'lost' and remain anonymous among the legal activities and actors. These black market hubs tend to be located in ports on major international sea lanes, in prime locations along traditional land-based trading routes, and in areas designated as free trade or economic zones.

These two types of hubs illustrate the two concepts that we have explored in this book—sovereignty and NEG. The hubs operated by ethnic groups seeking autonomy either within a state or by having their own state force us to rethink notions of sovereignty while the black market hubs capture the impact of economic agglomeration on the selection of places in which to engage in illicit activities. And these two types of hubs are controlled and governed by different types of organizations. The hubs focused on autonomy or some form of statehood are overseen by insurgent groups. They are engaged in a range of illicit activities to sustain their autonomy and to provide for citizens in an area often unrepresented or underrepresented in the government of the state within which they are located or, alternatively, controlled by ethnic groups that have been divided by a border and find themselves an 'enemy' in the state within which they reside. These black spots are most often found in Africa and Asia and appear to be the result of borders put into place during the periods of colonialization or de-colonialization. The black market hubs generally involve transnational criminal organizations (TCOs) who are focused on profit-maximizing businesses. They are most often found in Europe and Latin America. Like MNCs, these TCOs value places that offer them resources, employees, access to multiple transit routes, and markets. The economic advantages of agglomeration and anonymity are crucial.

There is a third group of black spots that is underrepresented in these two types of hubs. These are the black spots controlled by terrorist organizations. This set of black spots seems less well defined in our data, perhaps because some are co-located with TCOs and some are not. When terrorist organizations and TCOs co-locate, there is more emphasis on the diversity of activities and a business focus with fewer terrorist events. The TCOs appear to facilitate the terrorist organizations' activities by providing them with the kinds of financial support, weapons, and goods and services necessary for such organizations to pursue their goals while, in turn, the terrorist organizations become enamored with the TCOs' business model and focus more on making money than on engaging in terrorism.

The black spots also provide us with places to look for evidence of how those involved in illicit activities approach the task of transforming illegally gotten money into that regarded as legal. The organizations controlling the black spots take seriously the notion of layering in the money laundering process and are talented improvisers in exploiting the geography and level of development of the black spot in 'cleaning' their money. They use techniques that are readily available given that particular black spot's level of development. But here is where the black spots that are black markets become important, particularly the free trade zones (FTZs) and offshore financial centers, because they generally facilitate all types of money laundering from hawaladars to front companies to prepaid cards to international banking. And if they are geographically centrally located like a Dubai, they become a hub for the illicit economy. Such places thrive by providing a wide range of financial resources and an informal economy.

As often noted, money laundering is a complex process and generally involves engaging intermediaries who are not necessarily a part of the organization controlling a black spot. Consider the following list of such intermediaries: hawaladars, cash couriers, lawyers, accountants, real estate brokers, small business owners, prepaid card program managers and distributors, import/export businesses, to name a few. Even charities can get caught up in the money laundering enterprise. Such parties become vested in the black spots and the organizations operating them. Indeed, their livelihoods depend on the money laundering process and the organization employing them. As a result, organizations engaged in illicit activities are constantly on the lookout for intermediaries that offer diversified, innovative (hence, less detectable) money laundering services and black spots within which such activities can be concentrated.

With more and more of the world's population online, the internet and web have become a giant marketplace that spans the globe and have brought with them new opportunities for criminal activities. With an elaborate infrastructure, cyberspace leaves its users straddling a Westphalian state system, on one side, where established borders define sovereignty and the rule of law and a virtual transnational world, on the other, that lacks notions of sovereignty while emphasizing shared governance among state and non-state actors. Cyberspace poses a jurisdictional dilemma for states. And it offers those engaged in transnational criminal activities an essentially borderless environment, providing access to large numbers of potential intermediaries and customers where contact is instantaneous. Given the international character of cyberspace and the ease with which one can move across country borders, why not move criminal activities online? Certainly there is less risk of interdiction as exactly who is in charge of law enforcement is still in the process of being worked out.

The very nature of its infrastructure ensures that there are black spots in cyberspace. Fiber optic cables, cell towers, internet service providers (ISPs), browsers, computers, and software, for example, are necessary to be online. Here is where we find darknet markets, botnets, and rogue internet service providers. All reside in a geographic space as well as in virtual reality. Darknet markets are found in that part of the deep web that is kept hidden on purpose and, though business is done online, what is bought is shipped offline to the buyer. These are the Amazons of the Darknet. Botnets, their command and control centers, and botherders involve networks of computers and/or mobile devices that have been surreptitiously infected with software and, as a result, can be controlled remotely by criminals. The computers forming the botnet are geographically located as is the botherder and the command and control center. Rogue internet service providers (ISPs) facilitate the creation of bad neighborhoods in cyberspace. Such ISPs play host to cybercriminal operations by offering few contractual requirements; inadequate or lax fraud checking; integration with anonymous services such as Tor and paying by Bitcoin; and a location in a jurisdiction, province, or country lacking in resources, the predisposition to investigate, or laws permitting such actions. And they usually have at least one legitimate organization paying for their services to appear legal or above board. As we have observed, all three of these types of black spots have ties to the infrastructure of cyberspace even as they are also located in some particular geographic place. They each provide the characteristics of black spots that we have come to expect but cyberspace increases the scale of their impact and their ability to retain anonymity while at the same time decreasing their likelihood of being caught.

CHALLENGES

We have begun to understand the map of the world as viewed through the eyes of those involved in transnational criminal activities. In the process, we have made the discoveries discussed in this book. But we have also gained some insights into the challenges that this complex world poses. It is to elaborating these challenges that we turn now.

One such challenge is directed at us, the authors, and those involved in working on the project. This book has studied 80 black spots identified early on in our research and located in all regions of the world. In the process of trying to understand why these particular locations were selected and their impact on transnational criminal activities, we have identified many others. In effect, as we examined the flows of activities among the 80 black spots, we noticed other black spots that were involved in the production, transit, and/or distribution of trafficked items. One next task is to conduct in-depth case studies of these potential black spots and to add them to our 80. We have also learned what is common about the locations that insurgent, terrorist, and transnational criminal organizations select as black spots and where there are differences among the choices of these three types of organizations. Can we develop algorithms based on this information and identify other black spots that would make sense as part of our current map of the world and the illicit global economy? Toward this end, we have begun to build a relational database that allows us to study current linkages among the black spots across the variety of illicit activities that we have explored here. Such a process provides us with data on which to build maps like Figs. 4.1 and 4.2 but for all activities going to and from a black spot. This process enables us to more accurately trace where a particular illicit activity comes from and goes to as well.

A second challenge focuses on borders. International borders are clearly important in the decisions those involved in criminal operations make regarding where to locate. It is the change in the jurisdictional authority that appears to be the key to why borders—or borderlands—are critical in this choice. Laws and regulations change with international borders but because globalization has made such borders more fluid and less secure, it is as easy for illicit goods to flow over them as licit ones. It also has made thinking about becoming one's own state more prevalent. As Griffiths (2016: 7) has observed, "in an era of increasing globalization, small states can survive by plugging into the global economy to secure capital and resources and leverage their comparative advantage." And many of the insurgent organizations in control of black spots in this project have just such ideas in mind. Or, at the very least, they are interested in gaining or maintaining some autonomy within another state. They have been pushed to engage in illicit activities to provide the goods, services, and protection needed to retain control over a specific area. Were they granted the status they seek, would they remain a part of the illicit global economy? This issue is more complex than often portrayed. What about those borders that have been drawn separating particular ethnic groups (e.g., the Pashtuns) or drawn so that groups must navigate several borders in the course of doing business (the Kurds, for instance)? What about countries that have internationally recognized borders but include a number of black spots inhabited by different ethnic groups who have little in common with those in other parts of the same state (e.g., Somalia)? And what about a black spot governed by an insurgent group interested not necessarily in becoming a separate state but in gaining political influence and autonomy within an already recognized state (Hezbollah Territory in Lebanon, for instance)? All of these examples raise questions about borders and who gets to decide what borders count.

Then there is cyberspace where there are, in essence, no borders and, yet, the infrastructure needed to facilitate the internet and web add geographic location to what is supposedly a virtual world. It is an arena that facilitates criminal activity just as it has enlivened the legal global economy. With use of the darknet and The Onion Router, borders are overcome in seconds, almost as if they did not exist. At issue is who has jurisdiction and the ability to regulate cyberspace; who is in charge? It is easily possible to be physically in one location in one part of the world and sell goods, hack, send spam, phish, link computers into robots, and be attached to an internet service provider in another part of the globe. We have discovered black spots in cyberspace and those operating out of these places are intent on using the difficulties in defining who is in charge to their advantage.

A fourth challenge is encountered in what has been called the Robin Hood curse (Zartman and Aronson 2005). In effect, the insurgent, terrorist, and transnational criminal organizations operating from the black spots use their illicit activities to provide goods, services, employment, and protection to those residing there. In return, they benefit from the business income, taxes and fees, and loyalty of the residents as well as the various intermediaries that are needed to maintain their wealth and power. Were the insurgent, terrorist, and transnational criminal groups to disappear, all those involved in the maintenance of the black spot would suffer. And often this curse captures those in the government or regional and UN forces sent to try to deal with them. Robin Hood's Merry Men and their families and relatives as well as those enabling them lose if the largesse stops, particularly if the government of the state is unable to meet their needs and those operating in the black spot have different ethnic, political, and/or ideological interests. It is a curse difficult to overcome because many are benefiting from it remaining in place.

States have also added to the challenges we face in dealing with the global illicit economy by creating free trade zones (FTZs). These are "designated areas within a country in which incentives are offered to support the development of exports, foreign direct investment, and local employment," with the intention of improving the state's capability to provide goods and services to its citizenry (FATF 2010: 4). The dilemma is that to make FTZs successful, duties and quotas are removed on the re-export of items, customs duties and excise taxes are deferred on imports until they leave the FTZ and enter the country proper, customs procedures are streamlined, and the coordination between those in charge of the FTZ and central government officials is often lax. Moreover, these FTZs are usually on international borders. States, in effect, render it easier for legal and illegal activities to co-exist. And those engaged in transnational criminal activities have taken advantage of the opportunities such FTZs offer. Indeed, a number of these FTZs are found in our 80 black spots and there are roughly 3,000 in 135 countries around the world. These FTZs are a money launderer's paradise and their locations on borders means that it is conceivable to consider crisscrossing the globe using nothing but FTZs in getting one's product to market. It is to such places that those engaged in transnational criminal activities are especially drawn because they offer markets, anonymity, corruptible intermediaries, and relatively lax law enforcement. How do states take advantage of what FTZs have to offer in developing a country's economy without also providing a haven for illicit activity as well? Or is allowing for black markets to exist in FTZs the price governments pay for improving their own economies and being able to provide goods and services to areas that are relatively under-developed?

We have written about the 80 black spots in this book as if they were static and stable, as if there were no interdictions, no turf wars, no natural disasters, no armies sent in to take control. We know such is not the case and, in fact, we are continuously updating the in-depth case studies to check on the effects of such contingencies on the black spots. Of interest is how black spots change when certain events happen such as the changes that occurred in Abu Kamal on the Syria-Iraq border from the time UN sanctions were put in place on Iraq in the 1990s to the US invasion in 2003 to the takeover by ISIS in 2014. What about when the US and Colombia put Plan Colombia into place? What happened to the Wa State when Myanmar moved from being ruled by a military junta to taking steps toward becoming a democracy? We have learned in the process that it is to deal with such contingencies that those operating in black spots both diversify the illicit activities in which they engage and build in redundancies in transit routes and modes of transportation. It is also why they develop alternative black spots networks such as the various branches of the Balkan Route that can carry illicit goods into Europe. Moreover, successful attempts by law enforcement to capture or to kill the leaders of organizations involved in criminal activities has led them to become more horizontal than vertical as organizations, to build more diverse networks, and to proliferate. Such efforts have also led those involved in transnational criminal operations to look at cyberspace. The challenge here for those of us studying the illicit global economy and rethinking sovereignty is to move away from the usual focus on a single illicit activity, a single organization, or a particular region. If diversification and redundancy are the name of the game, we need to see the world as these organizations do and anticipate how regulations, interdictions, and economic plans are likely to reframe their world and how they are likely to innovate in order to deal with what is happening. Mapping the world as they do, what are their likely next steps?

The last challenge, but perhaps one of the most important, is the endemic nature of corruption and its use by those involved in transnational criminal activities to insure their black spot location and their livelihoods. As Shelley (2014: 67) has noted, "corruption is the Achilles' heel of the global economy." It provides the enabling environment for the selection and maintenance of a black spot and its ongoing activities and financing. Corruption facilitates the intermediaries that become useful in getting goods to market and in financing illicit activities. It is also important in keeping governments blind to the existence of a black spot and in insuring ease of movement across borders. Corruption, like the Robin Hood curse, can become a way of life and very difficult to eliminate. As recent empirical evidence suggests, we are more likely to engage in corrupt behavior when we perceive corruption as the norm (Kobis et al. 2016).

CONCLUSION

We return to what we said at the start of this volume. We have reported on 80 black spots found in all regions of the world, showing how they have led us to rethink sovereignty and the global economy. We have made discoveries about the nature of the global illicit economy as well as how globalization appears to be facilitating the development of smaller sovereign units rather than moving us toward global governance. But we have also come face-to-face with a set of challenges that confront those authorities engaged in understanding how the organizations involved in transnational criminal activities see the world and conduct their activities. These challenges raise issues that law enforcement as well as national, regional, and international governance structures are going to encounter in dealing with this black spots organized world. We are interested in ways others have thought about or studied the challenges that we have raised in this chapter. Indeed, this book has merely laid a foundation for future scholarly exploration of the black spots world. Our intention is to contribute to what others have done in rethinking sovereignty and the global economy by providing an initial map of the world as viewed through the eyes of insurgent, terrorist, and transnational criminal organizations.

REFERENCES

FATF. 2010. *Money Laundering Vulnerabilities of Free Trade Zones*. Paris: FATF/OECD.

Griffiths, Ryan. 2016. *Age of Secession: The International and Domestic Determinants of State Birth*. Cambridge: Cambridge University Press.

Kobis, Nils C., Jan-Willem van Prooijen, Francesca Righetti, and Paul A.M. Van Lange. 2016. "Who Doesn't?"—The Impact of Descriptive Norms on Corruption. *PLos One* 10 (6): e0131830.

Shelley, Louise I. 2014. *Dirty Entanglements: Corruption, Crime, and Terrorism*. Cambridge: Cambridge University Press.

Zartman, William, and Cynthia T. Aronson. 2005. *Rethinking the Economics of War: The Intersection of Need, Creed, and Greed*. Washington, DC: Woodrow Wilson Center Press.

APPENDIX A CODING MANUAL

MAPPING GLOBAL INSECURITY:
GLOBAL BLACK SPOTS RESEARCH PROJECT

Coding Manual
version 6.0
2017

Margaret G. Hermann
Catriona Standfield
Stuart S. Brown

**Moynihan Institute of Global Affairs,
Maxwell School, Syracuse University**

Reproduced with the permission of the Moynihan Institute of
Global Affairs

© The Author(s) 2020   177
S. S. Brown, M. G. Hermann, *Transnational Crime and Black
Spots*, International Political Economy Series,
https://doi.org/10.1057/978-1-137-49670-6

PRIMARY RESEARCH QUESTIONS

What are the conditions that lead to the development of Black Spots and their sustainability?
What are the factors contributing to the challenging/undermining of state authority within Black Spots?
What types of insecurity do the Black Spots export to the outside world?
What defensive moves do national and international authorities make to deal with Black Spots?

In order to address these questions, we will focus on the following four areas of analysis:

1. Fertile conditions
2. Challenges to state control
3. Export of insecurity
4. State and international responses

DEFINING AND DETECTING BLACK SPOTS

There are several indicators pointing to the existence or potential existence of a Black Spot in a particular area. Such indicators are based on information provided by one of the following sources:

- Host government reports that a part of its country falls outside effective governmental control
- Another government, institution, or organization reports increased criminal activity in a particular area threatening regional stability and/or security
- General warnings of evidence provided by a legitimate source (i.e., government, IGO, NGO, respectable mass-media outlet) of increased illicit activity that is clearly concentrated in or originating from a specific territory

Black Spot areas are defined based on the presence of the following features:

1. Lack of effective state governance
2. Dominance by illicit organizations
3. Transnational illicit activities that indicate involvement in the export of insecurity
4. Existence of informal rules governing the area
5. Interest in staying off legal and media radars

Part I: Fertile Conditions

What Are the Conditions That Lead to the Development of Black Spots and Their Sustainability?

Geopolitical Location
This variable looks at the distance of the Black Spot from international and internal borders as well as the nature of the terrain in which the Black Spot is located. The fact that the terrain is difficult for a government to control (e.g., jungle or high mountain) may make a difference for a government that is already weak.

0. Geographical Region of World Where Located

1. Europe
2. Middle East
3. Asia
4. Africa
5. Latin America
6. North America

1. Relation to Borders

1. Close to international border
2. Close to internal borders (e.g., natural, administrative)
3. Close to internal and international borders
4. Far from any borders

2. Population Type

1. Predominantly urban
2. Predominantly rural
3. Mixed urban/rural terrain

3. Predominant Terrain Features

1. Lowlands
2. Mountains
3. Mixed
4. Other (describe)

4. Vegetation

1. Predominantly desert
2. Predominantly jungle
3. Predominantly forest
4. None; urban environment

5. Climate Type

1. Arctic
2. Temperate
3. Tropical
4. Desert
5. Mixed (please specify which are involved)

Arctic climate: typically very cold in winter and cool temperatures in summer; low humidity, low precipitation.

Temperate climate: typically warm to hot temperatures in summer, cool to cold temperatures during winter. Higher humidity in summer, lower humidity in winter. Medium to high precipitation.

Tropical climate: typically hot temperatures throughout the year. High humidity and high precipitation.

Desert climate: typically cold or very cold at night and hot during day. Low humidity and low to very low precipitation.

6. Lines of Communication

6.1 Presence of formal and informal airfield/airports in Black Spot

Indicate the number of formal and informal airfields/airports
Kind (in terms of flights available)

1. International
2. National
3. Regional
4. Non-Operational

Nature of airport surface

1. Hard (asphalt or cement)
2. Soft (dirt or grass, etc.)

Indicate distance from Black Spot under analysis

6.2 Presence of roads in Black Spot
   1. Absent
   2. Present

      1. Highly developed (numerous)

         1. High quality (US/EU reference)
         2. Low quality (US/EU reference)

      2. Poorly developed (few)

         1. High quality (US/EU reference)
         2. Low quality (US/EU reference)

6.3 Presence of waterway system(s) in Black Spot, that is, waterways used
to transport goods/people

   1. Absent
   2. Present

   Indicate number
   Indicate kind (Are they operational? What are they used for?)
   Indicate distance from the Black Spot (in kilometers, NOT miles)

6.4 Presence of harbors in Black Spot
   1. Absent
   2. Present

   Indicate number
   Indicate kind

      1. Sea
      2. River

   Indicate number of docks
   Indicate distance from the Black Spot (in kilometers, NOT miles)

6.5 Presence of railroads in Black Spot
   1. Absent
   2. Present

1. Numerous

    1. High quality (US/EU reference)
    2. Low quality (US/EU reference)

2. Few

    1. High quality (US/EU reference)
    2. Low quality (US/EU reference)

6.6 Is Black Spot located on traditional/old trading route/area
    1. Yes (describe)
    2. No

7. Illicit Economy

This variable focuses on the nature of the *illicit* economy in the given area. Of interest is whether that economy is based on a single product/service (e.g., drugs) or whether it is based on a number of illicit products/services (e.g., drugs, weapons, and people). The purpose of this information is to determine whether or not Black Spots tend to be located in areas providing diverse sources of income. This may shed light on where to look for Black Spots. It could also indicate whether certain illicit economies are more likely to be associated with Black Spots or even lead to their emergence. In other words, it should reveal more information on whether there is any relationship between the Black Spot and the kind(s) of illicit economy in the area. Codes available for this variable include:

1. Single product/service dominates
2. Multiple products/services dominate
3. None

8. International (In)visibility Record

Does the particular location over the time period of the analysis enjoy significant or little attention from the international media? Of importance for this variable is whether Black Spots are, indeed, characterized by remaining in the shadows of media attention, a condition that they seem to relish. If that is true, then the more media attention a particular Black Spot receives, the less attractive it is as a spot for secret transnational organized criminal activity or residence. This variable has three possible codes:

1. Visible (picked up in media)
2. Invisible (not paid attention to)

3. Interval (sometimes in media and other times not)

9. Ethnic Composition and Conflict
What is the potential significance of the ethnic/national mixture in the area in which a given Black Spot appears? Is the population predominantly homogenous or heterogeneous? Is there conflict evident among the group(s) or not? To account for these possibilities, four codes are available to characterize the ethnic composition/conflict situation in the area:

1. Homogeneous conflicted
2. Homogeneous not conflicted
3. Heterogeneous conflicted
4. Heterogeneous not conflicted

10. Internal Cohesion
Does the Black Spot have informal rules or institutions that create internal cohesion among its people? Are such rules indigenous to the culture/history/religion or have they been imposed from the outside onto the area? These informal rules and institutions are separate from formal laws and government. Codes for this variable include:

1. Indigenous (cultural/historical/religious)
2. Imposed
3. Mixed
4. None

11. Black Spot Type
Based on the information available about the history of the Black Spot, is this a case of a stable or a pulsing Black Spot? Pulsing Black Spots have a tendency to show up and disappear (e.g., as a result of state or international reaction).

1. Stable
2. Pulsing
3. Both
4. None

Please incorporate a note on the causes if the Black Spot is considered to pulse.

12. Observed Life Span
When did the area under investigation become a Black Spot according to the definition we use?
   Date(s) of appearance (or reappearance) (dd/mm/yyyy)
   Date(s) of disappearance (unless it still exists) (dd/mm/yyyy)

PART II: CHALLENGES TO STATE CONTROL

How Is State Authority Challenged and/or Undermined in the Black Spot?

13. Host State's Government Type
Please use the CIA World Factbook (at www.cia.gov) for country reports and government types. If there are two or more host states involved (i.e., Black Spot is on an international border), please give the name of the country and then the government type code AND name in parentheses.

   1. Anarchy
   2. Authoritarian
   3. Commonwealth
   4. Constitutional democracy
   5. Constitutional monarchy
   6. Federal (Federation)
   7. Federal republic
   8. Parliamentary democracy
   9. Parliamentary monarchy
  10. Republic

14. Corruption in the Area Under Analysis
This variable describes whether there is strong evidence of corrupt practices in the area. Determining this is important because it could shed light on both the influence of corruptive potential on the fertility of the area under analysis to emerge as a Black Spot, and also demonstrate whether Black Spots, in fact, promote corruption or are based on it.

   1. Absent
   2. Present

15. Corruption in the Host State(s)
Use the Corruption Perceptions Index (CPI) from Transparency International at www.transparency.org. Use the following convention:
[STATE]-[CPI YEAR]: [POINTS] ([POSITION]/[NO. OF STATES IN REPORT])

Example: Austria-2008: 8.1 (12/180)

16. Area of a Recent Conflict
Was the Black Spot under analysis recently (last 20 years) a scene of a violent conflict?

1. Yes

   1. War
      Years/months [yyyy/mm-yyyy/mm]
   2. Civil war
      Years/months [yyyy/mm-yyyy/mm]
   3. Other
      [Describe]; Years/months [yyyy/mm-yyyy/mm]

2. No

17. Presence of a Recent Nearby Violent Conflict
Has there been a nearby (bordering state/province) violent conflict in the last 20 years?

1. Yes

   1. War
      Years/months [yyyy/mm-yyyy/mm]
   2. Civil war
      Years/months [yyyy/mm-yyyy/mm]
   3. Other
      [Describe]; Years/months [yyyy/mm-yyyy/mm]

Indicate the connection of the area to the conflict (trafficking of arms, soldiers, resupply route, regrouping ground, etc.)

1. Connection proved (clear evidence)
2. Connection likely (circumstantial evidence)
3. No evidence of a connection

2. No

18. Predominant Crime Types

This variable describes the types of crimes that were reported in the Black Spot. The point here is to determine whether Black Spots are necessarily characterized by organized criminal activities or whether they appear because of simpler types of crimes (or without any crime at all). Learning about such activity is important because it may shed light on what should be prevented (e.g., organized crime or all crime) to make sure that Black Spots do not bloom. Moreover, different crime types influence insecurity levels in the area in different ways, in addition to the particular area remaining outside of effective government control. Knowing what types are most common—if there is a pattern—may explain what makes or does not make a Black Spot. Codes used for this variable include:

1. Organized: they exhibit behaviors of *transnational* organized crime operations
2. Organized, but non-transnational organized crime
3. Ad hoc: there seems to be significant crime without the markings of organization behind it
4. Mixed: there is a combination of different kinds of crime (please enumerate the kinds)
5. None: there is no significant crime observed

19. Predominant Violence Motivation

This variable indicates whether particular patterns of violence by non-state actors may signal the existence of a Black Spot or whether no patterns in that regard can be established. If violence observed was generated predominantly or exclusively by the state (rather than a non-state actor), please indicate so in a short narrative description preceding the coding. This variable demonstrates whether:

1. Violent acts seem to be crime-related (theft, robbery, banditry, etc.)
2. Violent acts seem to be politically motivated (power struggle, etc.)
3. There was a combination of both (mixed)

4. Violence is mostly unrelated to crime, insurgency, or terrorism (random)
5. None—no violence at all

20. Nature of Predominant 'Bads' Present in the Area
It is important to establish whether Black Spots can be classified based on the actors operating in the area. This variable can shed light on the nature of Black Spots as safe havens for only a particular kind of 'bad' or as areas open to any kind of non-state structures avoiding state control. Thus, the aim of this variable is to reflect whether the Black Spot under analysis is observed to be dominated by:

1. Terrorist groups [NAMES if available]
2. Insurgent/guerilla groups (permanent presence in controlled territories) [NAMES if available]
3. Extremist, but non-violent groups [NAMES if available]
4. Transnational organized crime groups [NAMES if available]
5. Various kinds of actors (mixed) [NAMES if available]
6. None are present

CODING GUIDANCE: making an analytical distinction between terrorist groups and insurgents may prove difficult due to the blurring lines between the two phenomena. Thus, for the purpose of this coding exercise, insurgent groups are those that:

1. Perpetually or for long periods of time maintain permanent presence in and control over specific territories
2. Whose combat operations are limited to a specific region/area of operations
3. Are predominantly not known for international cell-like organizational structures

Terrorist organizations are those that:

1. Are generally internationally recognized as terrorist organizations (for instance as per the US State Department's and European Union's designations)
2. Are clearly organized based on international cell-like structures for both funding and combat operations, which may take place far away from the primary area of activities

3. Have engaged in terrorist attacks in faraway locations (bombings or suicide attacks targeting civilians and non-military targets as opposed to army-like tactical operations)

21. People of Interest Spotted in the Area (or Known to Have Been There)
Please list the names of known leaders or high-ranking members of terrorist, insurgent, or transnational criminal organizations that were spotted in the area.

[Transnational Criminals' NAMES]
[Terrorists' NAMES]
[Insurgents' NAMES]

22. Nexus of Crime and Terrorism
The purpose of this variable is to determine whether signs of interactions between transnational criminal and terrorist organizations have been observed in the studied area. Knowing whether such a nexus is present or absent may help classify Black Spots and lead to further research questions regarding conditions found in Black Spot areas and the impact of the criminal-terrorist nexus on international security. The two codes for this variable are:

1. Absent
2. Present

23. Organizational Types Present
Are Black Spots dominated by long-term entities or do they also appear as a result of activities conducted by short-term groups? Determining this may assist in answering the question whether there are pulsing Black Spots that appear and disappear with the arrival and departure of short-term bads, or whether Black Spots exist until they are somehow eliminated (either by another actor or due to lack of environmental incentives/fertile conditions). This variable aims to reflect whether the area is observed to be dominated by actors with:

1. Short-lived organizational structures (ad-hoc groups)
2. Highly organized actors (long-term structures)
3. A combination of both (mixed)

PART III: EXPORT OF INSECURITY

What, If Any, Insecurity Do the Black Spots Produce and Export to the Outside World?

24. *Kind of Insecurity Impact*
This variable describes the seemingly predominant security impact that the Black Spot is having. Available codes include:

1. Military
2. Economic
3. Political
4. Societal
5. Mixed (indicate which)

Military: all phenomena leading to military instability are considered a military threat. Examples include, but are not limited to, the use of military forces to eliminate threatening phenomenon, combat-motivated troop movements and buildup, creation of paramilitary armed groups by illegal non-state actors, evidence of or potential for terrorist attacks, potential of an illegal group to export violence (e.g., through people or products), or wide accessibility of weapons.

Economic: economic security encompasses phenomena leading to economic instability and inequality. Examples of such threats include, but are not limited to, money laundering (illicit financial transfers), economic booms and busts due to criminal activities, economic dependence on criminal activities, range of economic tentacles, high diversity of illicit economic income (e.g., racketeering, thefts, white-collar crime), or inflow of illegal money into the financial system.

Political: political security encompasses organizational stability of states, systems of government, and the ideologies that give governments and states their legitimacy. Examples of threats to political security include, but are not limited to, corrupt infiltration of political institutions, control over political figures through intimidation or blackmail, challenging state authority through violent means, undermining the functioning of democracy (e.g., unfair elections, assassination of key political figures), joint business activities between political figures and the criminal underworld, or criminal sponsorship of political campaigns.

Societal: societal security encompasses factors related to the security of society from the society's point of view. It, therefore, includes the general uncertainty, insecurity, and fear that people may feel due to potential or past terrorist attacks, lack of economic well-being, or political crises.

25. Range of Impact
This variable looks at the geographic range of the impact of the Black Spot in question as reported in open sources. Available codes include:

1. Local
2. National
3. Regional
4. Global
5. Multiple levels (describe; use sub-headings for each range of impact)

26. Role of the Location in Terms of Insecurity Flows (Illicit Products/ Services)
Insecurity flows: movement of assets, people, services, or know-how from one place to another in pursuit of illicit criminal or political gain with the intention of evading law enforcement, intelligence, and related agencies of the states being transited.

1. Source/Producer

Give destination of originating insecurity flows

2. Transit point

Give source: insecurity flows from
Give destination: insecurity flows to

3. Transit/Producer

Give source: insecurity flows from
Give destination: insecurity flows to

4. Destination point

Give source: insecurity flows from

5. All of the above (indicate how flows work)

27. Types of Insecurity
[Please list all that apply]

0. None
1. Illegal drugs
2. Conventional weapons
3. Transfers of illicitly obtained money
4. Money laundering
5. Elements involved in weapons of mass destruction (including dual-use technology)
6. Trafficking of people
7. Trade in human body parts
8. Know-how/sensitive know-how/illicit intelligence services
9. Trafficking of art and cultural objects
10. Smuggling of natural resources
11. Trafficking of animals and animal parts (e.g., endangered species, ivory)
12. Trafficking of household goods (e.g., CDs, computers, cigarettes, clothing, etc.)
13. Mercenary activities
14. Computer crime
15. Sea piracy
16. Terrorist activities (plotting, staging, execution)
17. Other (please specify)

If smuggling of natural resources was indicated, were the smuggled items:

1. Minerals (e.g., diamonds)
2. Timber
3. Other (please specify)

28. Role of Illicit Activity in the Area Under Analysis

1. Epicenter (central node)
2. Satellite location (sometimes used as an alternative to the epicenter, especially when the epicenter is blocked; sometimes used simultaneously with the epicenter but on a smaller scale)

3. Flat (dispersed epicenters of activity; for instance, villages or tribes within a particular area)
4. Mixed (specify which)

29. Relocation of Illicit Activities
Are there any signs that activities in the place under analysis were relocated from another area? For example, law enforcement agents may raid place A where drugs are grown, but that does not eliminate the issue, since the organization controlling the drug production will relocate to place B and continue growing the plants (in the fight against drugs this phenomenon is known as 'squeezing the balloon'). This refers to repeated activities, for instance, coca growing or illicit weapons production.

1. Activities relocated from another area
   Please give name(s) of the former area(s)
2. Activities did not relocate from another area
3. Activities are relocating to another area from the area under analysis
   Please give the name of where relocating to

30. Observed Frequency of Insecurity Flows
Please give *your best estimate* of the frequency of insecurity generated in the area (or transiting through the area). For instance, if the area is known for drug production, human trafficking, or illicit weapons production, which of the codes below would best describe it:

1. Close to permanent (daily)
2. Weekly
3. Monthly
4. Sporadic (very infrequent)
5. None

31. Perceived Level of Insecurity Flows According to the Media and Other Reports
How would you best characterize the level of insecurity flow that you observed (please describe EACH of the types of insecurity flows that you found) based *on the information that you have accessed* about the area under analysis:

1. Small/insignificant
2. Large
3. Very large

PART IV: STATE AND INTERNATIONAL RESPONSES

What Defensive Moves, in Response to the Black Spot, Have National and International Authorities Made?

32. National and International Responses
The purpose of this question is to gauge the nature of responses that a particular Black Spot required, provoked, caused, or made national and international authorities take. Such responses may reflect the scope of threats that authorities perceive (keeping in mind that both over-estimations and under-estimations do happen), but also reflect the capabilities and resources of given national and international authorities that were employed to tackle these perceived threats. Based on the research conducted so far it is believed that such responses may fall under one of the following categories (please make sure that you describe in the narrative sections *under each of the codes applied* what means were employed, by whom, over what time period, and to what effect). Please list all that apply.

1. Domestic peaceful solutions, such as negotiations, legalization, or cooptation
2. International cooperation, such as international foreign aid or external advising
3. Domestic confrontation, including operations conducted by law enforcement or armed forces
4. Outside soft intervention, for instance, shaming campaigns, media spotlights focusing on the area, or political/economic leverage
5. Outside hard intervention, including the use of formal military forces, special operations, or intelligence activities
6. Mixed (specify which)
7. None

33. Other Potential Black Spots Found in the Course of Coding
In the course of gathering information on the area under analysis, you are very likely to come across the names of other locations that may be potential Black Spots. Please:

- Enumerate all such locations, indicating area name (village, town, province, geographical area, etc.) and country (or countries, as appropriate) in which the area is located

- Next to each of the names of places listed, please briefly describe why that area may be a potential Black Spot

GUIDANCE FOR CASE WRITERS

Transparency

The most important principle in the case writing process is transparency. Be clear about why you have made your coding decision. Sometimes it will be a difficult choice or a borderline case, which is natural. In this case, provide the reasoning for your choice. If you cannot find enough information to be certain, discuss what code you think might be appropriate and note that more information is needed. Future case writers will be updating your work, so they need to know why you made particular decisions. Include your name and contact email on the cover page as well as the completion date of the coding and write-up so future case writers can contact you if necessary.

Research Strategies

This project uses open-source intelligence (OSInt). See Benavides' OSInt guide on the G drive for sources. Although Wikipedia is not recommended as a primary source, it is a great starting point that can lead you to more reliable sources.

If you are updating a case, you should try to find more recent sources to replace older ones. For instance, if all references to drug smuggling are from 2011–2012, you should try to find sources from the last year or two. If there are none, it may mean that media and law enforcement attention has shifted elsewhere or that this particular activity has ceased.

It is important to triangulate information. In other words, it is important to confirm the information that you are gathering from one source by locating it in a different, independent source. (Note that multiple news publications may report on the same issue, but that the original source may be the same, such as a newswire. This means that these are not independent sources.) Information that you can triangulate is more likely to be reliable than something you find in a one-off source. This procedure is less important for information that is common-sense or that is unlikely to change, such as geography.

Formatting

Use 12-point Times New Roman font. Proof-read for grammar and spelling errors.
Use plenty of white space and separate sub-codes on new lines. Items with one sub-code should be formatted like this:

19. Predominant Violence Motivation

19.1 *Violent acts seem to be crime-related*
     Then put your description

Items with more than one sub-code should be formatted like this:

6. Lines of Communication

6.1 *Presence of formal and informal airfields*
     Number, description

   6.1.1 *International*
        Description

        6.1.1.1 *Hard surface*
             Description

Referencing

Use footnotes to reference any source you use, especially websites. Zotero, EndNote, and other bibliographic software can help you do this. If you think a website link may break in the future, you can save the article in a folder marked 'Sources' under your Black Spot's folder on the G drive. If this folder does not already exist, you can create it. Be sure to save the articles with sensible filenames.

APPENDIX B SAMPLE CASE STUDY

MAPPING GLOBAL INSECURITY:
GLOBAL BLACK SPOTS RESEARCH PROJECT

Case Report: *Dubai, United Arab Emirates*
First Completed 2011; Current Update
January 2018

Moynihan Institute of Global Affairs
Maxwell School, Syracuse University

Reprinted with the permission of the Moynihan Institute of
Global Affairs

© The Author(s) 2020
S. S. Brown, M. G. Hermann, *Transnational Crime and Black
Spots*, International Political Economy Series,
https://doi.org/10.1057/978-1-137-49670-6

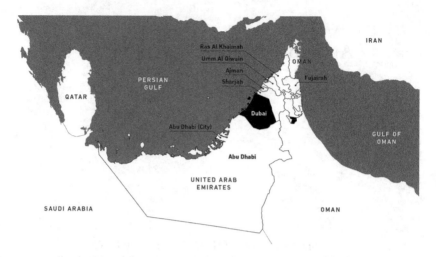

Fig. B.1   Division of Emirates in the United Arab Emirates

GEOPOLITICAL LOCATION

0. Geographical Region of World Where Located
0.2. Middle East

1. Relation to Borders
1.2. Close internal borders
Dubai (25°15′N 55°18′E) covers 4,114 square kilometers and is one of the seven emirates that make up the United Arab Emirates (UAE). Located along the Persian Gulf, Dubai is situated between the Emirates Abu Dhabi and Sharjah (see Fig. B.1).[1] The UAE is bordered by Saudi Arabia to the south and west and Oman to the east. The UAE shares maritime borders with Qatar and Iran and has a long-running, but relatively low-grade, conflict with Iran over two islands in the Gulf.[2]

---

[1] Adapted from "Download UAE Map with Cities." N.d. *Major Tourist Attractions Map.* Accessed from http://www.1830ndaytona.info/uae-map-with-cities/uae-map-with-cities-6-united-arab-emirates-maps-dubai-maps-uae-national/

[2] Henderson, Simon. "The Persian Gulf's 'Occupied Territory': The Three-Island Dispute." (Sept 2008). *The Washington Institute.* Accessed from http://www.washingtoninstitute.org/policy-analysis/view/the-persian-gulfs-occupied-territory-the-three-island-dispute

2. Population Type
2.1 Predominantly urban
Dubai is the second-largest emirate within the UAE in terms of geography, and the largest in terms of population. As of 2016, the emirate was estimated to have a population of 2,698,600, with only approximately 15% Emirati and the rest being expatriates or migrant workers.[3] Dubai is divided into 9 sectors, with sectors 1-6 being urban areas, while sectors 7-9 are considered rural. The rural sectors take up approximately 3885 square kilometers of the emirate's 4,114 square kilometers.[4] According to the most recent census data on rural versus urban living, which was taken in 2007, only 1.2% of Dubai's population lives in the rural sectors.[5] Additionally, census data from the same year reveals that men constitute 76.13% of the emirate's population.[6]

3. Predominant Terrain Features
3.1. Lowlands
Dubai is comprised of lowlands, lying approximately 16 meters above sea level.

4. Vegetation
4.1 Predominantly desert.
The Arabian Desert stretches across much of the United Arab Emirates. Therefore, rural areas of Dubai are desert with almost no vegetation.[7]

5. Climate Type
5.4. Desert
Dubai has a desert climate with temperatures reaching over 40°C in the summer months of June, July, and August. During the summer, strong winds known as "Shamal" blow across Saudi Arabia into Dubai, occa-

---

[3] "No. of Estimated Population by Sector and Community." (2016). *Dubai Statistics Center.* Accessed from https://www.dsc.gov.ae/Report/%20عدد%20السكان%20المقدر%20حسب%20القطاع%20والمنطقة 2016.pdf
"Moving to Dubai." N.d. *Expat Arrivals.* Accessed from http://www.expatarrivals.com/dubai/moving-to-dubai
[4] "Dubai Geography." N.d. *Dubai City Guide & Bookings.* Accessed from https://www.dubai.com/v/geography/
[5] "Population by Gender (Urban/Rural) – Emirate of Dubai." (2007). *Dubai Statistics Center.* Accessed from https://www.dsc.gov.ae/Report/49843600GC05-02-01.pdf#search=rural%20urban
[6] Ibid.
[7] "Arabian Desert." (Sep 2017). *Encyclopedia Britannica.* Accessed https://www.britannica.com/place/Arabian-Desert

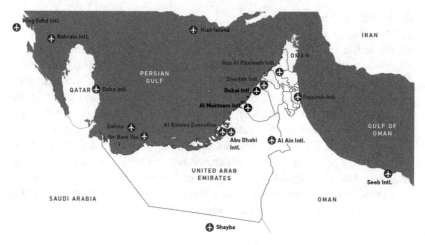

Fig. B.2   Airports in Dubai

sionally creating sand storms. Despite only receiving an average annual 150 mm of rainfall, Dubai often experiences high humidity. In the coldest month, January, temperatures rarely dip below 14°C.[8]

6. Lines of Communication (Airports, Roads, Waterways, Harbors, Railroads, on Traditional Trading Route)
6.1 Presence of formal and informal airfield/airports

6.1.1. International

6.1.1.1. Hard

There are two airports in the emirate of Dubai, both of which are international and have hard runways (see Fig. B.2 for a map of airports in Dubai).[9] Dubai International Airport (IATA code DXB) is one of the world's busiest airports, serving over 66 million people a year.[10] Located

---

[8] "Dubai Weather." N.d. *Travel Online.* Accessed from https://www.travelonline.com/dubai/weather.html
[9] Adapted from "Airports in UAE." (Jun 2014). *Maps of World.* Accessed from https://www.mapsofworld.com/international-airports/asia/uae.html
[10] Sahoo, Sananda. "Dubai airport remains world's busiest for international traffic despite slower 2016 growth." (Jan 2017). *The National.* Accessed from https://www.thenational.

within the city of Dubai, the airport has five runways, each of which is 4.5 kilometers long.[11] Meanwhile, Al Maktoum International Airport, while also in the emirate of Dubai, is approximately 37 kilometers southwest of the city. This airport services an estimated 7 million passengers annually, although an approved $32.67 billion expansion project will increase the capacity to handling over 220 million passengers per year.[12] As of 2017, the airport has two runways, although the approved expansion would include the construction of three more.[13]

6.2. Presence of roads in Black Spot

6.2.2 Present

6.2.2.1. Highly developed

6.2.2.1.1. High quality
Dubai has an extensive network of roads. Since 1993, 100% of the United Arab Emirates' roads have been paved.[14] Moreover, the United Arab Emirates frequently is ranked as having the best roads by various studies, although they suffer from congestion.[15] As of 2008, the UAE was estimated to have 4,080 kilometers of roads.[16]

ae/business/dubai-airport-remains-world-s-busiest-for-international-traffic-despite-slower-2016-growth-1.63673
"Dubai International (DXB)." N.d. *Dubai Airports.* Accessed from http://www.dubaiairports.ae/corporate/about-us/dubai-international-(dxb)
[11] "Dubai Airports." N.d. *Dubai Airports.* Accessed from http://www.dubaiairports.ae/corporate/media-centre/factsheets-list/detail/dubai-airports
[12] "Al Maktoum International Airport Expansion, Dubai." N.d. *Airport Technology.* Accessed from. http://www.airport-technology.com/projects/al-maktoum-international-airport-expansion-dubai/
[13] Ibid.
[14] "United Arab Emirates – Roads, paved (% of total roads). N.d. *Trading Economics.* Accessed from https://tradingeconomics.com/united-arab-emirates/roads-paved-percent-of-total-roads-wb-data.html
[15] "It's official, UAE has the best roads in the world." (Oct 2015). *Khaleej Times.* Accessed from https://www.khaleejtimes.com/nation/transport/its-official-uae-has-the-best-roads-in-the-world
Webster, Nick. "UAE has best road quality but could do better on congestion." (Feb 2017). *The National.* Accessed from https://www.thenational.ae/uae/transport/uae-has-best-road-quality-but-could-do-better-on-congestion-1.89870
[16] "Field Listing: Roadways." (2008). *Central Intelligence Agency.* Accessed from https://www.cia.gov/library/publications/the-world-factbook/fields/2085.html

6.3. Presence of waterway system (s) in Black Spot, that is, waterways used to transport goods/people

6.3.2. Present

There is one waterway system in Dubai: Dubai Creek. Situated in the city of Dubai, this saltwater creek was extended 10 kilometers inward in 2007.[17] In 1902, Sheikh Maktoum bin Hasher lifted all custom duties on imports, an act that caused Dubai to become a hub of trading. Although the economic value of the creek decreased when oil sales became a major source of revenue, the creek retains its cultural significance and is still used for some trade.[18]

6.4. Presence of harbors in Black Spot

6.4.2. Present

6.4.2.1. Sea

There are two ports in Dubai: Port Rashid and Jebel Ali Port, both of which are operated by the Dubai port authority.[19] Also known as Mina Rashid, Port Rashid is located along the coast of the city of Dubai; it has the greatest shipping capacity with 103 berths and can store approximately 20,000 standard containers.[20] The port also has a sizable cruise terminal capable of handling up to 7 mega cruise vessels at a time.[21]

---

[17] Baldwin, Derek. "Dubai Creek: It Just Got Longer." (Sep 2007). *Gulf News*. Accessed from http://gulfnews.com/news/uae/general/dubai-creek-it-just-got-longer-1.468911
[18] Al Zarooni, Mustafa. "Dubai Creek comes full circle." (Nov 2016). *Khaleej Times*. Accessed from https://www.khaleejtimes.com/nation/dubai/dubai-creek-comes-full-circle
[19] "Ports in Dubai." N.d. *Maps of World*. Accessed from https://www.mapsofworld.com/dubai/ports-in-dubai.html
[20] "Port Rashid, Dubai." N.d. (May 2011). *Global Security*. Accessed from https://www.globalsecurity.org/military/facility/port-rashid.htm
[21] "UAE – Mina Rashid." N.d. *DP World*. Accessed from http://web.dpworld.com/our-business/marine-terminals/middle-east-europe-africa/dubai-mina-rashid/

Although Port Rashid has a greater shipping capacity, Jebel Ali Port is the largest sized port in the Middle East. Located approximately 35 kilometers southwest of Dubai, the Jebel Ali Port spans 134 square kilometers and has 67 berths.[22] In 2005, a project to expand the port began, and the construction is projected to be complete in 2030.[23]

6.5. Presence of railroads in Black Spot

6.5.0. Absent

While the city of Dubai has a metro, there are no railroads within the emirate.[24] However, the UAE is currently working to build the Etihad Rail, a 1,200-kilometer railway network that will connect key cities in the UAE.[25] The railroad will extend to the borders of Saudi Arabia and Oman, states which are also in the process of constructing railroads.[26] In addition to transportation benefits, this will ease the cost of transporting goods, as freight trucks are currently being used.[27] Although initially projected to finish in 2018, the project's completion date was pushed back to 2021 after the sharp decline in oil prices.

6.6. Location on traditional trading route/area

6.5.1 Yes

Dubai has been a trading hub for the Gulf region for centuries. Archaeological findings from the Umm Al Nar Culture around 2600-2000 B.C. indicate that the civilization traded with civiliza-

[22] Jebel Ali Port, Dubai." N.d. *Ship Technology*. Accessed from http://www.ship-technology.com/projects/jebel-ali-port-dubai/
[23] Ibid.
[24] "Dubai Metro Map." N.d. *Dubai Online*. Accessed from https://www.dubai-online.com/transport/metro/map/
[25] John, Isaac. "Why GCC rail is a game-changer." (Aug 2017). *Khaleej Times*. Accessed from https://www.khaleejtimes.com/news/transport/why-gcc-rail-is-a-game-changer
[26] "Etihad Rail to link Dubai, Abu Dhabi, and Al Ain." (Jun 2013). *Emirates 24/7 News*. Accessed from http://www.emirates247.com/news/emirates/etihad-rail-to-link-dubai-abu-dhabi-and-al-ain-2013-06-17-1.510722
[27] John, Isaac. "Why GCC rail is a game-changer." (Aug 2017). *Khaleej Times*. Accessed from https://www.khaleejtimes.com/news/transport/why-gcc-rail-is-a-game-changer

tions in Mesopotamia and the Indus valley.[28] More recently, in the 1900s when Sheikh Mohammed bin Hasher made Dubai Creek a tax-free zone, the city became a major hub of trade.[29]

7. Illicit Economy
7.2. Multiple products/services

Dubai functions as a hub of trading for legal and illegal goods. Its lax trading regulations, compounded by the plethora of free trade zones make Dubai an attractive smuggling route for traffickers. The illicit economy has ties across the globe, with types of products varying from household goods to minerals to people—to mention a few categories. Among the most prominent illicit products are gold and diamonds.[30]Dubai has also been known for its money laundering services, although the UAE has increased financial system regulations recently, attempting to curb the flow of illegally obtained cash.[31]

---

[28] Baldwin, Derek. "Ancient UAE was Active Trading Hub." (Aug 2007). *Gulf News.* Accessed from http://gulfnews.com/news/uae/general/ancient-uae-was-active-trading-hub-1.467867

[29] Al Zarooni, Mustafa. "Dubai Creek comes full circle." (Nov 2016). *Khaleej Times.* Accessed from https://www.khaleejtimes.com/nation/dubai/dubai-creek-comes-full-circle

[30] "Gem smuggling thwarts revival of Central African Republic." (Dec 2017). *IOL.* Accessed from https://www.iol.co.za/business-report/gem-smuggling-thwarts-revival-of-central-african-republic-12192283

"Here's what not to do when smuggling diamonds." (Oct 2015). *The Economic Times.* Accessed from https://economictimes.indiatimes.com/magazines/panache/heres-what-not-to-do-when-smuggling-diamonds/articleshow/49182048.cms

"How Diamonds Fund Zimbabwe's Secret Police." (Sep 2017). *Bloomberg.* Accessed from https://www.bloomberg.com/news/articles/2017-09-10/diamonds-fund-zimbabwe-political-oppression-global-witness-saysInamdar, Nadeem. "Customs sleuths up airport vigil as gold smuggling on Pune-Dubai Route Rises." (Dec 2017). *Hindustan Times.* Accessed from http://www.hindustantimes.com/pune-news/customs-sleuths-up-airport-vigil-as-gold-smuggling-on-pune-dubai-route-rises/story-6dB1nEhVBvDkpuMfuxq5LI.html

Malhotra, Sarika. "Yellow Peril." (Dec 2013). *Business Today.* Accessed from http://www.businesstoday.in/magazine/features/gold-smuggling-resumes-in-india/story/200605.html

[31] "Anti Money Laundering (AML) in the United Arab Emirates (UAE)." N.d. *Bankers Academy.* Accessed from http://bankersacademy.com/resources/free-tutorials/57-ba-free-tutorials/608-aml-uae-sp-875

"War on drugs: UAE raises the stakes for traffickers and dealers." (Feb 2014). *The National.* Accessed from https://www.thenational.ae/uae/war-on-drugs-uae-raises-the-stakes-for-traffickers-and-dealers-1.605762

8. International (In)visibility Record
8.1 Visible

Prior to the September 11, 2001 attacks, illicit financial activity in Dubai seems to have attracted limited national and international attention. While US and Saudi officials warned the UAE that Dubai's banking system was being used to launder money, the admonitions to address the problem were largely ignored.[32] However, after the late 2001 revelations that the 9/11 hijackers laundered and received money through Dubai's financial system, the Black Spot attracted substantial international attention.[33] Since then, Dubai's role in the illicit economy has remained a focal point of the international community. The UAE consistently updates anti-money laundering regulations and increases its measures in its police in addressing the rampant smuggling.[34] The media routinely focuses on illegal activities occurring in Dubai, reporting on the smuggling of various illicit substances and goods.

9. Ethnic Composition and Conflict
9.4 Heterogeneous not conflicted

The United Arab Emirates has a highly diverse population, with only 11% believed to be Emirati; some other prominent ethnic groups present are Egyptian (10.2%), Bangladeshi (9.5%), Pakistani (9.4%), and Philippine (6.1%).[35] Although these data examine all of the UAE,

---

[32] Davidson, Christopher M. "Dubai and the United Arab Emirates: Security Threats." (Dec 2009). *British Journal of Middle Eastern Studies*, v.36 n.3., 431–447. *JSTOR.* Accessed from http://www.jstor.org/stable/40593284

[33] Breitweiser, Kristen. "UAE: Financial and Transit Hub of 9/11 Terror." (Sep 2017). *Huffington Post.* Accessed from https://www.huffingtonpost.com/entry/uae-financial-and-transit-hub-of-911-terror_us_59b9d4a2e4b06b71800c36a5

[34] "Anti Money Laundering (AML) in the United Arab Emirates (UAE)." N.d. *Bankers Academy.* Accessed from http://bankersacademy.com/resources/free-tutorials/57-ba-free-tutorials/608-aml-uae-sp-875

"War on drugs: UAE raises the stakes for traffickers and dealers." (Feb 2014). *The National.* Accessed from https://www.thenational.ae/uae/war-on-drugs-uae-raises-the-stakes-for-traffickers-and-dealers-1.605762

[35] "Middle East:: United Arab Emirates." (Dec 2017). *Central Intelligence Agency.* Accessed from https://www.cia.gov/library/publications/the-world-factbook/geos/ae.html

"Moving to Dubai." N.d. *Expat Arrivals.* Accessed from http://www.expatarrivals.com/dubai/moving-to-dubai

Dubai's population is also very cosmopolitan, as only approximately 15% of residents are Emirati.[36] Despite the discrimination faced by non-Emiratis, such as being barred from citizenship, the Emirates have experienced little internal conflict.[37]

10. Internal Cohesion (Informal Rules)
10.2 Imposed
The United Arab Emirate's penal code is partially derivative of Sharia. However, police operate relatively autonomously from the country.[38] While laws in Dubai remain conservative, there is an implicit acknowledgment that strict enforcement of some Emirati laws may harm tourism and international investment. For this reason, it appears that many police officers in Dubai are hesitant to enforce some of the more conservative laws—such as prohibitions on public displays of affection—unless there are complaints by locals.[39]

11. Potential Black Spot Type
11.1 Stable
Dubai's Black Spot potential stems from its long history as a free-wheeling regional trading hub and from its rapid growth over the past two decades as a major financial center. Dubai became a hub for Persian Gulf traders as far back as the early twentieth century and began attracting traders from South Asia by midcentury. Many of these traders increased their profits by using Dubai's light regulation to avoid taxes and other

---

[36] "No. of Estimated Population by Sector and Community." (2016). *Dubai Statistics Center*. Accessed from https://www.dsc.gov.ae/Report/عجمان%20بسكان%20جدد%20عدد%20مواليد%20بحسب%20السكان%20القطاع الوطني%202016.pdf
"Moving to Dubai." N.d. *Expat Arrivals*. Accessed from http://www.expatarrivals.com/dubai/moving-to-dubai

[37] Habboush, Mahmoud. "Call to naturalise some expats stirs anxiety in the UAE." (Oct 2013). *Reuters*. Accessed from https://uk.reuters.com/article/uk-emirates-citizenship-feature/call-to-naturalise-some-expats-stirs-anxiety-in-the-uae-idUKBRE99904J20131010

[38] "United Arab Emirates." N.d. *U.S. Department of State*. Accessed from https://www.state.gov/documents/organization/160079.pdf

[39] "Local Laws in Dubai." N.d. *Expat Arrivals*. Accessed from http://www.expatarrivals.com/article/local-laws-in-dubai
"Dubai: Strict morality laws behind Western appearance." (May 2010). *The Telegraph*. Accessed from http://www.telegraph.co.uk/news/worldnews/middleeast/dubai/7443280/Dubai-strict-morality-laws-behind-Western-appearance.html

trade restrictions.[40]Dubai's popularity has only increased, with Dubai's airports and ports servicing millions annually.[41] According to the World Bank's June 2017 rankings, the United Arab Emirates ranks 21st out of all countries for ease of doing business.[42]
Given the ease of doing business, compounded by the lax regulations, Dubai attracts sizable illicit transactions. While the UAE has imposed stricter banking laws, trying to curb illicit financial transactions, money laundering persists—albeit to a lesser degree.[43] Despite the international community's continued expressions of concern over illicit trade in Dubai, customs officials have proven incapable of sufficiently addressing the illicit transportation of goods through the emirate's free trade zone.[44]

12. Observed Life Span
Date of Appearance: 1840s
Historically, Dubai functioned as a port of call for slave traders. In the 1840s, the British, through peace agreements, increased restrictions on the slave trade in Gulf States. It became illegal to traffic Somalis, and the British further banned the exportation of slaves from Africa on Arab ships.[45] Still, traders operating out of the UAE—among other locations—did not heed the new regulations, attempting to evade British inspection ships in the Gulf. This appears to be the origin of Dubai as a Black Spot, although as the years went by Dubai's illicit economy diversified, incorporating smuggled arms, diamonds, and gold—to a name a few goods.[46] The popularization of free trade zones in Dubai in the late

---

[40] Davidson, Christopher. "Dubai: The Security Dimensions of the Region's Premier Free Port." (2008). *Middle East Policy Council*, volume XV, number 2. Accessed from http://www.mepc.org/dubai-security-dimensions-regions-premier-free-port
[41] "Doing business in the United Arab Emirates: UAE trade and export guide." (Dec 2015). *Gov.UK*. Accessed from https://www.gov.uk/government/publications/exporting-to-the-united-arab-emirates/exporting-to-the-united-arab-emirates
[42] "Economy Rankings." (Jun 2017). *The World Bank*. Accessed from http://www.doing-business.org/rankings
[43] Al Kuttab, Jasmine. "Tougher banning laws in UAE to counter terrorist activities." (Sep 2016). *Khaleej Times*. Accessed from https://www.huffingtonpost.com/entry/uae-financial-and-transit-hub-of-911-terror_us_59b9d4a2e4b06b71800c36a5
[44] Reinl, James. "UN raises concern over Dubai port." (Jul 2009). *The National*. Accessed from https://www.thenational.ae/uae/un-raises-concern-over-dubai-port-1.486868
[45] Davidson, Christopher M. (2008) Dubai: The Security Dimensions of the Region's Premier Free Port. *Middle East Policy*, v.15 n.2, 143–160.
[46] Ibid.

twentieth century increased the appeal for illicit trade within the Black Spot.[47]

13. Host State's Government Type
13.6. Federal (Federation)
More specifically, the United Arab Emirates is a federation of monarchies.[48]

14. Corruption in the Area under Analysis
14.1 Present
Although, according to Transparency International's Corruption Perception Index, the UAE has the least corruption of any country in the Middle East and North Africa, corruption still remains a problem in the country.[49] Public procurement and internal company corruption—especially in Dubai—are two of the most common types of corruption in the UAE.[50] Additionally, although the country's legal system is based off a strict interpretation of Sharia, the law is only imposed occasionally, with some foreigners jailed for holding hands, while others have no interaction with Emirati law enforcement.[51] Thus, although the legal system is not highly corrupt, its application can appear indiscriminate. There are numerous examples of high-level government officials and businessmen being involved in corrupt schemes. For example, Damas revealed in October 2009 that its chief executive engaged in unauthorized transactions worth $165 million.[52] Another example comes from

[47] Reinl, James. "UN raises concern over Dubai port." (Jul 2009). *The National.* Accessed from https://www.thenational.ae/uae/un-raises-concern-over-dubai-port-1.486868

[48] "United Arab Emirates." (Nov 2017). *Central Intelligence Agency.* Accessed from https://www.cia.gov/library/publications/the-world-factbook/geos/ae.html

[49] "Corruption Perceptions Index 2016." (2016). *Transparency International.* Accessed from https://www.transparency.org/news/feature/corruption_perceptions_index_2016

[50] Oteify, Rania. "Corruption 'unusually high' in Dubai – police chief." (Dec 2009). *Arabian Business.* Accessed from http://www.arabianbusiness.com/corruption-unusually-high-in-dubai-police-chief-27479.html

"United Arab Emirates Corruption." N.d. *Business Anti-Corruption Portal.* Accessed from http://www.business-anti-corruption.com/country-profiles/united-arab-emirates

[51] Nordland, Rod. "Holding Hands, Drinking Wine, and Other Ways to Go to Jail in Dubai." (Nov 2017). *The New York Times.* Accessed from https://www.nytimes.com/2017/11/11/world/middleeast/dubai-crimes-united-arab-emirates-jail.html?_r=0

[52] Parasie, Nicolas and Dinesh Nair. "Analysis: Gulf reforms key to private equity regaining allure." (Aug 2010). *Reuters.* Accessed from https://www.reuters.com/article/us-gulf-privateequity-analysis-idINTRE67B1JA20100812

the development of the Dubai International Financial Center (DIFC)—the Emirate's high-profile effort to build an international financial services hub with world-class regulatory and legal standards. Property development rights in DIFC were awarded to local businessmen outside of the established auction process, leading two high-profile British-national DIFC officials (who had been brought in to help oversee the center) to object. When the dispute became public, the British officials were quickly dismissed.[53]

The drive for profit extends high into the government of Dubai, with many members of the ruling family developing extensive commercial interests. An interesting, and perhaps telling, example of this is Al-Fajer Properties, owned by Hasher Al Maktoum, the brother of Dubai's ruling emir. In 2008, Maktoum installed his son as president of the company, replacing Shahram Abdullah Zadeh, an Iranian-born businessman. The Maktoums claimed that Zadeh forged contracts and fraudulently transferred money between Al-Fajer and his other companies, leaving Al-Fajer a financial mess. Zadeh, on the other hand, claims that he is the sole rightful owner of Al-Fajer, and that the Maktoums pushed him out to gain control of a profitable firm; he also says he is owed $1.9 billion by Al-Fajer.[54]

There have also been suspicions that Dubai authorities target expatriates for financial crime prosecutions while protecting local Emiratis from punishment. Prosecutors charged seven foreigners in connection to a $500 million fraud investigation at Dubai Islamic Bank, but no Emiratis. Observers find it unlikely that foreigners could have perpetrated such a crime without the help of well-placed local stakeholders.[55] Along with the DIFC example discussed previously, this suggests the presence of opaque networks of local businessmen that can protect each other from public scrutiny.

[53] Spindle, Bill. "Dubai faces hurdles in quest to build financial center." (Mar 2006). *Daily Report Online.* Accessed from https://www.law.com/almID/1202552537758/

[54] "Dubai shaikh's lawyer rejects lawsuit as baseless." (May 2009). *Khaleej Times.* Accessed from https://www.khaleejtimes.com/article/20090504/ARTICLE/305049951/1036

[55] Spencer, Richard. "End of a glittering Dubai dream: three Britons in jail accused of $500 million 'fraud'." (Jun 2009). *The Telegraph.* Accessed from http://www.telegraph.co.uk/news/worldnews/middleeast/dubai/5588310/End-of-a-glittering-Dubai-dream-three-Britons-in-jail-accused-of-500-million-fraud.html

210 APPENDIX B SAMPLE CASE STUDY

15. Corruption in the Host State
United ArabEmirates-2016: 66 (24/176).[56]

16. Area of a Recent Conflict
16.2 No

17. Presence of a Recent Nearby Violent Conflict
17.1 Yes

17.1.2. The Civil War in Yemen [2004/06–present][57]
The civil war in Yemen began as a series of conflicts between the Houthis—an advocacy group for a religious sect of Shi'a Islam known as the Zaidis—and is widely regarded as transforming into a civil war in early 2015, when the Houthis took control of Sanaa and ousted the Yemeni president, Abrabbuh Mansur Hadi.[58] Although the conflict does not border the UAE, it has occasionally spilled over into neighboring Saudi Arabia, and the Emiratis' role in the war warrants its mention. The UAE has had a small contingent of troops in Yemen, focusing on countering al-Qaeda in the Arabian Peninsula. Working in conjunction with US special operations forces, the troops have been successful in retaking vital Yemeni cities and weakening the terrorist organization.[59] Although the conflict has not appeared to impact Dubai specifically, the Houthis have threatened to attack Saudi and Emirati airports, leaving open the possibility of a terrorist attack in Dubai.[60]

[56] "Corruption Perceptions Index 2016." (2016). *Transparency International.* Accessed from https://www.transparency.org/news/feature/corruption_perceptions_index_2016
[57] Boucek, Christopher. "War in Saada: From Local Insurrection to National Challenge." (April 2010). *Carnegie Endowment for International Peace.* Accessed from http://carnegieendowment.org/files/war_in_saada.pdf
[58] "Yemen profile – Timeline." (July 2017). *BBC News.* Accessed from http://www.bbc.com/news/world-middle-east-14704951
[59] Ryan, Missy. "U.S. forces kill 7 suspected al-Qaeda militants in new Yemen raid." (May 2017). *The Washington Post.* Accessed from https://www.washingtonpost.com/news/checkpoint/wp/2017/05/23/u-s-forces-kill-7-suspected-al-qaeda-militants-in-new-yemen-raid/?utm_term=.1868f281cca1
Wagner, Daniel and Giorgio Cafiero. "The UAE's High Stakes in Yemen." N.d. *Huffington Post.* Accessed from https://www.huffingtonpost.com/daniel-wagner/the-uaes-high-stakes-in-y_b_8170042.html
[60] "Yemen Houthi rebels threaten to attack UAE and Saudi airports." (Nov 2017). *The New Arab.* Accessed from https://www.alaraby.co.uk/english/news/2017/11/8/houthis-threaten-to-attack-uae-and-saudi-airports

18. Predominant Crime Types
18.1 Organized transnational crime

Dubai functions as a hub of transnational crime with illicit goods following from, to, and through the emirate. For example, acacia trees grown in southern Somalia are made into charcoal and then shipped out of various port cities along the country's coast.[61] One of the destinations is Dubai, where the charcoal is exchanged for sugar, typically coming from Brazil. The sugar is then transported back to Somalia and often makes its way to Kenya.[62] This is just one transnational criminal network, although Dubai has a myriad of others that span the globe.

19. Predominant Violence Motivation
19.1 Crime related (though minimal)

Despite Dubai's size and high level of illicit activity, the emirate experiences minimal crime. The US Department of State considers the city of Dubai a low-threat location, and the crime that does occur generally happens in expatriate and migrant worker communities.[63] As of December 2017, both the US and UK governments had posted messages on their travel safety sites, warning their citizens about the potential for a terrorist attack in the UAE.[64] Overall, though, the UAE has

---

[61] Baxter, Zach. "Somalia's Coal Industry." (May 2007). *Mandal Projects*. Accessed from http://mandalaprojects.com/ice/ice-cases/somalia-coal.htm
Monitoring Group on Somalia and Eritrea. "Somalia." (Nov 2017). *United Nations Security Council*. Accessed from http://daacad.com/wp-content/uploads/2017/11/SEMG_REPORT_SOMALIA.pdf
"Somali charcoal production, transport and stockpiles." (Nov 2017). *Mareeg*. Accessed from https://mareeg.com/somali-charcoal-production-transport-and-stockpiles/
[62] Jorgic, Drazen. "Kenya wages war on smugglers who fund Somali militants." (Jun 2015). *Reuters*. Accessed from https://www.reuters.com/article/us-kenya-security-somalia-insight/kenya-wages-war-on-smugglers-who-fund-somali-militants-idUSKBN0P105320150621
[63] "United Arab Emirates 2017 Crime & Safety Report: Dubai. (2017). *Bureau of Diplomatic Security, U.S. Department of State*. Accessed from https://www.osac.gov/pages/ContentReportDetails.aspx?cid=21353
[64] "Foreign Travel Advice: United Arab Emirates." (Dec 2017). *Gov.UK*. Accessed from https://www.gov.uk/foreign-travel-advice/united-arab-emirates/terrorism
"United Arab Emirates." (Feb 2017). *Bureau of Consular Affairs, U.S. Department of State*. Accessed from https://travel.state.gov/content/travel/en/international-travel/International-Travel-Country-Information-Pages/UnitedArabEmirates.html

not experienced many terrorist attacks on their soil, with searches for terrorism in the UAE only detailing the government's condemnations for terrorist attacks elsewhere.

20. Nature of Predominant "Bads" in the Area
20.5. Various kinds of actors

While news articles discuss the prominence of Dubai for transnational criminal organizations, terrorist organizations, and guerilla groups to smuggle goods and launder money, there are no recent reports detailing the specific actors that utilize Dubai for illicit transactions. Although al-Qaeda used Dubai to launder money and supply funds to the hijackers of 9/11, the UAE has tightened financial regulations, and there have been no recent reports on terrorist organizations using Emirati banks to launder money. However, it remains to be seen whether this is due to the success of anti-money laundering regulations or terrorist organizations' skillful evasion of detection. Ultimately then, while a variety of actors are involved in Dubai's illicit economy, the names of the groups are not recorded in media reports.

21. "People of Interest" Spotted in the Area
Sarah Panitzke—one of the UK's most wanted criminals, Panitzke has laundered over £1 billion pounds. Although she is believed to be hiding in Spain, Panitzke has visited Dubai in the past, presumably laundering money in the emirate.[65]

22. Nexus of Crime and Terrorism
22.1 Present

While transnational criminal operations dominate the illicit activity in Dubai, the emirate is still a nexus of crime and terrorism. Investigations after 9/11 revealed strong ties between the hijackers and money laundering in Dubai, causing the UAE and the US to examine the financial system's ties to terrorist financing.[66] Since then, the UAE has imposed

---

[65] "Sarah Panitzke." N.d. *National Crime Agency*. Accessed from http://www.national-crimeagency.gov.uk/most-wanted-hub/item/66-sarah-panitzke
[66] Breitweiser, Kristen. "UAE: Financial and Transit Hub of 9/11 Terror." (Sep 2017). *Huffington Post*. Accessed from https://www.huffingtonpost.com/entry/uae-financial-and-transit-hub-of-911-terror_us_59b9d4a2e4b06b71800c36a5

stricter banking laws to try and curb the illicit financial transactions. However, the UAE has frequently had to update and expand the scope of the laws to address new methods.[67] Thus, it is highly probable that Dubai remains a nexus of crime and terrorism, although the ease with which terrorist groups can operate, as well as the number of illicit financial transactions, has likely decreased.

23. Organizational Types Present
23.3 A combination of both (mixed)
Although there is a dearth of recent information available on the specific groups that run smuggling operations to, from, and through Dubai, the consistency of smuggling as well as the size of shipments suggest that long-term structures with highly organized actors are in place. For example, the United Nations has repeatedly condemned the UAE for not cracking down on massive charcoal shipments that come from al-Shabaab in Somalia and are exchanged for sugar in Dubai and other Emirati ports.[68] These massive shipments necessitate highly organized actors in order to facilitate the exchange and evade authorities. Additionally, *hawala* networks—ancient international transaction systems built upon trust that leave no digital trace or record of financial transfers—are known to operate in Dubai.[69] These ancient networks require significant organization and commitment on behalf of those operating the *hawala* networks.

At the same time, there appear to also be short-lived organizational structures—ad-hoc groups that emerge to meet the demand of a certain illicit good, but have little to no over-arching organizational structure.

[67] Al Kuttab, Jasmine. "Tougher banning laws in UAE to counter terrorist activities." (Sep 2016). *Khaleej Times.* Accessed from https://www.huffingtonpost.com/entry/uae-financial-and-transit-hub-of-911-terror_us_59b9d4a2e4b06b71800c36a5

[68] Baxter, Zach. "Somalia's Coal Industry." (May 2007). *Mandal Projects.* Accessed from http://mandalaprojects.com/ice/ice-cases/somalia-coal.htm
Monitoring Group on Somalia and Eritrea. "Somalia." (Nov 2017). *United Nations Security Council.* Accessed from http://daacad.com/wp-content/uploads/2017/11/SEMG_REPORT_SOMALIA.pdf
Somali charcoal production, transport and stockpiles." (Nov 2017). *Mareeg.* Accessed from https://mareeg.com/somali-charcoal-production-transport-and-stockpiles/

[69] Seftel, Bennett. "Hawala Networks: The Paperless Trail of Terrorist Transactions." (Mar 2017). *The Cipher Brief.* Accessed from https://www.thecipherbrief.com/hawala-networks-the-paperless-trail-of-terrorist-transactions

Alternately, individuals may smuggle goods into Dubai on their own accord, having no role in a larger smuggling network.

24. Kind of Security Impact
24.5. Mixed (military, economic, and political)

Military

Although not impacting Dubai militarily, some illicit financial transactions that occur in Dubai fund terrorist organizations and criminal activity in other countries, thereby generating military insecurity.[70] Since 2001, the UAE has taken steps to counter money laundering; however, it is still an endemic problem in the country.[71]

Economic

The security impact of this Black Spot is primarily economic. Dubai has a high volume and frequency of smuggling, causing economic dependence on illicit activity.[72]

Political

The UAE occasionally experiences international pressure due to the smuggling and money laundering that takes place in Dubai. Most notably, following the 9/11 attacks when the US learned that the hijackers received money through Dubai, the US put pressure on the UAE to implement stricter laws on financial transactions.[73] Additionally, Dubai

[70] Al Shouk, Ali. "Money from fake goods trade funds terrorism, drugs, officer says." (Dec 2017). *Gulf News*. Accessed from http://gulfnews.com/news/uae/emergencies/money-from-fake-goods-trade-funds-terrorism-drugs-officer-says-1.2139827
Mathiason, Nick. "Dubai's dark side targeted by international finance police." (Jan 2010). *The Guardian*. Accessed from https://www.theguardian.com/business/2010/jan/24/dubai-crime-money-laundering-terrorism
[71] "Anti Money Laundering (AML) in the United Arab Emirates (UAE)." N.d. *Banker's Academy*. Accessed from http://bankersacademy.com/resources/free-tutorials/57-ba-free-tutorials/608-aml-uae-sp-875
[72] Davidson, Christopher. "Dubai: The Security Dimensions of the Region's Premier Free Port." (2008). *Middle East Policy Council*, volume XV, number 2. Accessed from http://www.mepc.org/dubai-security-dimensions-regions-premier-free-port
[73] Ibid.

has had a political impact due to the sanctions imposed on Iran for their nuclear program. Smugglers transporting to Iran weakened the effectiveness of the sanctions and endangered the UAE's reputation with other pro-sanction states.[74]

25. Range of Impact
25.5 All

The influence Dubai has in the global community has continued to rise over the past several years as Dubai becomes an ever more important player on the global financial and trade stage. The impact of Dubai's financial regulations and free trade policies are clearly visible at the global level, as terrorist organizations have capitalized on the ability to use Dubai for transfers of illicit money and goods, financing operations like the 9/11 attacks in the US.[75] While, undoubtedly, the 9/11 attacks would have been conducted through other means had Dubai prevented the financial transactions of al-Qaeda, the absence of serious anti-money laundering legislation in the UAE at the time certainly aided terrorist organizations in raising and transferring funds.[76] Additionally, since many of the terrorist groups that have utilized Dubai's financial networking system are located regionally, this Black Spot has a regional impact.

The national and local impact of the illicit economy is more opaque. Still, Dubai has a high volume and frequency of smuggling, causing eco-

[74] Sharma, Gaurav. "Dubai: The Perfect Gateway to a Post Sanctions Iran." (Sep 2015). *Forbes.* Accessed from https://www.forbes.com/sites/gauravsharma/2015/09/28/dubai-the-perfect-gateway-to-a-post-sanctions-iran/#6e7c6d635e30

Walt, Vivienne. "To Pressure Iran, the U.S. Leans on Dubai." (Apr 2010). *Time.* Accessed from http://content.time.com/time/world/article/0,8599,1977352,00.html

"Iran smuggles $1 billion in cash through Dubai, Turkey to doge sanctions." (Feb 2015). *The Japan Times.* Accessed from https://www.japantimes.co.jp/news/2015/02/26/world/iran-smuggles-1-billion-in-cash-through-dubai-turkey-to-dodge-sanctions/#.Wjcp9LbMxmA

[75] Breitweiser, Kristen. "UAE: Financial and Transit Hub of 9/11 Terrorists." (Sep 2017). *Huffington Post.* Accessed from https://www.huffingtonpost.com/entry/uae-financial-and-transit-hub-of-911-terror_us_59b9d4a2e4b06b71800c36a5

[76] "US and GCC sign agreement to cut off terrorism funding." (May 2017). *The National.* Accessed from https://www.thenational.ae/world/us-and-gcc-sign-agreement-to-cut-off-terrorism-funding-1.34260

nomic dependence on illicit activity.[77] Thereby, some locals are highly reliant on the continuation of smuggling, profiting from transnational criminal networks. Moreover, Dubai brings in sizable revenue for the small Gulf state, and the continuing pressure to increase restrictions to combat smuggling—such as more inspections—may cause the use of the port to decrease, thereby shrinking the income it generates for the UAE. Thus, at the local and national level, the Black Spot impacts the economic security of the UAE; intense measures to expose and dismantle smuggling networks could have serious implications for the historic trading center.

26. Role of the Location in Terms of Insecurity Flows
26.5. All of the above (source/producer, transit point, destination)
Dubai has a booming illicit economy, with goods being smuggled from across the globe. While the emirate functions as a source/producer and destination, its biggest role is as a transit point. The main illegal services and products found in Dubai are counterfeit documents, shell companies, and money laundering. Dubai serves as a transit point for a plethora of smuggled goods. The most reported are ivory, pangolins, rhinoceros horns, charcoal, cigarettes, drugs, wood from red sanders, gold, diamonds, and humans. Although Dubai primarily functions as a transit point, some of the trafficked goods remain in the emirate. Gold, diamonds, cigarettes, charcoal, and humans are among such smuggled items that are often sold within the UAE, in addition to being exported elsewhere.

Dubai has been known as an area where smugglers can procure the necessary documentation for illicit goods. This has been especially true in the case of diamond smugglers, who have obtained fake Kimberley Process certificates in Dubai, which certify that the diamonds have originated from conflict-free zones.[78] With this paperwork, smugglers can easily sell their diamonds to jewelry store owners in Dubai.

Additionally, Dubai is filled with shell companies—that is, companies that appear real but offer no real goods or services. Instead, they are used for

---

[77] Davidson, Christopher. "Dubai: The Security Dimensions of the Region's Premier Free Port." (2008). *Middle East Policy Council*, volume XV, number 2. Accessed from http://www.mepc.org/dubai-security-dimensions-regions-premier-free-port

[78] Sharife, Khadija and John Grobler. "Kimberley's Illicit Process." (Jan 2014). *World Policy*. Accessed from http://www.worldpolicy.org/blog/2014/01/13/kimberleys-illicit-process

tax evasion, or created to steal funders' money. Shell companies in Dubai often have ties to India.[79] The Guptas, an Indian billionaire family with business operations in South Africa, have a plethora of shell companies in Dubai.[80] Dubai is known for its financial system, which has historically allowed criminals and terrorists to launder large sums of money without investigation. However, following the 9/11 terrorist attacks and the revelation that much of the funds flowed through Dubai, the UAE has tightened financial regulations, enacting anti-money laundering laws that appear to have curbed the illicit activity. Still, it remains to be seen whether these measures have been effective or if they have simply driven the money laundering further underground.[81] Reports on ivory smuggling indicate that it is sourced from a host of African nations and trafficked to various East Asian countries after transiting through Dubai. Articles detailing recent interceptions have most commonly cited Kenya as the country of origin, although the Ivory Coast has been mentioned as well.[82] Meanwhile, destinations have ranged from Sri Lanka to Vietnam to Hong Kong.[83]

[79] Ghosh, Sugata. "As Dubai prepares to change tax laws, Indians scramble to hide undeclared wealth." (Mar 2017). *The Economic Times.* Accessed from https://economictimes. indiatimes.com/wealth/tax/as-dubai-prepares-to-change-tax-laws-indians-scramble-to-hide-undeclared-wealth/articleshow/57621994.cms

[80] Serrao, Angelique and Pieter-Louis Myburgh. "Dubai: The Guptas' City of Shells." (Oct 2017). *News 24.* Accessed from https://www.news24.com/SouthAfrica/News/dubai-the-guptas-city-of-shells-20171027

[81] Miko, Francis T. "Removing Terrorist Sanctuaries: The 9/11 Commission Recommendations and U.S. Policy." (Aug 2004). *Congressional Research Service.* Accessed from https://fas.org/irp/crs/RL32518.pdf

Seftel, Bennett. "Hawala Networks: The Paperless Trail of Terrorist Transactions." (Mar 2017). *The Cipher Brief.* Accessed from https://www.thecipherbrief.com/hawala-networks-the-paperless-trail-of-terrorist-transactions

[82] Al Jandaly, Bassma. "Elephant ivory tusk smuggling trough Dubai to be stopped." (May 2013). *The National.* Accessed from http://gulfnews.com/news/uae/general/elephant-ivory-tusk-smuggling-through-dubai-to-be-stopped-1.1184632

Malek, Caline. "Hundreds of pieces of raw elephant ivory seized in Dubai." (May 2013). *The National.* Accessed from https://www.thenational.ae/uae/hundreds-of-pieces-of-raw-elephant-ivory-seized-in-dubai-1.255274

Oueiti, Rezan. "More than 10 tonnes of illegal ivory destroyed in Dubai." (Apr 2015). *The National.* Accessed from https://www.thenational.ae/uae/more-than-10-tonnes-of-illegal-ivory-destroyed-in-dubai-1.78057

[83] Ibid.

Like ivory, pangolin scales transiting through Dubai often come from countries in Africa, destined for East Asia—particularly Malaysia, Vietnam, China, and Hong Kong.[84] One article traced a smuggling network originating in the Democratic Republic of the Congo's capitol city, Kinshasa, that passed through Nairobi, Kenya, and Dubai before ending in Kuala Lumpur, Malaysia.[85] Other articles have pointed to the countries of origin as Ghana and Cameroon.[86]

Similarly, rhinoceros horns tend to originate in Africa and flow to East Asia. Articles have cited Mozambique, Dubai, and Angola as origin countries; Dubai, Singapore's Changi airport, Laos, and Bangkok as transit points; and Vietnam and Loas as destinations.[87]

Smuggled charcoal comes from acacia trees grown between the Juba and Shabelle rivers in southern Somalia.[88] It is often trafficked through

[84] "More than 100 endangered pangolins seized in Thailand." (Aug 2017). *Daily Mail.* Accessed from http://www.dailymail.co.uk/wires/ap/article-4839712/Thai-customs-seize-smuggled-pangolins-scales.html

[85] "KLIA Customs seizes Hong Kong-bound Pangolin scales worth RM4.4m." (Nov 2017). *Customs News.* Accessed from http://customsnews.vn/klia-customs-seizes-hong-kong-bound-pangolin-scales-worth-rm44m-5291.html

"Malaysia seizes smuggled African pangolin scales worth millions." (May 2017). *The Asahi Shimbun.* Accessed from http://www.asahi.com/ajw/articles/AJ201705080034.html

[86] "Malaysian authorities seize 700 kg of pangolin scales smuggled from Africa." (May 2017). *The Telegraph.* Accessed from http://www.telegraph.co.uk/news/2017/05/08/malaysian-authorities-seize-700kg-pangolin-scales-smuggled-africa/

"Press Releases." (Jun 2016). *Hong Kong Government.* Accessed from http://www.info.gov.hk/gia/general/201606/23/P201606231001.htm

[87] Chong, Elena. "Vietnamese jailed for 15 months for smuggling rhino horns worth more than $1 million." (Jan 2014). *The Straits Times.* Accessed from http://www.straitstimes.com/singapore/vietnamese-jailed-for-15-months-for-smuggling-rhino-horns-worth-more-than-1-million

Vu, Vi. "Vietnamese man arrested in Thailand for smuggling rhino horn from Angola." (Aug 2017). *VN Express.* Accessed from https://e.vnexpress.net/news/news/vietnamese-man-arrested-in-thailand-for-smuggling-rhino-horn-from-angola-3625921.html

"8 pieces of illegal rhino horn seized at Changi Airport." (Sep 2017). *Channel News Asia.* Accessed from https://www.channelnewsasia.com/news/singapore/8-pieces-of-illegal-rhino-horn-seized-at-changi-airport-9177800

[88] Baxter, Zach. "Somalia's Coal Industry." (May 2007). *Mandal Projects.* Accessed from http://mandalaprojects.com/ice/ice-cases/somalia-coal.htm

Monitoring Group on Somalia and Eritrea. "Somalia." (Nov 2017). *United Nations Security Council.* Accessed from http://daacad.com/wp-content/uploads/2017/11/SEMG_REPORT_SOMALIA.pdf

Somali charcoal production, transport and stockpiles." (Nov 2017). *Mareeg.* Accessed from https://mareeg.com/somali-charcoal-production-transport-and-stockpiles/

Kismayo, Somalia (another Black Spot in our database) to the United Arab Emirate's ports, including those in Dubai.[89] While some charcoal remains in Dubai, it is often trafficked to other Gulf nations that also prize the Somali charcoal. In exchange for the trafficked charcoal, the UAE often provides licit sugar that originates in Brazil and is illicitly trafficked to Kismayo, Somalia before it is distributed to black markets in Dabaab and Garissa Town, Kenya.[90] Smuggled cigarettes often flow in from other countries in the Middle East, particularly Iraq, Iran, and Syria, transit through Dubai, and then are resold in India.[91] Meanwhile, drugs tend to flow into Dubai from various European countries, with the UAE serving as a gateway to the Middle East.[92] Qatar and Saudi Arabia are particularly common destinations for the illicit substances, although some cigarettes remain in Dubai, available for purchase.[93]

Red Sanders trees in Andhra Pradesh, India, are smuggled out of the country, typically transiting through Dubai and then Pakistan before reaching their end destination in China, or occasionally another East Asian country.[94] Smugglers in India typically use the Chennai Port or

[89] Ibid.

[90] Opala, Ken. "Dreaded Somali terrorist group taps into sugar racket." (Apr 2009). *Daily Nation.* Accessed from http://www.nation.co.ke/news/1056-559404-k5wbyxz/index. html

Rasmussen, Jacob. "Sweet Secrets: Sugar smuggling and State Formation in the Kenya-Somalia Borderlands." (Nov 2017). *Danish Institute for International Studies.* Accessed from http://pure.diis.dk/ws/files/1269212/DIIS_WP_2017_11.pdf

[91] Tiwari, Siddharth. Counterfeit, smuggled cigarettes thriving in India." (May 2017). *Sunday Guardian Live.* Accessed from http://www.sundayguardianlive.com/ news/9347-counterfeit-smuggled-cigarettes-thriving-india

[92] Al Ramahi, Nawal. "Hollow bananas and heroin chocolates: Dubai Police help bust elaborate drug smuggling attempts." (Nov 2017). *The National.* Accessed from https:// www.thenational.ae/uae/hollow-bananas-and-heroin-chocolates-dubai-police-help-bust-elaborate-drug-smuggling-attempts-1.675309

Gysin, Christian. "Go to jail for ever, drug-smuggling Briton told." N.d. *Daily Mail.* Accessed from http://www.dailymail.co.uk/news/article-47645/Go-jail-drug-smuggling-Briton-told.html

[93] Al Amir, Salam. "'GCC drug smugglers caught with 2.2 kg of heroin in Dubai." (Jul 2017). *The National.* Accessed from https://www.thenational.ae/uae/gcc-drug-smugglers-caught-with-2-2kg-of-heroin-in-dubai-1.609323

[94] Sivanl, Jayaraj. "Red sanders smugglers have links with Dubai underworld: Sleuths." (Apr 2015). *The Times of India.* Accessed from https://timesofindia.indiatimes.com/india/ Red-sanders-smugglers-have-links-with-Dubai-underworld-Sleuths/article-show/46843404.cms

Nhava Sheva port—India's two largest ports—to traffic the wood out of the country.[95] Meanwhile, gold is trafficked into India, often through the port of Chennai.[96] Traffickers purchase gold in Dubai's booming gold market, smuggle it into India, thereby avoiding the tax levied on it by the Indian government, and then resell the gold in India for a sizable profit. While not all gold in Dubai is trafficked into the port city, some of it is—often coming from conflict zones or illegal mining operations in South or Central America.[97] In particular, companies in Dubai have been accused of purchasing illegally mined gold from operations in the Madre de Dios region of Peru.[98] Therefore, Dubai serves as both a transit point and destination for gold.

Umashanker, K. "Deathblow to red sanders smuggling network." (Nov 2016). *The Hindu.* Accessed from http://www.thehindu.com/news/national/andhra-pradesh/Deathblow-to-red-sanders-smuggling-nework/article16441670.ece

"Notorious red sanders smuggler among 11 held, banned timber worth Rs one crore seized." (Nov 2017). *The New Indian Express.* Accessed from http://www.newindianexpress.com/states/andhra-pradesh/2017/nov/01/notorious-red-sanders-smuggler-among-11-held-banned-timber-worth-rs-one-crore-seized-1688750.html

[95] Kumar, Praveen. "The great forest robbery: How Andhra's rare red sanders are smuggled around the world." (Nov 2017). *The News Minute.* Accessed from https://www.thenewsminute.com/article/great-forest-robbery-how-andhra-s-rare-red-sanders-are-smuggled-around-world-72089

Pachouly, Manish. "Smugglers chopped 1200 red sanders trees: Customs officials." (Jan 2011). *Hindustan Times.* Accessed from http://www.hindustantimes.com/mumbai/smugglers-chopped-1-200-red-sanders-trees-customs-officials/story-euD1C8tLf3q1x-UN1163D7L.html

[96] "Dubai jeweler held for smuggling 50 kg of gold into India." (Dec 2017). *Gulf News.* Accessed from http://gulfnews.com/xpress/news/dubai-jeweller-held-for-smuggling-50kg-of-gold-into-india-1.2147878

[97] Smith, Michael and Jonathan Franklin. How to Become an International Gold Smuggler." (Mar 2017). *Bloomberg.* Accessed from https://www.bloomberg.com/news/features/2017-03-09/how-to-become-an-international-gold-smuggler

[98] Castilla, Oscar. Nelly Luna Amancio, and Fabiola Torres Lopez. "The Companies Accused of Buying Latin America's Illegal Gold." (Aug 2015). *InSight Crime.* Accessed from https://www.insightcrime.org/news/analysis/the-companies-accused-of-buying-latin-america-illegal-gold/

Dupraz-Dobias, Paula. "US Companies Importing Dirty Gold from Illegal Mining Operations in Peru." (Jan 2015). *Earth Island Journal.* Accessed from http://www.earthisland.org/journal/index.php/elist/eListRead/us_companies_importing_dirty_gold_from_illegal_mining_operations_in_peru/

Diamonds trafficked into Dubai generally originate in African conflict zones. News reports have mentioned a variety of locations, such as the Central African Republic and Zimbabwe's Marange field.[99] Once in Dubai, counterfeit documents are produced, certifying them as not originating in conflict zones.[100] Then, a majority of the gems are transported to other countries for sale, although some remain in Dubai. It appears that there is no single destination, as reports have noted India, Belgium, Hong Kong, China, and Qatar as some of the final locations.[101] Persons trafficked through Dubai originate from a host of Southeast Asian countries. Often times, the individuals are recruited under the pretext of a better life working abroad. However, they are stripped of their passports and often forced into labor or prostitution, working for low wages that are split between the trafficker and the victim. Human traffickers sell their victims throughout the Middle East, often using Dubai as a transit point.[102] Still, some workers—both in prostitution and in other forms of labor—are forced to work in Dubai.

Although other illicit goods are trafficked to and through Dubai, only the aforementioned products have been written about enough to have a credible indication of their flow.

[99] Bax, Pauline. "Gem Smuggling Thwarts Revival of Central African Republic." (Nov 2017). *Bloomberg.* Accessed from https://www.bloomberg.com/news/articles/2017-11-28/gem-smuggling-thwarts-drive-to-revive-central-african-republic

"How Diamonds Fund Zimbabwe's Secret Police." (Sep 2017). *Bloomberg.* Accessed from https://www.bloomberg.com/news/articles/2017-09-10/diamonds-fund-zimbabwe-political-oppression-global-witness-says

[100] Ibid.

[101] "A Game of Stones." N.d. *Global Witness.* Accessed from https://www.globalwitness.org/en/campaigns/central-african-republic-car/game-of-stones/?accessible=true

Bax, Pauline. "Gem Smuggling Thwarts Revival of Central African Republic." (Nov 2017). *Bloomberg.* Accessed from https://www.bloomberg.com/news/articles/2017-11-28/gem-smuggling-thwarts-drive-to-revive-central-african-republic

"How Diamonds Fund Zimbabwe's Secret Police." (Sep 2017). *Bloomberg.* Accessed from https://www.bloomberg.com/news/articles/2017-09-10/diamonds-fund-zimbabwe-political-oppression-global-witness-says

[102] Al Amir, Salam. "Three human traffickers who fooled women into prostitution in Dubai are jailed." (Jan 2017). *The National.* Accessed from https://www.thenational.ae/uae/three-human-traffickers-who-fooled-women-into-prostitution-in-dubai-are-jailed-1.2695

"United Arab Emirates: 2017 Trafficking in Persons Report." (2017). *U.S. Department of State.* Accessed from https://www.state.gov/j/tip/rls/tiprpt/countries/2017/271307.htm

27. Types of Insecurity

27.1. Illegal drugs[103]

27.2. Conventional weapons[104]

27.3. Transfers of illicitly obtained money[105]

27.4. Money laundering[106]

27.6. Trafficking of people[107]

[103] Al Amir, Salam. "'GCC Drug Smugglers Caught with 2.2 kg of Heroin in Dubai." (Jul 2017). *The National.* Accessed from https://www.thenational.ae/uae/gcc-drug-smugglers-caught-with-2-2kg-of-heroin-in-dubai-1.609323

Al Ramahi, Nawal. "UAE Customs find Children as Young as 11 Used as Drug Mules for Smuggling." (Apr 2017). *The National.* Accessed from https://www.thenational.ae/uae/uae-customs-find-children-as-young-as-11-used-as-drug-mules-for-smuggling-1.81844

Nammour, Marie. "Man smuggles a tonne of narcotics pills in sheep intestines." (Aug 2017). *Khaleej Times.* Accessed from https://www.khaleejtimes.com/news/crime/Man-caught-smuggling-1-tonne-of-pills-in-sheep-intestines

[104] Issa, Wafa. "16,000 Pistols Bound for Yemen Seized in Dubai." (Mar 2011). *The National.* Accessed from https://www.thenational.ae/uae/16-000-pistols-bound-for-yemen-seized-in-dubai-1.429028arms

Rasheed, Abdullah. "'Group Smuggled Weapons into UAE." (Nov 2015). *Gulf News.* Accessed from http://gulfnews.com/news/uae/courts/group-smuggled-weapons-into-uae-1.1620936

Spencer, Richard. "UAE moves on illegal nuclear and weapons trade." (Jul 2010). *The Telegraph.* Accessed from http://www.telegraph.co.uk/news/worldnews/middleeast/dubai/7863884/UAE-moves-on-illegal-nuclear-and-weapons-trade.html

[105] Mathiason, Nick. "Dubai's Dark Side Targeted by International Finance Police." (Jan 2010). *The Guardian.* Accessed https://www.theguardian.com/business/2010/jan/24/dubai-crime-money-laundering-terrorism

Saul, Jonathan. Parisa Hafezi, and Louis Charbonneau. "Exclusive: Iran smuggles in $1 billion of bank notes to skirt sanctions – sources." (Feb 2015). *Reuters.* Accessed from https://www.reuters.com/article/us-iran-dollars-exclusive/exclusive-iran-smuggles-in-1-billion-of-bank-notes-to-skirt sanctions sources idUSKBN0LS1LV20150224

"Woman held for trying to smuggle cash to Dubai." (Jun 2017). *The Indian Express.* Accessed from http://indianexpress.com/article/cities/mumbai/woman-held-for-trying-to-smuggle-cash-to-dubai-4720573/

[106] Al Shouk, Ali. "Money from fake goods trade funds terrorism, drugs, officer says." (Dec 2017). *Gulf News.* Accessed from http://gulfnews.com/news/uae/emergencies/money-from-fake-goods-trade-funds-terrorism-drugs-officer-says-1.2139827

Ziady, Hanna. "UAE Central Bank probes Gupta Money Laundering." (Oct 2017). *Business Day.* Accessed from https://www.businesslive.co.za/bd/national/2017-10-31-uae-central-bank-probes-gupta-money-laundering/

[107] Olaleye Aluka, Abuja. "Nigerian Woman Jailed in Dubai for Human Trafficking Flees." (Nov 2017). *Punch.* Accessed from http://punchng.com/nigerian-woman-jailed-in-dubai-for-human-trafficking-flees/

Human trafficking in Dubai encompasses forced labor and sex trafficking.

27.10. Smuggling of natural resources

27.10.1. Minerals

There are two primary minerals smuggled into Dubai: diamonds and gold. Diamonds flow from South African countries, where they typically are resold.[108] Meanwhile, Dubai is most frequently used as a transit point for gold, before it is smuggled into India to avoid import taxes.[109]

27.10.2. Timber

Red Sanders trees in Andhra Pradesh, India, are smuggled out of the country, typically transiting through Dubai and then Pakistan before reaching their end destination in China.[110]

Skaf, Sarah. "Two Arrested in Dubai for Human Trafficking." (May 2017). *Gulf News*. Accessed from http://gulfnews.com/news/uae/crime/two-arrested-in-dubai-for-human-trafficking-1.2034869

Twaha, Matovu Abdallah. (Oct 2017). "Breather for Trafficking Victims." *The Gulf Today*. Accessed from http://gulftoday.ae/portal/be6c47e5-6589-4b84-abf7-8cced2f280b9.aspx

[108] "Gem smuggling thwarts revival of Central African Republic." (Dec 2017). *IOL*. Accessed from https://www.iol.co.za/business-report/gem-smuggling-thwarts-revival-of-central-african-republic-12192283

"Here's what not to do when smuggling diamonds." (Oct 2015). *The Economic Times*. Accessed from https://economictimes.indiatimes.com/magazines/panache/heres-what-not-to-do-when-smuggling-diamonds/articleshow/49182048.cms

"How Diamonds Fund Zimbabwe's Secret Police." (Sep 2017). *Bloomberg*. Accessed from https://www.bloomberg.com/news/articles/2017-09-10/diamonds-fund-zimbabwe-political-oppression-global-witness-says

[109] Inamdar, Nadeem. "Customs sleuths up airport vigil as gold smuggling on Pune-Dubai Route Rises." (Dec 2017). *Hindustan Times*. Accessed from http://www.hindustantimes.com/pune-news/customs-sleuths-up-airport-vigil-as-gold-smuggling-on-pune-dubai-route-rises/story-6dB1nEhVBvDkpuMfuxq5LI.html

Malhotra, Sarika. "Yellow Peril." (Dec 2013). *Business Today*. Accessed from http://www.businesstoday.in/magazine/features/gold-smuggling-resumes-in-india/story/200605.html

[110] Sivanl, Jayaraj. "Red sanders smugglers have links with Dubai underworld: Sleuths." (Apr 2015). *The Times of India*. Accessed from https://timesofindia.indiatimes.com/india/Red-sanders-smugglers-have-links-with-Dubai-underworld-Sleuths/articleshow/46843404.cms

Umashanker, K. "Deathblow to red sanders smuggling network." (Nov 2016). *The Hindu*. Accessed from http://www.thehindu.com/news/national/andhra-pradesh/Deathblow-to-red-sanders-smuggling-nework/article16441670.ece

"Notorious red sanders smuggler among 11 held, banned timber worth Rs one crore seized." (Nov 2017). *The New Indian Express*. Accessed from http://www.newindianex-

27.10.3. Other—Charcoal[111]

The smuggled charcoal comes from acacia trees grown between the Juba and Shabelle rivers in southern Somalia. The United Arab Emirate's ports, including those in Dubai, are major destinations for charcoal, with the United Arab Emirates providing sugar in exchange.

27.11. Trafficking of animal and animal parts[112]

This has ranged from the trafficking of live exotic animals to ivory, rhino horns, and pangolin scales.

27.12. Trafficking of household goods[113]

Although various household goods are trafficked through, to, or from Dubai, jewelry is especially prominent.

press.com/states/andhra-pradesh/2017/nov/01/notorious-red-sanders-smuggler-among-11-held-banned-timber-worth-rs-one-crore-seized-1688750.html

[111] Baxter, Zach. "Somalia's Coal Industry." (May 2007). *Mandal Projects*. Accessed from http://mandalprojects.com/ice/ice-cases/somalia-coal.htm

Monitoring Group on Somalia and Eritrea. "Somalia." (Nov 2017). *United Nations Security Council*. Accessed from http://daacad.com/wp-content/uploads/2017/11/SEMG_REPORT_SOMALIA.pdf

Somali charcoal production, transport and stockpiles." (Nov 2017). *Mareeg*. Accessed from https://mareeg.com/somali-charcoal-production-transport-and-stockpiles/

[112] Al Jabry, Amal. "Craziest animals smuggled into Dubai." (Jan 2015). *Emirates 24/7 News*. Accessed from http://www.emirates247.com/news/emirates/craziest-animals-smuggled-into-dubai-2015-01-26-1.578045

Chayutworakan, Sutthiwit. "Three held after B50m rhino horn bust." (Dec 2017). *Bangkok Post*. Accessed from https://www.bangkokpost.com/news/crime/1378183/three-held-after-b50m-rhino-horn-bust

Todorova, Vesela. "Dubai 'major hub' for wildlife trafficking: report." (Dec 2013). *The National*. Accessed from https://www.thenational.ae/uae/environment/dubai-major-hub-for-wildlife-trafficking-report-1.325484

"Malaysian Authorities Seize 700 kg of Pangolin Scales Smuggled from Africa." (May 2017). *The Telegraph*. Accessed from http://www.telegraph.co.uk/news/2017/05/08/malaysian-authorities-seize-700kg-pangolin-scales-smuggled-africa/

[113] "Smugglers caught at Dubai airport with Dh3 million worth of watches strapped to limbs." (Jul 2017). *The National*. Accessed from https://www.thenational.ae/uae/smuggler-caught-at-dubai-airport-with-dh3-million-worth-of-watches-strapped-to-limbs-1.614067

"The Nuclear Deal's Other Winner." (Jul 2015). *The Economist*. Accessed from https://www.economist.com/news/middle-east-and-africa/21659760-many-firms-looking-do-business-iran-will-go-through-dubai-nuclear-deals

27.16. Terrorist activities

Terrorist activities in Dubai, and in The UAE in general, center around money laundering to fund terrorist organizations. While the UAE cracked down on terrorist support after 9/11, the use of unregistered *hawalas*—ancient, informal trading networks grounded in trust—and the frequency of money laundering cases in Dubai suggests that the funding of terrorist activities remains a problem in the UAE.[114] Furthermore, in a 2014 report, the US State Department acknowledged continued concern over terrorism funds emanating from the UAE.[115]

27.17 Other—Shell Companies

Dubai is filled with shell companies—that is, companies that appear real but offer no real goods or services. Instead, they are used for tax evasion, or created to steal funders' money. Shell companies in Dubai often have ties to India.[116] The Guptas, an Indian billionaire family with business operations in South Africa, have a plethora of shell companies in Dubai.[117]

27.17 Other—Diesel

The UAE has seen sizable diesel smuggling in the past decade. Although the majority of it has occurred in Abu Dhabi, there have been dozens of cases in Dubai.[118] Actors engaged in smuggling have been driving pas-

---

[114] Miko, Francis T. "Removing Terrorist Sanctuaries: The 9/11 Commission Recommendations and U.S. Policy." (Aug 2004). *Congressional Research Service.* Accessed from https://fas.org/irp/crs/RL32518.pdf

Seftel, Bennett. "Hawala Networks: The Paperless Trail of Terrorist Transactions." (Mar 2017). *The Cipher Brief.* Accessed from https://www.thecipherbrief.com/hawala-networks-the-paperless-trail-of-terrorist-transactions

[115] "Countries/Jurisdictions of Primary Concern – United Arab Emirates." (2014). *U.S. Department of State.* Accessed from https://www.state.gov/j/inl/rls/nrcrpt/2014/vol2/222842.htm

[116] Ghosh, Sugata. "As Dubai prepares to change tax laws, Indians scramble to hide undeclared wealth." (Mar 2017). *The Economic Times.* Accessed from https://economictimes.indiatimes.com/wealth/tax/as-dubai-prepares-to-change-tax-laws-indians-scramble-to-hide-undeclared-wealth/articleshow/57621994.cms

[117] Serrao, Angelique and Pieter-Louis Myburgh. "Dubai: The Guptas' City of Shells." (Oct 2017). *News 24.* Accessed from https://www.news24.com/SouthAfrica/News/dubai-the-guptas-city-of-shells-20171027

[118] Sadafy, Mohammad Al. "85 Cases of Diesel Smuggling in UAE." (Apr 2014). *Emirates 24/7.* Accessed from http://www.emirates247.com/news/emirates/85-cases-of-diesel-smuggling-in-uae-2014-04-15-1.545707

senger vehicles, as well as tankers.[119] Companies have frequently been implicated in crime.[120]

27.17 Other—Forged documents

Numerous recent news stories detail accounts of individuals forging documents for monetary gain.[121] While the criminals appear to be working solitarily in most instances, Dubai has been known as an area where smugglers can procure necessary documentation. This has been especially true in the case of diamond smugglers, who have obtained fake Kimberley Process certificates in Dubai, which certify that the diamonds have originated from conflict-free zones.[122]

28. Illicit Activity Role of the Area under Analysis

28.3. Flat

Dubai functions as a hub of illicit trade, with a wide array of illicit goods available. Pangolin, drugs, weapons, conflict diamonds, gold—all can be purchased in the port city.[123] While the UAE has imposed greater restrictions aimed at curbing the flow of illegal goods and stopping money

[119] Shabaan, Ahmad. "Diesel smugglers fined Dh6,000 each." (Feb 2016). *Khaleej Times*. Accessed from https://www.khaleejtimes.com/nation/crime/diesel-smugglers-fined-dh6000-each

[120] Baldwin, Derek. "Illegal diesel sale in Dubai: 12 companies raided in joint sting operation." (Mar 2016). *Gulf News*. Accessed from http://gulfnews.com/news/uae/environment/illegal-diesel-sale-in-dubai-12-companies-raided-in-joint-sting-operation-1.1683094
Rahman, Fareed. "UAE government takes steps to curb petrol smuggling." (Aug 2015). *Gulf News*. Accessed from http://gulfnews.com/news/uae/government/uae-government-takes-steps-to-curb-petrol-smuggling-1.1560742

[121] Al Amir, Salam. "Man releases two dogs from quarantine using fake government stamp." (Dec 2017). *The National*. Accessed from https://www.thenational.ae/uae/man-releases-two-dogs-from-quarantine-using-fake-government-stamp-1.683809
Al Amir, Salam. "Pair jailed for forging documents to steal Dh2.7 m from local bank." (Nov 2017). *The National*. Accessed from https://www.thenational.ae/uae/pair-jailed-for-forging-documents-to-steal-dh2-7m-from-local bank-1.676115
Nammour, Marie. "Dubai driver, petrol station workers jailed for Dh73,000 fuel fraud." (Dec 2017). *Khaleej Times*. Accessed from https://www.khaleejtimes.com/news/crime/dubai-driver-petrol-station-workers-jailed-for-dh73000-fuel-fraud

[122] Sharife, Khadija and John Grobler. "Kimberley's Illicit Process." (Jan 2014). *World Policy*. Accessed from http://www.worldpolicy.org/blog/2014/01/13/kimberleys-illicit-process

[123] "Malaysian Authorities Seize 700 kg of Pangolin Scales Smuggled from Africa." (May 2017). *The Telegraph*. Accessed from http://www.telegraph.co.uk/news/2017/05/08/malaysian-authorities-seize-700kg-pangolin-scales-smuggled-africa/

laundering, both remain a central problem in this Gulf country. Despite the magnitude of illicit trade that daily flows through Dubai, the smuggled goods are not concentrated in one central node. Instead, there are dispersed centers of activity throughout the city, ranging from shell companies to ports to shops that sell conflict diamonds—to name a few.

29. Relocation of Illicit Activities
29.2 Activities did not relocate from another area

Despite the increasing regulations, daily media reports of smuggled goods indicate the scope of the networks and frequency of transport, revealing no noticeable decline in the illicit economy.[124] Thus, it appears that Dubai remains an epicenter with no indication of illicit trade relocating elsewhere.

30. Observed Frequency of Insecurity Flows
30.1 Close to permanent (daily)

Illicit activity in Dubai appears to occur on a daily basis. A basic search on smuggling in Dubai brings up dozens of recent reports on gold, drugs, and household goods—among other things—being transported illegally into and out of Dubai. While the UAE has made steps to address most of the types of illicit activity, the frequency of the media writing on smuggling in Dubai indicates that insecurity flows occur daily.[125]

31. Perceived Level of Insecurity Flows According to Media and Other Reports
31.3 Very large

Dubai is a hub of illicit activity with a wide variety of illicit goods and services available. A basic search on smuggling in Dubai brings up dozens

Davidson, Christopher M. (2008) Dubai: The Security Dimensions of the Region's Premier Free Port. *Middle East Policy*, v.15 n.2, 143–160.

[124] Claus, Liz. "In Pictures: The fight against smuggling in the UAE." (May 2014). *The National.* Accessed from https://www.thenational.ae/business/in-pictures-the-fight-against-smuggling-in-the-uae-1.247452

[125] Arnold, Tom. "Smuggling in the UAE: Counterfeit goods seeping into ports daily." (May 2014). *The National.* Accessed from https://www.thenational.ae/business/smuggling-in-the-uae-counterfeit-goods-seeping-into-ports-daily-1.247451

of recent reports on gold, drugs, and household goods—among other things—being transported illegally into and out of Dubai. While the UAE has cracked down on financial crimes in recent years, arresting over 6,800 in the first eight months of 2014 and instituting new laws aimed at complicating illicit transactions of money, financial crimes are still prominent in the emirate.[126] Additionally, in the US Department of State's 2017 report on trafficking in persons, the UAE was noted as not meeting the required standards for eliminating human trafficking. Moreover, the report acknowledged the prevalence of human trafficking for forced labor and sex trafficking within the country.[127]

32. National and International Responses
32.6. Mixed (domestic peaceful solutions, international cooperation, domestic confrontation, and outside soft intervention)

Despite the scope and gravity of smuggling, money laundering, and human trafficking that occurs in Dubai, national and international responses have avoided confrontation. The international community has applied soft power, pressuring the UAE to reform financial regulations to curb money laundering.[128] Additionally, the US shamed the UAE for their failure to address human trafficking, placing them on tier 3 (of 3) in the US State Department's Trafficking in Person's report in 2001, 2002, and 2003.[129] In 2003, the UAE placed increased effort on curbing human trafficking, and their actions were rewarded with a move to tier 2 in the 2004 Trafficking in Persons report.

While the international community has shamed and used soft power to shape the UAE's response to the Black Spot, the UAE has relied on domestic peaceful solutions and domestic confrontation, instituting new

---

[126] Bedirian, Razmig. "Over 6800 arrested for financial crimes." (Sep 2014). *Gulf News.* Accessed from http://gulfnews.com/news/uae/crime/over-6-800-arrested-for-financial-crimes-1.1386391

"New Law to Protect Dubai's Economy from Financial Crimes." (Apr 2016). *Khaleej Times.* Accessed from https://www.khaleejtimes.com/nation/government/new-law-to-protect-dubais-economy-from-financial-crimes

[127] "Trafficking in Persons Report 2017." (2017). *U.S. Department of State.* Accessed from https://www.state.gov/documents/organization/271345.pdf

[128] Mathiason, Nick. "Dubai's dark side targeted by international finance police." (Jan 2010). *The Guardian.* Accessed from https://www.theguardian.com/business/2010/jan/24/dubai-crime-money-laundering-terrorism

[129] Kakande, Yasin. *Slave States: The Practice of Kafala in the Gulf Arab Region.* (2015). *Zero Books.*

regulations to address Dubai's illicit economy, and arresting those who fail to adhere to the new laws. These internal reforms have pacified international criticisms of inaction, although their success in stopping the flow of illicit goods to and through Dubai appears to be minimal, as new reports continue to daily publish accounts of smuggled goods in the Emirate.[130]

33. Potential Other Black Spots Found

Lahore, Pakistan—This major city appears in a plethora of news articles regarding organ trafficking.[131]

Marange diamond fields, Zimbabwe—While diamond trafficking appears to be the predominant illicit activity in the area, there is also a sizable amount of forced labor.[132]

Hamriyah, United Arab Emirates—This port city has been implicated in the charcoal smuggling perpetrated by Somalia's al-Shabaab.[133]

Liboi, Garissa Town, and Dabaab Refugee Camp in Kenya—All these towns are referred to as part of the sugar smuggling network that has ties to al-Shabaab and charcoal smuggling.[134]

---

[130] Arnold, Tom. "Smuggling in the UAE: Counterfeit goods seeping into ports daily." (May 2014). *The National*. Accessed from https://www.thenational.ae/business/smuggling-in-the-uae-counterfeit-goods-seeping-into-ports-daily-1.247451

[131] "Pakistan uncovers illegal organ trade ring: official." (May 2017). *The National*. Accessed from https://www.thenational.ae/world/pakistan-uncovers-illegal-organ-trade-ring-official-1.59016

"Watch: Wealth and Poverty keep Pakistan's Illegal Organ Trafficking Trade alive." (Jun 2017). *First Post*. Accessed from http://www.firstpost.com/world/watch-wealth-and-poverty-keep-pakistans-illegal-organ-trafficking-trade-alive-3751427.html

[132] Manayiti, Obey and Elias Mambo. "How Marange diamonds looting started." (Dec 2016). *Zimbabwe Independent*. Accessed from https://www.theindependent.co.zw/2016/12/23/telone-reels-us378m-debts/

"Diamonds in the Rough: Human Rights Abuses in the Marange Diamond Fields of Zimbabwe." (2009). *Human Rights Watch*. Accessed from https://www.hrw.org/report/2009/06/26/diamonds-rough/human-rights-abuses-marange-diamond-fields-zimbabwe

[133] Baxter, Zach. "Somalia's Coal Industry." (May 2007). *Mandal Projects*. Accessed from http://mandalaprojects.com/ice/ice-cases/somalia-coal.htm

Monitoring Group on Somalia and Eritrea. "Somalia." (Nov 2017). *United Nations Security Council*. Accessed from http://daacad.com/wp-content/uploads/2017/11/SEMG_REPORT_SOMALIA.pdf

Somali charcoal production, transport and stockpiles." (Nov 2017). *Mareeg*. Accessed from https://mareeg.com/somali-charcoal-production-transport-and-stockpiles/

[134] Rasmussen, Jacob. "Sweet Secrets: Sugar Smuggling and State Formation in the Kenya-Somalia Borderlands." (Dec 2017). *Danish Institute for International Studies*. Accessed from

Khasab, Oman—This small coastal town is home to Iranian merchants known for their smuggling to Iran.[135] Goods smuggled into Iran have typically been household goods, especially cigarettes.[136] These smugglers have thrived during the Iranian sanctions.

Madre de Dios, Peru—This region is known for its illegal gold mining operations, although there are also reports of human smuggling networks, too.[137]

An earlier coder noted:

"Sharjah, the neighboring emirate of the UAE, is a potential satellite Black Spot for illicit financial activity. The UAE seems to have several Black Spots that would warrant additional research. Specifically, its capitol city. Abu Dhabi and two other ports, Mina' Saqr and Khawr Fakkan."

http://pure.diis.dk/ws/files/1269212/DIIS_WP_2017_11.pdf

Monitoring Group on Somalia and Eritrea. "Somalia." (Nov 2017). *United Nations Security Council.* Accessed from http://daacad.com/wp-content/uploads/2017/11/SEMG_REPORT_SOMALIA.pdf

Somali charcoal production, transport and stockpiles." (Nov 2017). *Mareeg.* Accessed from https://mareeg.com/somali-charcoal-production-transport-and-stockpiles/

[135] "Iranian smugglers set up shop in coastal Oman." (Jul 2013). *The Observer.* Accessed from http://observers.france24.com/en/20130711-oman-haven-iranian-smugglers-khasab

[136] Muller, Quentin and Sebastian Castelier. "Hard times for Oman's Strait smugglers." (Sep 2016). *Al Jazeera.* Accessed from http://www.aljazeera.com/news/2016/09/hard-times-oman-strait-smugglers-160926114325822.html

von Mittelstaedt, Juliane. "Iran Sanctions Good for Business in Tiny Omani Port." (Jan 2012). *Spiegel Online.* Accessed from http://www.spiegel.de/international/world/smuggler-s-paradise-iran-sanctions-good-for-business-in-tiny-omani-port-a-810165.html

[137] Daley, Suzanne. "Peru Scrambles to Drive Out Illegal Gold Mining and Save Precious Land." (Jul 2016). *New York Times.* Accessed from https://www.nytimes.com/2016/07/26/world/americas/peru-illegal-gold-mining-latin-america.html

Gurney, Kyra. "New Peru Human Smuggling Groups Points to New Migration Patterns." (Jun 2014). *InSight Crime.* Accessed from https://www.insightcrime.org/news/brief/new-human-smuggling-groups-peru-points-changes-migration-patterns/

Taj, Mitra. "Peru crackdown on illegal gold leads to new smuggling routes." (Nov 2014). *Reuters.* Accessed from https://www.reuters.com/article/us-peru-gold/peru-crackdown-on-illegal-gold-leads-to-new-smuggling-routes-idUSKCN0J90E720141125

BIBLIOGRAPHY

Abraham, Itty, and Willem van Schendel. 2005. Introduction. In *Illicit Flows and Criminal Things: States, Borders, and the Other Side of Globalization*, ed. Willem van Schendel and Itty Abraham. Bloomington: Indiana University Press.

Adams, Devin M. 2017. The 2016 Amendment to Criminal Rule 41: National Search Warrants to Seize Cyberspace, "Particularly" Speaking. *University of Richmond Law Review* 51: 721–773.

Adams, Jackson, and Mohamad Albakajai. 2016. Cyberspace: A New Threat to the Sovereignty of the State. *Management Studies* 4 (6): 256–265.

Adams, Jonathan. 2008. In Basilan, Philippines, a US Counterterrorism Model Frays. *Christian Science Monitor*, December 11.

Adelman, Jonathan. 2014. Modeling Insecurity Flow Dynamics in Response to Degradation of Illicit Groups' Safe Havens. Paper Presented at the Annual Meeting of the International Studies Association, Toronto, Canada, March 26–29.

Agnew, John. 2009. *Globalization and Sovereignty*. New York: Roman and Littlefield.

Allen, Ernie. 2010. Domestic Minor Sex Trafficking. Testimony Before the Subcommittee on Crime, Terrorism, and Homeland Security, Committee on the Judiciary, US House of Representatives, September 15.

Al-Tamimi, Aymenn Jawad. 2013. The Factions of Aba Kamal. *Middle East Forum*, December 18.

Anderson, Nate. 2011. LulzSec Manifesto: "We Screw Each Other Over for a Jolt of Satisfaction." *Ars Technica*, May 17.

Andreas, Peter. 2000. *Border Games: Policing the US-Mexico Divide*. Ithaca: Cornell University Press.

© The Author(s) 2020
S. S. Brown, M. G. Hermann, *Transnational Crime and Black Spots*, International Political Economy Series,
https://doi.org/10.1057/978-1-137-49670-6

Assl, Nima Khorrami. 2011. Hezbollah: A State Above the State. *Foreign Policy Journal*, February 3.

Associated Press. 2011. Prepaid Cards Attract Money Launderers. *Post Standard*, May 20.

Audretsch, David B. 1998. Agglomeration and the Location of Innovative Activity. *Oxford Review of Economic Policy* 14 (2): 18–29.

Ayaz, Erum. 2012. Peace and Development in FATA Through Economic Transformation. *TIGAH: A Journal of Peace and Development* 1 (2): 74–95.

Baldwin, Richard. 2016. *The Great Convergence: Information Technology and the New Globalization*. Cambridge, MA: Belknap Press.

Bariyo, Nicholas. 2013. Inside Congo's Link in the Gold Chain. *Wall Street Journal*, April 14.

Basu, Gautam. 2013. The Role of Transnational Smuggling Operations in Illicit Supply Chains. *Journal of Transportation Security* 6 (4): 315–328.

BBC News. 2005. Spain Cracks $300m Money Racket, March 13.

Becerra, Robert J. 2015. The Black Market Peso Exchange and the Small Exporter. *International Law Quarterly* 32 (3): 10–11, 34–37.

Benavides, E. Ben. 2015. *Open Source Intelligence (OSInt) 2ool Kit on the Go*. Online Book, Creative Commons.

Bevir, George. 2017. Cost of Online Piracy to Hit $52bn. *IBC 365*, October 30.

Bhattacharjee, Yudhijit. 2011. Welcome to Hackerville: The Romanian Cybercriminal Hotspot. *Wired*, March.

Bischoff, Paul. 2016. Guide: How to Access the Deep Web and Darknet. *VPN & Privacy*, May 31.

Blas, Javier. 2014. Reporting Back: Equatorial Guinea. *Financial Times*, January 23.

Blum, Jack A., Michael Levi, R. Thomas Naylor, and Phil Williams. 1998. *Financial Havens, Banking Secrecy, and Money Laundering*. New York: United Nations.

Booth, William, and Nick Miroff. 2010. 'Cartels' Cash Flows Across Border. *Washington Post*, August 26.

Bowers, Charles B. 2009. Hawala, Money Laundering, and Terrorism Finance: Micro Lending as an End to Illicit Remittance. *Denver Journal of International Law and Policy* 37: 379–419.

Bran, Mirel. 2013. In Romania, a Quiet City Has Become the Global Hub for Hackers and Online Crooks. *Le Monde* (English Edition), January 7.

BrightPlanet. 2012. *Deep Web: A Primer*. brightplanet.com, June 4.

Broad, William J., David E. Sanger, and Raymond Bonner. 2004. A Tale of Nuclear Proliferation: How Pakistani Built His Network. *New York Times*, February 12.

Broadhurst, Roderic, Peter Grabosky, Mamoun Alazab, and Steve Chon. 2014. Organizations and Cybercrime: An Analysis of the Nature of Groups Engaged in Cybercrime. *International Journal of Cyber Criminology* 8 (1): 1–20.

Broadhurst, Roderic, Peter Grabosky, Mamoun Alazab, Brigitte Bohours, Steve Chon, and Chen Da. 2013. Crime in Cyberspace: Offenders and the Role of Organized Crime Groups Working Paper, Australian National University Cybercrime Observatory, May 15.

Brown, Stuart S., and David Levey. 2015. The Global Innovation System: A New Phase of Capitalism. *International Journal of Business, Humanities, and Technology* 5 (1): 6–10.

Burnett, John. 2014. A Wash in Cash, Drug Cartels Rely on Big Banks to Launder Profits. *NPR*, March 20.

Buscaglia, E., and Jan Van Dijk. 2003. Controlling Organized Crime and Corruption in the Public Sector. *Journal on Crime and Society* 3 (1 & 2): 3–34.

Byman, Daniel. 2007. *Understanding Proto-Insurgencies*. Santa Monica: RAND Corporation.

Caldwell, Leslie R. 2016. Highlighting Cybercrime Enforcement. Speech at Center for Strategic and International Studies, December 7.

Calvery, Jennifer Shasky. 2012. Combating Transnational Organized Crime: International Money Laundering as a Threat to Our Financial System. Statement Before the Subcommittee on Crime, Terrorism, and Homeland Security, Committee on the Judiciary, United States House of Representatives, February 8.

Cardenas, Alvarao A., Svetlana Radosavac, Jens Grossklags, John Chuang, and Chris Hoofnagle. 2009. An Economic Map of Cybercrime. Paper Presented at the 37th Research Conference on Communication, Information, and Internet Policy, George Mason University.

Carless, Will. 2014. Welcome to Paraguay's 'Wild West', a Bastion for Bootleggers, Organized Crime, and Maybe Even Islamic Extremists. *GlobalPost*, September 16.

Caspersen, Nina, and Gareth Stansfield, eds. 2011. *Unrecognized States in the International System*. New York: Routledge.

Cassara, John A. 2015. *Trade-Based Money Laundering*. Hoboken: John Wiley & Sons.

Chacos, Brad. 2013. Meet Darknet: The Hidden Anonymous Underbelly of the Searchable Web. *PC World*, August 12.

Chawki, Mohamed. 2006. Anonymity in Cyberspace: Finding the Balance. Computer Crime Research Center, July 9.

Choo, Raymond, and Peter Grabosky. 2013. Cyber Crime. In *Oxford Handbook of Organized Crime*, ed. Letizia Paoli. Oxford: Oxford University Press.

Choucri, Nazli, and David D. Clark. 2012. Integrating Cyberspace and International Relations. Paper presented at ECIR Workshop on Who Controls Cyberspace, MIT and Harvard University, November 6–7.

Cirnio, John A., Silvano L. Elizondo, and Geoffrey Wawro. 2004. Latin American Security Challenges: A Collaborative Inquiry from North and South. In *Latin*

America's Lawless Areas and Failed States: An Analysis of the New Threats, ed. Paul D. Taylor. Newport: Naval War College Press.

Clayton, Richard. 2009. *How Much Did Shutting Down McColo Help?* Cambridge: Cambridge Computer Laboratory, Cambridge University.

Cohen-Almagor, Raphael. 2012. Freedom of Expression, Internet Responsibility, and Business Ethics: The Yahoo Saga and Its Implications. *Journal of Business Ethics* 106 (3): 353–365.

Collins, Catherine, and Douglas Frantz. 2018. The Long Shadow of A.Q. Khan. *Foreign Affairs*, January 31.

Correll, Sean-Paul. 2010. Inside Mariposa—The Largest Botnet Takedown in History. *ISSA Magazine*, May.

Costa, Antonio Maria. 2010. Preface. In *The Globalization of Crime: A Transnational Organized Crime Threat Assessment*. Vienna: UNODC.

Couch, Robbie. 2014. 70 Percent of Child Sex Trafficking Victims Are Sold Online: Study. *The Huffington Post*, July 25.

Crane, David M. 2008. Dark Corners: The West African Joint Criminal Enterprise. *International Studies Review* 10: 387–391.

Crawford, Leslie. 2005. Hot Money in Spain's Costa del Crime. *House Price Crash Forum*, March 22.

CyberBunker. 2016. Spamhaus Blackmail War. http://cyberbunker.com/web/spamhaus.php. Accessed 24 July 2018.

Davidson, Christopher. 2008. *Dubai: The Vulnerability of Success*. London: Hurst & Co.

Di Natala, Leandro. 2012. *Usury: The Bank System of Camorra*. Brussels: European Strategic Intelligence and Security Center Briefing, December 20.

Duaij, Abdulrahman. 2009. Hawala: The Main Facilitator for Middle Eastern Organized Crime Groups. Unpublished Paper, George Mason University.

Duhaime, Christine. 2016. The Anti-Money Laundering Lawyer's Primer on Beneficial Ownership and Numbered, Shelf, and Shell Companies. *AML Law in Canada*, April 24.

Dunn, Stephen J. 2014. Bank Deposits, Structuring, and Asset Forfeitures. *Forbes Magazine*, April 19.

Ellingwood, Ken, and Tracy Wilkinson. 2011. Mexico Sets Its Sights on Cartels' Cash. *Los Angeles Times*, November 27.

Emerson, Steven. 2016. Report: German Refugee Program Money Given to Hezbollah Operatives. *Algemeiner*, April 21.

Europol Financial Intelligence Group (EFIG). 2015. *Why Is Cash Still King?* The Hague: European Police Office.

Eventon, Ross, and Dave Bewley-Taylor. 2016. *An Overview of Recent Changes in Cocaine Trafficking Routes into Europe*. Lisbon: European Monitoring Centre for Drugs and Drug Addiction.

FATF. 2006. *The Misuse of Corporate Vehicles Including Trust and Company Service Providers*. Paris: FATF/OECD.

————. 2010a. *Financial Action Task Force Annual Report 2009–2010*. Paris: FATF/OECD.

————. 2010b. *Money Laundering Vulnerabilities of Free Trade Zones*. Paris: FATF/OECD.

————. 2012. *International Standards on Combating Money Laundering and the Financing of Terrorism and Proliferation*. Paris: FATF.

————. 2013. *Guidance for a Risk-Based Approach: Prepaid Cards, Mobile Payments, and Internet-Based Payment Services*. Paris: FATF.

————. 2014. *Financial Flows Linked to the Production and Trafficking of Afghan Opiates*. Paris: FATF/OECD.

FATF/APG. 2015. *Money Laundering and Terrorist Financing Risks and Vulnerabilities Associated with Gold*. Paris/Sydney: FATF/APG.

Fielding, Sarah. 2018. Craigslist Has Banned Personal Ads Thanks to a New Trafficking Law—Here's How Sex Workers Say It Could Put Them in Huge Danger. *INSIDER*, March 20.

Fischer, Sabine. 2016. Russian Policy in Unresolved Conflicts. In *Not Frozen*, ed. Sabine Fischer. Berlin: German Institute for International and Security Affairs.

Fitzpatrick, Derek R. 2017. *Greed and Grievance and Drug Cartels: Mexico's Commercial Insurgency*. Fort Leavenworth: US Army Command and General Staff College.

Florea, Adrian. 2014. De Facto States in International Politics (1945–2011): A New Data Set. *International Interactions* 40 (5): 788–811.

Fontinelle, Amy. 2012. *The Mechanics of the Black Market*. Investopedia.com.

Ford, Christopher M. 2007. Of Shoes and Sites: Globalization and Insurgency. *Military Review*, May–June: 85–91.

Franceschi-Bicchierai, Lorenzo. 2015. Inside "Hackerville," Romania's Infamous Cyber Crime Hub. *Motherboard*, June 17.

Freed, Anthony M. 2010. An Interview with UN Cybersecurity Expert Raoul Chiesa. *The Huffington Post*, April 15.

Fujita, Masahisa, and Paul Krugman. 2004. The New Economic Geography: Past, Present and the Future. *Papers in Regional Science* 83: 139–164.

Fujita, Masahisa, and Tomoya Mori. 2005. *Frontiers of the New Economic Geography*. Kyoto: Institute of Economic Research, Kyoto University.

Fund for Peace. 2015. *2015 Fragile States Index*. Washington, DC: Fund for Peace.

Gambill, Gary C. 2003. Ain al-Hilweh: Lebanon's "Zone of Unlaw". *Middle East Intelligence Bulletin* 5 (6), June.

Gaspareniene, Ligita, and Rita Remeikiene. 2015. Digital Shadow Economy: A Critical Review of the Literature. *Mediterranean Journal of Social Sciences* 6 (6): 402–409.

George, Alexander L. 1979. Case Studies and Theory Development: The Method of Structured, Focused Comparison. In *Diplomacy: New Approaches to History, Theory, and Policy*, ed. P.G. Lauren. New York: Free Press.

George, Alexander L., and Andrew Bennett. 2005. *Case Studies and Theory Development in the Social Sciences.* Cambridge, MA: MIT Press.

Glaser, Daniel L. 2010. Testimony on Charities. Testimony Before Subcommittee on Oversight and Investigations, Committee on Financial Services, US House of Representatives, May 26.

Glenny, Misha. 2009. *McMafia: A Journey Through the Global Criminal Underworld.* New York: Vintage Books.

Global RADAR. 2017. US Government Stopping Piracy Across the Globe. *Global RADAR*, December 25.

Gold, Zack. 2014. *Security in the Sinai: Present and Future.* The Hague: International Centre for Counter-Terrorism, March.

Greenberg, Andy. 2016. The Silk Road's Dark Web Dream Is Dead. *Wired*, January 14.

Griffiths, Ryan. 2016. *Age of Secession: The International and Domestic Determinants of State Birth.* Cambridge: Cambridge University Press.

Guell, Oriol. 2016. Turf War Between Irish Mafias Spills Over into Marbella. *El Pais*, March 10.

Guttmann, Jean. 1973. *The Significance of Territory.* Charlottesville: University of Virginia Press.

Hall, Tim. 2012. Geographies of the Illicit: Globalization and Organized Crime. *Progress in Human Geography* 37 (3): 366–385.

Herman, Lyndall. 2016. Sisi, the Sinai, and Salafis. *Middle East Policy* 23 (2): 95–107.

Hoffman, Bruce. 1998. *Inside Terrorism.* New York: Columbia University Press.

Holt, Thomas J., and Adam M. Bossler. 2014. Cybercrime. *Oxford Handbooks Online*, Oxford University Press, June.

Holt, Thomas J., April M. Zeoli, and Kathleen Bohner. 2013. Examining the Decision-Making Processes of Sex Tourists Using Online Data. *Journal of Qualitative Criminal Justice and Criminology* 1: 122–155.

Hubbard, Ben, Robert F. Worth, and Michael R. Gordon. 2014. Power Vacuum in Middle East Lifts Militants. *New York Times*, January 4.

ICE. 2006. Prepaid Cards an Emerging Threat. *The Cornerstone Report* 3 (1): 4.

Insulza, Jose Miguel. 2013. *The OAS Drug Report: 16 Months of Debates and Consensus.* Washington, DC: Organization of American States.

Internal Revenue Service. 2006. *Internal Revenue Manual.* Washington, DC: Treasury Department.

International Chamber of Commerce. 2013. *Controlling the Zone: Balancing Facilitation and Control to Combat Illicit Trade in World's Free Trade Zones.* Paris: International Chamber of Commerce.

International Telecommunications Union (ITU). 2017. *ICT Facts and Figures 2017.* Geneva: ITU.

Jenkins, Quentin. 2011. Dutch ISP Attempts False Police Report. *Spamhaus News*, October 14.

Jost, Patrick M., and Harjit Singh Sandhu. 2006. The Hawala Alternative Remittance System and Its Role in Money Laundering. Financial Crimes Enforcement Network, US Department of the Treasury and INTERPOL/FOPAC.

Keefe, Patrick Radden. 2013. The Geography of Badness: Mapping the Hubs of the Illicit Global Economy. In *Convergence: Illicit Networks and National Security in the Age of Globalization*, ed. Michael Miklaucic and Jacqueline Brewer. Washington, DC: National Defense University Press.

Khan, Raza Rayman. 2012. FATA Political Regime: Changing Legal-Administrative Status of Tribal Areas. *TIGAH: A Journal of Peace and Development* 1 (1): 115–134.

Kiguolis, Ugnius. 2017. Koobface Worm Proliferates and Makes Astounding Profit for Its Owners. *2SpyWare*, February 7.

King, Douglas. 2013. *Have Anti-Money Laundering Measures Kept Pace with the Rapid Growth of GPR Prepaid Cards?* Retail Payments Risk Forum Working Paper. Atlanta: Federal Reserve Bank of Atlanta, January.

Kobis, Nils C., Jan-Willem van Prooijen, Francesca Righetti, and Paul A.M. Van Lange. 2016. "Who Doesn't?"—The Impact of Descriptive Norms on Corruption. *PLoS One* 10 (6): e0131830.

Kopp, Pierre. 2004. *The Political Economy of Illicit Drugs*. London: Routledge.

Krebs, Brian. 2007a. Shadowy Russian Firm Seen as Conduit for Cybercrime. *Washington Post*, October 13.

———. 2007b. Russian Business Network: Down, But Not Out. *Washington Post*, November 7.

———. 2008. Host of Internet Spam Groups Is Cut Off. *Washington Post*, November 12.

———. 2010. Naming and Shaming 'Bad' ISPs. *Krebs on Security*, March 19.

———. 2014. How a Car Wreck in a Moscow Square Affected the Spam We Receive Everyday. *Krebs on Security*, December 29.

———. 2016. Inside "The Attack That Almost Broke the Internet". *Krebs on Security*, August 26.

Krugman, Paul. 1991. *Geography and Trade*. Cambridge, MA: MIT Press.

Lahrichi, Kamilia. 2015. Counterfeit Goods Are Big Business in Paraguay. *USA Today*, May 18.

Lally, Conor. 2016. Who Is the Kingpin Behind Irish-Led Cartel Based in Spain? *Irish Times*, February 7.

Lamb, Robert D. 2008. *Ungoverned Areas and Threats from Safe Havens*. Washington, DC: Office of the Under Secretary of Defense.

Latonero, Mark. 2011. *Human Trafficking Online: The Role of Social Networking Sites and Online Classifieds.* Los Angeles: Center on Communication Leadership and Policy, Annenberg School for Communications and Journalism, University of Southern California, September.

Laville, Sandra. 2009. India Arrests Hawala Money Laundering Suspect Naresh Jain. *The Guardian*, December 8.

Levitsky, Melvyn. 2008. Dealing with Black Spots of Crime and Terror: Conclusions and Recommendations. *International Studies Review* 10: 392–395.

Levitt, Matthew. 2004. Charitable Organizations and Terrorist Financing: A War on Terror Status Check, Stein Program on Counterterrorism and Intelligence. Washington Institute for Near East Policy, Washington, DC, March.

———. 2005. Hezbollah: Financing Terror Through Criminal Enterprises. Testimony Before Committee on Homeland Security and Government Affairs, US Senate, May 25.

———. 2007. Hezbollah Finances: Funding the Party of God. In *Terrorism Financing and State Responses: A Comparative Perspective*, ed. Jeanne Giraldo and Harold Trinkunas. Stanford: Stanford University Press.

———. 2013. *Hezbollah: The Global Footprint of Lebanon's Party of God.* Washington, DC: Georgetown University Press.

Leyden, John. 2012. Five Koobface Botnet Suspects Named by New York Times. *The Register*, January 18.

Litvin, Kate. (2011) *Does Charitable Aid Fund Social Services or Suicide Bombers? Exploring Hezbollah's and Hamas' Involvement in US Charities.* University Honors in International Studies, American University, Spring.

Loewenstein, Antony. 2016. How Not to Fix an African Narco-State. *Foreign Policy*, January 6.

Lyons, John. 2008. Colombia Says FARC Sought to Make "Dirty Bomb". *Wall Street Journal*, March 5.

Martinez, Michael, Priscilla Riojas, and Jacqueline Hurtado. 2014. Los Angeles "Epicenter" of Cartel Money Laundering, Feds Say. *CNN*, September 12.

Mathiason, Nick. 2010. Dubai's Dark Side Targeted by International Finance Police. *The Guardian*, January 23.

Mayyasi, Alex. 2014. Hawala: The Working Man's Bitcoin. *Priceonomics*, February 7.

McAfee. 2018. *The Economic Impact of Cybercrime—No Slowing Down.* Washington, DC: McAfee and Center for Strategic and International Studies.

McKinley, James C., Jr., and Marc Lacey. 2009. Along the US-Mexico Border a Torrent of Illicit Cash. *New York Times*, December 25.

McLean, Alan, Guilbert Gates, and Archie Tse. 2013. How the Cyberattack on Spamhaus Unfolded. *New York Times*, March 30.

MENA FATF. 2015. *Money Laundering Through the Physical Transportation of Cash.* Paris: FATF and MENAFATF, October.

Metz, Steven. 2007. *Rethinking Insurgency*. Carlisle: Strategic Studies Institute, US Army War College.

Michaletos, Ioannis. 2010. An Outlook of Radical Islamism in Bosnia. *Serbianna*, September 25.

Miklaucic, Michael, and Jacqueline Brewer, eds. 2013. *Convergence: Illicit Networks and National Security in the Age of Globalization*. Washington, DC: National Defense University Press.

Miraglia, P., R. Ochoa, and I. Briscoe. 2012. Transnational Organised Crime and Fragile States. OECD Development Cooperation Working Papers, Paris.

Morris, Michael. 2005. *Al Qaeda as Insurgency*. Fort Belvoir: Defense Technical Information Center.

Morrisey, Deborah. n.d. *Shells, Trusts, and Similar Entities in International Money Laundering*. Miami: ICE.

Moura, Giovane C.M. 2013. Internet Bad Neighborhoods. The Netherlands Center for Telematrics and Information Technology, University of Twente.

Moura, Giovane C.M., Ramin Sadre, and Aiko Pras. 2014. Bad Neighborhoods on the Internet. *IEEE Communications Magazine* 52 (7) preprint.

Mozingo, Joe, Tiffany Hsu, and Victoria Kim. 2014. LA Fashion District Firms Raided in Cartel Money Laundering Probe. *Los Angeles Times*, September 10.

Mueller, Milton, Andreas Schmidt, and Brenden Kuerbis. 2013. Internet Security and Networked Governance in International Relations. *International Studies Review* 15 (1): 86–104.

Mylonas, Harris, and Ariel I. Abrams. 2015. De Facto States Unbound. PONARS Eurasia, Elliott School of International Affairs, George Washington University.

Nadeau, Barbie Letza. 2015. Is the Mafia Saving Italy from ISIS or Just Profiting from Them? *Daily Beast*, December 11.

Naim, Moises. 2005. *Illicit: How Smugglers, Traffickers, and Copycats Are Hijacking the Global Economy*. New York: Anchor Books.

———. 2012. Mafia States: Organized Crime Takes Office. *Foreign Affairs*, May/June.

Naylor, R. Thomas. 2002. *Wages of Crime: Black Markets, Illegal Finance, and the Underworld Economy*. Ithaca: Cornell University Press.

———. 2004. *Hot Money and the Politics of Debt*. Montreal: McGill-Queen's University Press.

Negi, Yogita. 2011. Pragmatic Overview of Hacking & Its Counter Measures. Proceedings of the 5th National Conference; INDIACom, New Delhi. March 10–11.

Neocleous, Mark. 2003. *Imagining the State*. Maidenhead: Open University Press.

Neumann, Jeff. 2015. Wealth and War in Middle East Fuel Appetite for Amphetamines. *Newsweek UK*, November 3.

Neuwirth, Robert. 2011. *Stealth of Nations: The Global Rise of the Informal Economy*. New York: Pantheon Books.

Nordstrom, Carolyn. 2011. Extra-Legality in the Middle East. *Middle East Review* 41 (Winter): 10–13.

O'Brien, Craig. 2007. *Hawala and Western Business Principles.* Master's Thesis, National Intelligence College.

O'Loughlin, John, Vladimir Kolossov, and Gerard Toal. 2014. Inside the Post-Soviet De Facto States: A Comparison of Attitudes in Abkhazia, Nagorno-Karabakh, South Ossetia, and Transnistria. *Eurasian Geography and Economics* 55 (3): 423–456.

Office of the United States Trade Representative. 2017. *2017 Out-of-Cycle Review of Notorious Markets.* Washington, DC: Executive Office of The President.

Overseas Security Advisory Council. 2017. *Indonesia 2017 Crime and Safety Report: Surabaya.* Washington, DC: US Department of State.

Pagnucco, Ray, and Jennifer Peters. 2015. Backed by China, a Massive Narco-Army Angles for More Power in Myanmar. *Vice News*, June 12.

Passas, Nikos. 2001. Globalization and Transnational Crime: Effects of Criminogenic Asymmetries. In *Global Crime Today: The Changing Face of Organized Crime*, ed. M. Galeotti. London: Routledge.

Peters, Gretchen. 2012. Haqqani Network Financing: The Evolution of an Industry. Harmony Program, The Combatting Terrorism Center, West Point.

Pfanner, Eric, and Kevin J. O'Brien. 2013. Provocateur Comes into View After Cyberattack. *New York Times*, March 29.

Primi, Annalisa. 2013. The Evolving Geography of Innovation: A Territorial Perspective. In *Global Innovation Index 2013: The Local Dynamics of Innovation*, ed. Soumitra Dutta and Bruno Lanvin. Geneva: Cornell-INSEAD-WIPO.

Prince, Brian. 2010. How The Koobface Botnet Made $2 Million in a Year. *eWeek*, November 13.

Prince, Matthew. 2013. The DDoS That Almost Broke the Internet. *The Cloudflare Blog*, March 27.

Rabasa, Angel, Christopher M. Schnaubelt, Peter Chalk, Douglas Farah, Gregory Midgette, and Howard J. Shatz. 2017. *Counternetwork: Countering the Expansion of Transnational Criminal Networks.* Santa Monica: RAND Corporation.

Rabkin, Jeremy A. 2004. *The Case for Sovereignty: Why the World Should Welcome American Independence.* Washington, DC: AEI Press.

Rastler, John. 2013. *Don't Forget the Drugs: The Impact of Plan Colombia's Cocaine. Flows on US National Security.* Master's Thesis, Hertie School of Governance, Berlin.

Realuyo, Celina. 2015. The Future Evolution of Transnational Criminal Organizations and the Threat to US National Security. Defense and Technology Paper 107, National Defense University Press.

Reuter, Peter, and Edwin M. Truman. 2004. *Chasing Dirty Money.* Washington, DC: Peterson Institute of International Economics, November.

Reyes, Richard R. 2011. Latin America Special Economic Zones and Their Impacts on Regional Security. Unpublished Doctoral Dissertation, Naval Postgraduate School, Monterey.

Roberts, Elise. 2016. Notes from Marseille, Rotterdam, and Marbella. Memo, Mapping Global Insecurity Project, Moynihan Institute of Global Affairs, July 23.

Roeder, Phillip G. 2017. National Succession. In *Oxford Encyclopedia of Politics*. Oxford: Oxford University Press.

Roig-Franzia, Manuel. 2008. Mexico's Drug Cartels Take Barbarous Turn: Targeting Bystanders in Sinaloa Brings Widespread Carnage and Terror. *Washington Post*, July 30.

Rosenberg, Mica, and Brett Wolf. 2016. Money Laundering Rule on Prepaid Cards Stalled After Industry Pushback. *Reuters*, August 10.

Schmid, Alex P. 2011. Academic Consensus Definition of Terrorism. In *Handbook of Terrorism Research*, ed. Alex P. Schmid. London: Routledge.

Schneider, Friedrich, Konrad Raczkowski, and Bogdan Mroz. 2015. Shadow Economy and Tax Evasion in the EU. *Journal of Money Laundering Control* 18 (1): 34–51.

Schumpeter. 2016. The Crime Families of Naples Are Remarkably Good at Business. *The Economist*, August 27.

Sedgwick, Kai. 2018. These Are the Most Popular Darknet Marketplaces Right Now. *Bitcoin News*, May 1.

Serrano, Monica, and Maria Celia Toro. 2002. From Drug Trafficking to Transnational Organized Crime in Latin America. In *Transnational Organized Crime and International Security*, ed. Mats Berdal and Monica Serrano. Boulder: Lynne Reiner.

Shaw, Mark. 2016. "We Pay, You Pay": Protection Economics, Financial Flows, and Violence. In *Beyond Convergence: World Without Order*, ed. Hilary Matfess and Michael Miklaucic. Washington, DC: National Defense University Press.

Shelley, Louise I. 2014. *Dirty Entanglements: Corruption, Crime, and Terrorism*. Cambridge: Cambridge University Press.

Shelley, Louise I., John T. Picarelli, Allison Irby, Douglas M. Hart, Patricia A. Craig-Hart, Phil Williams, Steven Simon, Nabi Abdullaev, Bartosz Stanislawski, and Laura Covill. 2005. *Methods and Motives: Exploring Links Between Transnational Organized Crime and International Terrorism*. Washington, DC: US Department of Justice.

Siboni, Gabi, and Ram Ben-Barack. 2014. *The Sinai Peninsula Threat Development and Response Concept*. Washington, DC: Brookings Institution, January.

Sienkiewicz, S.J. 2007. Prepaid Cards: Vulnerable in Money Laundering? Payment Cards Center Discussion Paper 07-02, Federal Reserve Bank of Philadelphia.

Silverstein, Ken. 2012. Keep the Dictators Out of Malibu. *New York Times*, July 2.

Smith, Jack D. 2009. Disrupting Terrorist Financing with Civil Litigation. *Case Western Reserve Journal of International Law* 41: 67.

Smith, Michael. 2010. Banks Financing Mexican Drug Gangs Admitted in Wells Fargo Deal. *Bloomberg News*, June 29.

Soska, Kyle, and Nicolas Christin. 2015. Measuring the Longitudinal Evolution of the Online Anonymous Marketplace Ecosystem. Proceedings of the 24th USENIX Security Symposium, Washington, DC, August 12–14.

Spencer, Bree. 2011. Akwesasne: A Complex Challenge to US Northern Security. *National Strategy Forum* (Special Issue), 20 (3 Summer): 45–50.

Speth, James Gustave, and Peter M. Haas. 2006. *Global Environmental Governance*. Washington, DC: Island Press.

Staniland, Paul. 2015. Every Insurgency Is Different. *New York Times*, February 15.

Stanislawski, Bartosz H. 2006. Black Spots: Insecurity Beyond the Horizon. Unpublished Doctoral Dissertation, Maxwell School, Syracuse University (Retrieved from ProQuest Political Science. UMI Number: 3251822).

———. 2011. Black Spots: Breeding Grounds for Terrorism and Transnational Crime. *National Strategy Forum* (Special Issue), 20 (3 Summer): 5–10.

Stiles, Nicole. 2013. Theft and Money Laundering: The Dark Side of Prepaid Cards. *NW3C News*, August 8.

Stone-Gross, Brett, Christopher Kruegel, Kevin Almeroth, Andreas Moser, and Engin Kirda. 2009. FIRE: Finding Rogue Networks. Paper Presented at the 25th Annual Conference on Computer Security Applications, Honolulu, December 7–9.

Stoutzenberger, Timothy, and Marc Barnett. 2016. *Trafficking Trends in the Migrant Market*. Paper Presented at the Annual Meeting of the International Studies Association, Atlanta, March.

Strange, Susan. 2010. *The Retreat of the State: The Diffusion of Power in the World*. Cambridge: Cambridge University Press.

Sullivan, Clare, and Evan Smith. 2011. Trade-Based Money Laundering: Risks and Regulatory Responses. Research and Public Policy Series 115, AIC Reports, Australian Institute of Criminology.

Sullivan, John P. 2013. How Illicit Networks Impact Sovereignty. In *Convergence: Illicit Networks and National Security in the Age of Globalization*, ed. Michael Miklaucic and Jacqueline Brewer. Washington, DC: National Defense University Press.

Sullivan, John P., and Robert J. Bunker. 2011. Rethinking Insurgency: Criminality, Spirituality, and Societal Warfare in the Americas. *Small Wars and Insurgences* 22 (5): 742–763.

Sung, H.E. 2004. State Failure, Economic Failure, and Predatory Organized Crime: A Comparative Analysis. *Journal of Research in Crime and Delinquency* 41 (1): 111–129.

Tax Justice Network. 2018. *Financial Secrecy Index 2018: Narrative Report on the United Arab Emirates (Dubai)*. Chesham: Tax Justice Network.

Taxin, Amy. 2014. Fashion District Raid Funds $100 Million of Laundered Mexican Cartel Ransom Money. *The Christian Science Monitor*, September.

The Economist. 2012. An Unsettling Settlement—Standard Chartered v New York, August 18.

———. 2014. The Amazons of the Darknet, November 1.

———. 2015. Dubai's Bright Prospects: The Nuclear Deal's Other Winner, July 23.

———. 2016a. Getting Rid of Big Banknotes Is Not as Easy as It Looks, March 3.

———. 2016b. Shedding Light on the Dark Web, July 16.

Thompson, Edwina A. 2006. The Nexus of Drug Trafficking and Hawala in Afghanistan. In *Afghanistan Drug Industry*, ed. Doris Buddemberg and William A. Byra. Vienna: UNODC/World Bank.

Toal, Gerard, and John O'Loughlin. 2014. How People in South Ossetia, Abkhazia and Transnistria Feel About Annexation by Russia. *Washington Post Monkey Cage*, March 20.

Tollefsen, Andreas F., and Halvard Buhaug. 2015. Insurgency and Inaccessibility. *International Studies Review* 17 (1): 6–25.

UNEP-MONUSCO-OSESG. 2015. *Experts' Background Report on Illegal Exploration and Trade in Natural Resources Benefiting Organized Criminal Groups in Eastern DR Congo. Final Report*. Nairobi: UN Environment Programme, April 15.

United Nations Office on Drugs and Crime (UNODC). 2010. *The Globalization of Crime: A Transnational Organized Crime Threat Assessment*. Vienna: UNODC.

———. 2011. *World Drug Report 2011*. New York: United Nations.

———. 2012. *Transnational Organized Crime in Central America and the Caribbean: A Threat Assessment*. Vienna: UNODC.

———. 2013. *Comprehensive Study on Cybercrime*. Vienna: UNODC.

———. 2014. *World Drug Report 2014*. New York: United Nations.

———. 2017. *Country Programme 2017–2020 Indonesia: Making Indonesia Safer from Crime, Drugs, and Terrorism*. Vienna: UNODC.

US Department of Homeland Security. 2012. *Guide to the Analysis of Insurgency*. Washington, DC: US Government Printing Office.

Van de Bunt, Henk. 2008. A Case Study on the Misuse of Hawala Banking. *International Journal of Social Economics* 35 (9): 691–702.

Van der Sar, Ernesto. 2017. US Government Teaches Anti-Piracy Skills Around the Globe. *Torrent Freak*, December 17.

Van Dijk, Jan. 2008. *World of Crime: Breaking the Silence on Problems of Crime, Justice, and Development Across the World*. Thousand Oaks: Sage Publications.

Van Dijk, Jan, and Toine Spapens. 2014. Transnational Organized Crime Networks. In *Handbook of Transnational Crime and Justice*, ed. Philip Reichel and Jay Albanese, 2nd ed. Los Angeles: Sage Publications.

Van Eeten, Michel, Johannes M. Bauer, Hadi Asghari, Shirin Tabatabaie, and Dave Rand. 2010. *The Role of Internet Service Providers in Botnet Mitigation: An Empirical Analysis Based on Spam Data*. Paper Presented at the Ninth Workshop on the Economics of Information Security, George Mason University, June 7–8.

Van Schendel, Willem. 2005. Spaces of Engagement: How Borderlands, Illicit Flows, and Territorial States Interlock. In *Illicit Flows and Criminal Things: States, Borders, and the Other Side of Globalization*, ed. Willem van Schendel and Itty Abraham. Bloomington: Indiana University Press.

Vernetti, Gianmaria. (2010) *The Power of Networking: An Insight of the Russian Business Network*. United Nations Interregional Crime and Justice Research Institute, July.

Wainwright, Tom. 2016. *Narconomics: How to Run a Drug Cartel*. New York: Public Affairs.

Walker, Jane. 2005. Police Crack Huge Racket in South of Spain. *Irish Times*, March 14.

Walker, Philip. 2011. The World's Most Dangerous Borders: Afghanistan and Pakistan. *Foreign Policy*, June 24.

Wall, David S. 2005. *Cybercrime, Deviance, and the Internet*. Cambridge: Polity.

Weinbaum, Marvin G. 2017. Insurgency and Violent Extremism in Pakistan. *Small Wars and Insurgencies* 28 (1): 34–56.

Williams, Phil. 1994. Transnational Criminal Networks. In *Networks and Netwars: The Future of Terror, Crime, and Militancy*, ed. John Arquilla and David Ronfeldt. Santa Monica: RAND Corporation.

———. 2001. Crime, Black Markets, and Money Laundering. In *Managing Global Issues: Lessons Learned*, ed. Chaneal de Jonge Oudraat and P.J. Simmons. New York: Carnegie Endowment for International Peace.

Winstock, Adam R., Monica I. Barratt, Larissa J. Maier, and Jason A. Ferris. 2018. *Global Drug Survey 2018: Key Findings Report*. London: Global Drug Survey.

Wood, Geoffrey. 2004. Business and Politics in a Criminal State: The Case of Equatorial Guinea. *African Affairs* 103: 547–567.

World Bank Group. 2016. *Responses to Illicit Financial Flows: A Stocktaking*. Washington, DC: World Bank, March 22.

Zarate, Juan. 2013. *Treasury's War: The Unleashing of a New Era of Financial Warfare*. New York: Public Affairs.

Zartman, William, and Cynthia T. Aronson. 2005. *Rethinking the Economics of War: The Intersection of Need, Creed, and Greed*. Washington, DC: Woodrow Wilson Center Press.

Zdanowicz, John S. 2009. Mitigating the Risks of International Trade Transactions through Effective Monitoring. Paper Presented at the 2009 Mid-Atlantic Anti-Money Laundering Conference, September 22–24.

Zickuhr, Kathryn. 2010. *Generations 2010*. Pew Internet & American Life Project, December 16.

INDEX

© The Author(s) 2020
S. S. Brown, M. G. Hermann, *Transnational Crime and Black Spots*, International Political Economy Series,
https://doi.org/10.1057/978-1-137-49670-6

245

91, 98, 99, 112, 130, 166, 167,
171, 173, 175
Ein el-Hilweh, Lebanon, 89–91, 93, 94
El Arish, Egypt, 23, 54, 63–65, 67
Equatorial Guinea, 59
Erzurum/Kars/Igdir Triangle, Turkey,
69
Europe
black spots, 2, 8, 24, 35, 36, 42, 53,
56, 69–72, 74, 86, 99
hubs, 64, 67, 71, 86
illicit activities, 53, 86
insurgent organizations, 86
terrorist organizations, 99, 187
transnational criminal organizations,
99

F
FARC Territory, Colombia, 35, 70
Federally Administered Tribal Areas
(FATA), Pakistan, 1–3, 15, 21,
60, 61, 79, 105, 132–134
Fergana Valley, 19
Financial Action Task Force (FATF),
63, 113, 116, 119, 121–123,
127, 130–132, 173
Fitzpatrick, Derek, 62
Fujita, Masahisa, 34–36, 38, 40

G
George, Alexander L., 5
Glenny, Misha, 118
Globalization, 7, 10, 18–20, 27, 29,
59, 143
Goma, DRC, 26, 122, 133, 134
Grabosky, Peter, 144, 146
Griffiths, Ryan, 61, 172
Gudauta, Abkhazia, 63, 105
Guinea-Bissau, 71, 72
Guttmann, Jean, 17

H
Hackerville (Ramnicu Valcea),
152–153
Hakkari-Van Provinces, Turkey, 68,
69, 79
Hall, Tim, 38–40
Hezbollah, 22, 26, 42, 61, 62, 66–68,
82–83, 115, 126, 130
Hezbollah Territory, Lebanon, 15, 61,
62, 67, 68, 74, 82–84, 86, 88,
89, 104, 126, 134, 172
Hoffman, Bruce, 80, 89
Holt, Thomas J., 147, 148, 150, 151

I
Illicit activities
animals/animal parts, 50, 64
counterfeit money/documents, 50,
112
drugs, 1, 5, 50, 52, 53, 64, 82, 86,
101, 111, 192, 226–228
household goods, 1, 50, 53, 86,
227, 228
mercenary/terrorism, 50, 53, 86
money laundering, 50, 53, 107,
205, 212, 217, 226–227
natural resources, 1, 50, 52, 86
people, 1, 50, 52, 53, 86
weapons, 1, 50, 52, 53, 86, 107,
111, 226
Insulza, Jose Miguel, 38
Insurgent organizations
definition, 1
examples, 52, 87, 88
geopolitical locations, 85
goals of black spots, 87
illicit activities, 1, 52, 86, 94
national and international
government reactions, 88
Islamic State of Iraq and Syria (ISIS),
20, 37, 72, 90, 91, 104, 174

248 INDEX